The Seven Deadly Virtues

and Other Lively Essays

The Seven Deadly Virtues

and Other Lively Essays

Coming of Age as a Writer, Teacher, Risk Taker

Lynn Z. Bloom

The University of South Carolina Press

© Lynn Z. Bloom

Published by the University of South Carolina Press
Columbia, South Carolina 29208

www.sc.edu/uscpress

Manufactured in the United States of America

17 16 15 14 13 12 11 10 09 08   10 9 8 7 6 5 4 3 2 1

Library of Congress Cataloging-in-Publication Data

Bloom, Lynn Z., 1934–
   The seven deadly virtues and other lively essays : coming of age as a writer, teacher,
risk taker / Lynn Z. Bloom.
      p. cm.
Includes bibliographical references.
ISBN 978-1-57003-730-6 (alk. paper)
   1. Bloom, Lynn Z., 1934– 2. English teachers—United States—Biography. 3. College
teachers—United States—Biography. 4. Authorship. 5. Creative writing. I. Title.
   PE64.B595A3 2008
   814'.6—dc22   2007048828

This book was printed on Glatfelter Natures, a recycled paper with 50 percent
post consumer waste content.

Martin
Laird
Lynn
Sara
To the Bloom family, with love.
Bard
Paul
Vicki
Beth
Rhys

Contents

Illustrations

Acknowledgments

I would like to thank my undergraduate violin teacher, Gilbert Ross, professor of music, University of Michigan, who advised me—in midlesson—to become a writer, though he had read nothing of my work, and other Michigan English professors for reinforcing his judgment: Sheridan Baker, Kenneth Rowe, A. K. Stevens, Austin Warren, John Weimer, and especially Arthur Eastman, who taught me to listen to the words, the music, the sounds of silence. Benjamin Spock, M.D., provided the same advice that he used in *Baby and Child Care* for my writing in *Doctor Spock: Biography of a Conservative Radical:* "If you don't write clearly, someone could die." He also taught me how to write as one friend speaking to another.

The Aetna Endowment and the University of Connecticut, where I have held the Aetna Chair of Writing throughout the writing of this book, have provided a series of superb research assistants: Kathrine Aydelott, Denise M. Lovett, Matthew Simpson, Valerie Smith, and Jenny Spinner. Their exacting work, including unerring research accuracy, unsparing critical sense, and their own experience as writers of fiction and nonfiction, has made my work infinitely easier and much better. Lori Corsini-Nelson, writing programs specialist, has helped throughout in keeping the paper flow on target and on time. Among writing colleagues at UConn and throughout the country, Penelope Pelizzon, poet and essayist, has been the cheerleader par excellence for this book, which she read with a keen eye and generous spirit. "Send it in!" she said. And so I did.

Editors of journals and books in which some of these pieces have appeared—essay lovers all—include Rachel Hile Bassett, John Boe, Brenda Brueggemann, Linda Calendrillo, Robert Con Davis, Suzanne Diamond, Kristie Fleckenstein, Sheryl Fontaine, Doug Hesse, Cynthia Huff, Susan Hunter, Sherrie Inness, Walter Levy, Marian E. Lupo, Irene Paupolis, Louise Z. Smith, Michelle Tokarczyk, and Joe Trimmer. They were willing to publish work risky and radical, that challenged conventional academic sensibility; their advice, from the macro ("Get to the point!") to the micro (tiny tweaks), made it better.

Staff members at the University of South Carolina Press have been a pleasure to work with. Linda Haines Fogle, assistant director, a kindred spirit in sense, sensibility, and style, has been the ideal readers as well as acquistions editor for this manuscript. Jonathan Haupt, also assistant director, has exercised creative ingenuity in many ways, and many media, to help this book fly off the shelves! Bill Adams, managing editor, has made *The Seven Deadly Virtues and Other Lively Essays* even more lively through the various stages of editing—with perspicacity, precision, and wit.

M. F. K. Fisher has observed that "our three basic needs, for food and security and love, are so mixed and mingled and entwined that we cannot straightly think of one without the others (*Gastronomical Me*, 53)." Martin, Bard, and Laird Bloom, and later Vicki (Bard's wife) and Sara (Laird's wife), have provided Fisher's sustaining matrix for the life reflected and refracted throughout this book, and much of the food as well, since we are a family of cheerful cooks. Paul and Beth for a decade and more, and now Rhys, four as this goes to press, help to keep us all happy, just by being themselves.

Martin (aka Saint-Martin-in-the-Fields), social psychologist, professor, and now artist, has been my best critic and best friend even before we married at the beginning of our doctoral work. Twenty years ago he was diagnosed with a rare brain tumor, thought to be malignant. That it was benign put the universe into a new perspective, and ourselves into a new orbit with new jobs, world travels, friends of all ages from many places. As a writer I have felt newly free to take chances, run risks in subject, form, and style, to have fun, and fun yet again. Out of jeopardy has come great joy, high energy, and peace even in this turbulent world. Every day is a gift, which I offer here to you.

Essays in *The Seven Deadly Virtues* that have been previously published are listed below. Some were greatly revised for this book.

"Academic Essays and the Vertical Pronoun." *Literature Interpretation Theory* 16 (Winter 2005): 417–30.

"Coming of Age in the Field That Had No Name." Lynn Bloom, *Composition Studies as a Creative Art.* Logan: Utah State Univesity Press, 1998, 143–57.

"The Dinner Hours." *CEA Critic* 69 (Fall 2006–Winter 2007): 3–13. (forthcoming spring or summer 2007).

"(Im)Patient." *Prose Studies* 27 (April–August 2005): 186–95.

"Living to Tell the Tale: The Complicated Ethics of Creative Nonfiction." *College English* 65 (January 2003): 276–89.

"The Seven Deadly Virtues." *Journal of the Assembly for Expanded Perspectives on Learning* 10 (Winter 2004–5): 1–13.

"Subverting the Academic Master Plot." *Narration as Knowledge: Tales of the Teaching Life.* Ed. Joseph F. Trimmer. Portsmouth, N.H.: Heinemann, 1997, 116–26.

"Teaching College English as a Woman." *College English* 54 (November 1992): 818–25.

"The Two-Thousand-Mile Commute." *Parenting and Professing: Balancing Family Work with an Academic Career.* Ed. Rachel Mile Bassett. Nashville: Vanderbilt University Press, 2005, 151–60.

"Voices." *Prose Studies* 26 (special issue on women's life writings and imagined communities; April–August 2003): 265–77.

"Writing and Cooking, Cooking and Writing" *Pilaf, Pozole, and Pad Thai: American Women and Ethnic Food.* Ed. Sherrie Inness. Amherst: University of Massachusetts Press, 2001, 69–83.

"Writing *Blue Berries:* Once More to My Summer Vacation." *Writing on the Edge* 9 (Spring/Summer 1998): 43–59.

Introduction

The Girl Scouts, Huck Finn, and Benjamin Franklin Weigh In on Virtue

When I was a child I thought as a child. I believed that if I were perfect my virtue would illuminate the world as I knew it and inspire not only reciprocity but appreciation. My parents would love me better than my brother, as became the eldest child. I would be the teacher's pet, still innocent of its loathsome status. I would be the most popular kid in the class, despite the fact that, gawky and geeky, I lacked the requisite social assurance or athletic grace. People would remember my birthday, as they did that of my archrival, Hester Prynne (do you suspect a pseudonym?), born on Valentine's Day; or my brother, Burke, born on the Fourth of July. Since none of this happened, I assumed it was because—as I knew all too well—I wasn't perfect.

The Girl Scouts offered a safe haven, and I joined as soon as I could, at ten. The gray-green uniform became my favorite dress, worn to school every meeting day, and I flung myself into numerous merit-badge projects involving nature—"Bird Finder," "Wild Flower Finder"—and cooking; the best combined both—"Outdoor Cooking." Scouting had an oath that supplanted the ones I already knew, the "zounds" and "odds bodkins" of fictional pirates, and laws that provided troublesome new concepts of virtue even more unattainable than my vague notion of perfection. For this credo, I now realize, incorporated variations of the Seven Deadly Virtues, which I discuss in a later—duty, rationality, conformity/conventionality, efficiency, order, economy, and punctuality. These constitute a plague on academic life, for they discourage the risk taking that is the essence of creativity. The Girl Scouts' version, like the virtues of their elders, an assemblage of behaviors guaranteed to give fits and the fantods, as Huck Finn would have said, to anyone trying to practice them in earnest.

Here's what the Scouts were up against. At the beginning of each meeting, even on the cookouts and campouts, we recited the oath: "On my honor I will try to do my duty to God and my country, to help other people at all times, and to obey the Girl Scout Laws." Then we recited the laws (operative from 1920 to 1970), which I know by heart to this day: A Girl Scout's Honor Is to Be Trusted; A Girl Scout Is Loyal; A Girl Scout's Duty Is to Be Useful and to Help Others; A Girl Scout Is a Friend to All, and a Sister to Every Other Girl Scout; A Girl Scout Is Courteous; a Friend to Animals; Obeys Orders; Is Cheerful; Thrifty; and Clean in Thought, Word, and Deed. On seeing these after many years' absence, my first reaction is that of a writer. These laws are slovenly. Although they exhort the Scouts to be neat and orderly, the laws themselves are afflicted by anarchy of the grammar. All Scouts could use a brisk march to a catchy tune, but the laws are out of parallel, and they straggle along with no sense of rhythm or sound. And Why All the Capital Letters? Where is Moses, who reserved capitals for God and LORD, when we need him? If form followed function, the Scouts would have been in Big Trouble—though by the 1996 version they finally got it right.

Then I started pondering the laws themselves, ordained not by God himself but certainly by God's handmaiden, so we Scouts believed, Girl Scout founder Juliette Gordon Low. In 1912, adapting Lord Baden-Powell's 1908 oath and laws of the British Boy Scouts, Low eliminated the promise (still operative in the Boy Scouts today) "to keep myself physically strong, mentally awake, and morally straight." In actual fact, in the absence of elucidation, I interpreted "Clean in Thought, Word, and Deed" to mean not to peep at the dirty drawings Hester surreptitiously passed around in school (but who could resist "DO NOT LOOK"), certainly not to discuss them with anybody (you are my first audience for this taboo subject), and to keep my room clean. Hardly a license for girls to embrace slackness, sloth, or sexuality, this omission nevertheless allowed the Girl Scouts to welcome girls with disabilities (Low herself was deaf and suffered from back pain and breast cancer) and, unlike the Boy Scouts, be a "sister" to gays and "every other Girl Scout no matter to what Social Class she May Belong." Although the latter qualifier was dropped in 1917, it was nevertheless practiced in my troop, which without fanfare provided scholarships and free uniforms as needed. "Bravery," another Boy Scout virtue, was also deleted for what might have been, in E. B. White's parlance, "secret reasons"—though the need for bravery remained very much alive as I discovered the fortitude it took to live with my mother's clinical depression, an unacknowledged family secret.

What remained in the Girl Scout Laws was an emphatic admonition to Duty, Helpfulness, and Obedience. Louisa May Alcott's *Little Women*, heroines of my childhood, embodied these virtues, abetted by "Precious Marmee." This exemplar of maternal patience and humility, preternaturally devoid of anger, was given to admonitions such as "Watch and pray, dear; never get tired of trying, and never think it is impossible to conquer your fault"—in this case, Jo's "dreadful temper" (Alcott, 69). I loved that book for my own secret reasons. I could never admit to anyone my fear that something, anything, I might do would set off my own mother's hair-trigger temper and she would leave home for good, as she had threatened. Nevertheless, as an aspiring writer myself, I thought that Jo, summoned to Duty incarnate, should never have given up a burgeoning literary career to marry that musty, too-old German, Professor Bhaer.

Duty, Helpfulness, and Obedience are key words of the oath and reiterated in the laws, as befits a collection of precepts that seem more oriented to good manners and good conduct—the virtues du jour—than to a pervasive system of ethics that Scouts, doing their "duty to God," could learn about in church. Now that I am interrogating what I took for granted as a child, I realize that the laws exactly reinforce the rules, implicit and explicit, of the household I grew up in, except for Friendliness, where as the only sociable family member I was the outlier, the "family white sheep," my husband says. As the eldest child of another professor of Prussian origin, Oswald Theodore Wilhelm Zimmerman, who claimed omniscience and was always reminding me to do my Duty, I was expected "to be Useful and to Help Others" at all times. "You *must* do what you *ought* to do!" was his all-encompassing order, more a law of the universe than a specific command. I struggled to Obey, to be Helpful, as you will read in the first chapter, "Writing *Blue Berries:* Once More to My Summer Vacation." Except for my championing of stylistic parsimony (Strunk and White's "Omit needless words"), you won't read much about Thrift, a prevailing post–Depression era virtue embedded in the ethos of the small New Hampshire college town I grew up in, because it was as taken for granted as breathing. Durham's motto could have been that of the World War II poster, "Use it up, wear it out, make it do." But you will read a lot about Loyalty, Friendship, Courtesy, and Good Cheer in the family Martin and I created, a bulwark against professional struggle and harassment, also a prevailing theme. And you will read even more about disobedience, anger, violation of Duty, which I understood over time to be lifesaving virtues.

Breaking the Law

I started, as most lawbreakers do, in a small way. Although I doted on Shag, our energetic border collie, I could never be a sincere Friend to all animals. Perhaps Juliette Low knew only cats, dogs, and horses in Savannah, but in New Hampshire I had to keep a safe distance from random skunks, porcupines, foxes, and the occasional blacksnake that populated the woods behind our house and the rats that raided the chicken coop, devouring our insurance against meat rationing. Although I would have liked to be a sincere Friend to all people, the propaganda and politics of World War II, McCarthyism, and the Cold War made this impossible. Enemies lurked in submarines off the coast; spies in the skies meant blackout curtains at night. Durham also harbored suspicious outsiders: migrant apple pickers from Jamaica, French-Canadian immigrants, New Yorkers wearing conspicuous jewelry and make-up who came for UNH summer school and cheap vacations at our pristine beaches. Although my parents said to keep my distance from "those people" (read blacks, Catholics, and Jews) and from UNH men as well, I could feel the virtues crumbling as I trudged through high school. For the last two years, I dated an Elvis look-alike from the neighboring mill town, whose blue suede shoes, tight jeans, and chronic violation of the rules of grammar implied another sort of license calculated to offend my parents with every swiveling step he took. Loyalty to my parents' supercilious values dissipated, then disappeared, in tandem with Obedience.

By then I had traded in all four of the Little Women, who seemed too Goody Two-Shoes as I got older, for Huck Finn, whose grammar was none too precise either, but whose heart, I knew, was full of Loyalty and Honor. Like Huck, perhaps like all American adolescents with gumption and guts (the Girl Scouts should have kept bravery), I knew I would have to light out for the territory. So I went to the University of Michigan, a thousand miles from home (though honesty compels me to confess that this was my parents' alma mater), out of sight and generally away from the parental mind. In the absence of e-mail, instant messaging, and even phone calls (long distance was reserved for death and disaster), communication was confined to the dutiful, superficial weekly letter, which I often wrote in class under the guise of taking notes.

Many of my values changed, as is inevitable in the course of a decade of growing up, some emerging during my undergraduate and graduate education, others in the process of coming out as a human being, as a wife, mother, scholar, professor, and especially writer, the prevailing themes of this book. The grammar of this statement makes the progression sound logical, rational, inevitable. It was not. The Girl Scout Virtues went up in flames when, at twenty-three, I agreed to marry Martin. Ignoring his intelligence and kindness, my parents treated his Courtesy as a vice rather than a virtue: "He can't be much of a man," sneered my father, "he's too nice to you." Disregarding my fiancé's egalitarianism—in an era when most women were Putting Hubby Through (PHT), we both planned to earn Ph.D.s—my parents saw Martin as a Jew and only as a Jew: "If you marry him, we will have nothing to do with you, or him, or any children you may have." So much for Duty. I leapt to the choice that was no choice at all—and in this book I tell you about that, and its consequences as well.

Many of the essays in *The Seven Deadly Virtues* are thus attempts to probe the assumptions and values—intellectual, social, aesthetic, ethical—of what I have found to be the most complicated, challenging, satisfying, and problematic aspects of love and work. Thus I examine the family and the culture I grew up in, including peers and old boyfriends; my education, informal and formal, through graduate school and beyond; the profession of teaching English and the practices of writing as they have unfolded over the past half century. These subjects involve a mixture of pleasure (marriage, parenthood, writing, teaching, cooking, and travel) and pain (injury, our son's near-fatal auto accident, ostracism, exile); they incorporate success, failure, perplexity.

I am not out to supplant virtue with vice, though that is always tempting, but to propose, in essay after essay, an alternative set of lively virtues to replace the deadly. (Duty and Helpfulness have their place, though I have busted up more than one romance and quit more than one job over issues of servility, sexism, and second-class citizenship; I would augment these with *anger* and *defiance*.) First among my alternative virtues is *honesty*. That this is missing—except with some stretching—from the Ten Commandments, the Girl Scout Laws, and Benjamin Franklin's autobiographical list of virtues (which emphasizes temperance, order, frugality, industry, moderation, and cleanliness—harbingers of the Girl Scouts) surprises me. Other virtues include *risk-taking; independence of mind and spirit* (particularly in overturning precedent or ignoring advice I don't want to hear); *originality; rigor,* as applied to myself and my work; *energy;* and *having fun,* an idiosyncratic virtue that entails a lot of hard work, especially when it comes to enjoying life on the edge, which is where I feel the most comfortable, a writer without borders.

1

Coming to Life

Writing *Blue Berries*

Once More to My Summer Vacation

My mantra for teaching writing, and for writing about teaching writing, is now and always Robert Scholes's assertion, "The response to a text is itself always a text. . . . Our job is not to produce 'readings' for our students but to give them the tools for producing their own" (*Textual Power,* 20, 24). This philosophy is paramount in how I teach students to read and write personal essays. As I tell my students in every course, every semester, "Through the act(s) of reading and rereading, writing and rewriting, I hope you'll come to understand—among other things that writers know:

1. That a particular experience, common or unusual, can be rendered in innumerable versions, voices, modes.

2. That nominally personal writing can send numerous messages with social, political, cultural, ethical (and many other) implications.

3. That style is intimate kin to substance and to self.

4. That the unsaid—reemphasis, omissions, gaps, erasures—is potentially as significant as what is said.

5. That dishonesty can destroy a piece, ethically and aesthetically.

6. That nothing is insignificant—every word, every syntactic structure, every punctuation mark—counts; the format, as well as the form, sends a host of messages.

7. That critical rigor undergirds writing well.

8. That most writing benefits from rewriting, and rewriting, and rewriting. . . .

9. That it is important to read literature, as well as to write it, with an understanding of the writer's craft, the writer's art" (Bloom, "Textual Terror, Textual Power," 58).

To remind myself of the truth and toughness of these precepts, when I teach any form of creative nonfiction—freshman or advanced composition, as well as graduate workshops in the subject—I always try to write an essay I can share, first with my students while we're all struggling with works in progress, and ultimately with a wider audience. How, as a teacher, can I ask my students to lay their lives on the line without being willing to do so myself?

This essay has been coming to life for eighteen years, ever since my husband and I moved to Connecticut to take new teaching jobs and have been able to spend summers out of doors instead of sequestered in air-conditioned Virginia. I tried in vain for the first three years to write an essay that would capture the essence of summertime, O summertime, as I was learning to re-experience it in New England. Although I had grown up in New Hampshire, my parents had evicted me from the family when I married Martin, and their unwavering anti-Semitism made our brief visits during our children's summer vacations a tense reminder that there was no home there to go to anymore. I tried to cram the whole history into ten elliptical pages and could never get it right—too much, too little, too fast. That essay languishes on my computer to this day.

So I decided to try a different tack in my search for my own version of "Once More to the Lake," aka "What I Did on My Summer Vacation." Since I write all the time in my head when I'm doing repetitive tasks—swimming, cooking, sometimes (I hate to admit) even while I'm driving—I knew that sooner or later the perfect subject would appear. What, I finally decided, extracting just a single word from my earlier paper, could be better than blueberries—as actual fruit, as metaphor? I'd write a page or two and see what happened. I did not know at the outset, or even during the first two years of intermittent forays into writing about the blueberry patch, where the tension so necessary to any narrative, even this low-key one, would come from. But when blackberries finally inserted their thorny toughness into the blueberry patch, I knew then that I would have to plunge into the tangled thicket of another, much earlier, summer vacation. It would be hard, perhaps impossible, to tell the truth of a story I do not fully understand even to this day, but it would be worth the effort to try.

Blueberries

As I leave our house in northeastern Connecticut on those soft summer evenings when there's still a good two hours of daylight before dusk, I am dressed for my destination—almost entirely in blue. My holey navy gardening sneakers. Blue jeans, blue T-shirt, a faded blue madras long-sleeved overshirt if the wind's not strong enough to blow the mosquitoes away. And a big-brimmed blue straw hat with a white ribbon that was once elegant enough to consider wearing to our son's wedding, five years ago.

I usually go blueberrying by myself at Crooke's Orchard, the nearby family farm where the public can pick blueberries from July 15 to Labor Day. This summer they were $1.00 a pound—a generous quart, large and lush and so abundant that we could grab them by the handfuls. The quadruple rows of shoulder-high bushes embrace a pond too small for waves; only the occasional frog splash disturbs its tranquil surface. Their submerged energy is mirrored in the speed pickers who rush along the rows, snatching clusters as they pass. The fruit, firm and smooth like young human skin, spills into my hands, and the light-and-leaf patterns of the slowly setting sun glow through the latticed twigs. Although I, like the speed pickers, race through life with stopwatch timing, in the blueberry patch I wear no watch and tell time only by the circuit of the setting sun.

So I mostly sit under the bushes and search for buried treasure, the biggest and bluest berries out of sight of casual browsers. I am out of sight as well, invisible under my hat, all the better to eavesdrop on other pickers. In the visible world I've been accused of talking too much. My mother complains, "You're always trying to organize everyone's life. Stop telling me what to do." She's right. I do give her advice, more than ever when she's 86-87-88: "You should stop shoveling your own driveway." "Get a dated pillbox so you can keep track of your medicine." Like her advice to me until she stopped, cold, when I got married, it's all for her own good. She ignores what I say. Among the rows of well-tended bushes, I listen.

The stories I overhear in this berry patch are as a rule more joyous than the tales of trauma people spill over the vegetable counter at the Super Stop and Shop fourteen miles away—"I've been laid off and the only times I can shop are on food stamp days." "My wife died last month; how do I cook for one person?" Here parents and grandparents discuss at leisure what they'll do with all those blueberries, and exchange good recipes, offhandedly teaching their children to take good care of the bushes as they pick the fruit. They plan and reflect on vacations, and share information about good places in the area to hike, good beaches, good colleges to send those children. Once, best of all, I broke my habit of silence for a long conversation with the biographer of Edwin Way Teale, the area's renowned naturalist, concealed under bushes on the opposite side of the row. When we'd finished talking and picking we stood up and stretched to shake hands, without spilling a berry.

Recently the talk turned from the chances of beating the slots at the Mashantucket Pequot casino at Ledyard ("Consider it recreation, not income," advises a man who plays the slots twice a month, every payday) to the country fairs that abound in rural New England during August and

September. I'm so surprised by one woman's claim that she goes to a fair every weekend that I must ask her why. "My husband and I breed champion stud horses. We have a ranch in Willington"—surely a rarity in rocky Connecticut—"and every weekend during fair season we show the horses." "Why here, instead of, say, Colorado?" I ask. "We got into it six years ago when our son developed leukemia. We had to have something to think about besides his health, something that would get us outdoors, out of the hospital, and exercising"—she breathes deeply—"something our daughter, she was seven and he was five, could do and he could watch. We couldn't let him get the slightest scratch; an infection might be fatal." Berries cascade efficiently into her pail. "After three years we were able to let him into the ring. Last year he showed a horse, but he was very clumsy. The chemo for so long had knocked out his coordination. He has a very short attention span, and he just couldn't get it all together." "Did he ever go to Hole-in-the-Wall Gang Camp?" I ask. Just down the road from Crooke's Orchard, Paul Newman has established a state-of-the-art summer ranch for critically ill children; the facilities range from a pond with heated gazebo for frail swimmers to a helipad for medical airlifts. "He was eligible, but we didn't let him go." She pauses, "We couldn't bear to have him away from us for even one night; we never knew whether he'd be alive in the morning." Then, smiling, "It's been nine months since the treatments ended; he practiced hard and just won a ribbon for showmanship. We are so proud." I fight the impulse to tell her about our son Laird's auto accident at fifteen, the sixty-four stitches across his face and forehead concealing the wires and plastic supports that will as long as he lives hold his face together and his left eye in place. Nor do I discuss the medical crisis that impelled Martin and me to move abruptly to Connecticut, around the time her son's leukemia began. This is her story. "Come and see our ranch, the Rocking M, anytime," she says. "I'll bring our grandson when he's a little older," I promise.

In season Crooke's has apples that Martin and I pick together. McIntosh, first in September, surprisingly tart and firm if they're picked before they've had time to mellow on the tree. These are so hard we can skip Rhode Island Greenings, the real pie apples. Then we pick Cortlands. And by October, Red Delicious. Golden Delicious, always looking slightly green and freckled. Ida Reds. Finally our favorite, Empire, a cross of McIntosh and Red Delicious, bright red skin covering crisp white flesh. This year there is a medium-sized mystery apple for sampling, later identified as Gala, a cross between Kidd's Orange Red and Golden Delicious; at 25 cents apiece or $3.25 a peck, we splurge on the peck.

Lynn and Martin at a Connecticut lake, 2004

To reach the apples we pass a field of pumpkins, bright orange suns shining through fading foliage. Most are the right size for decorating front porches or carving as jack-o'-lanterns; one splendid specimen, waist high, would make a fitting coach for Cinderella. Then we stride past the young trees, braced to ramrod posture by horizontal wires that stretch the length of the rows. Their espaliered branches look as if a holdup is in progress, with the promise of pies as ransom.

Finally we reach the mature trees, each surrounded by a carpet of fragrant, fallen fruit that will be pressed into cider. The vigorous, gray-haired woman who hands us the plastic white-and-green-checked "Crooke's Orchard" bags, decorated with red apples, for picking reiterates the message of a sign attached to the portable scale, "Twenty pounds minimum," that's half a bushel, "at 40 cents a pound." I think because of her friendly gravity and her posture, slender and erect, that she must be Mrs. Crooke's mother, but she seems too reserved to ask. She assigns us to a row. "Empire down this way."

We know that if we walk a very long way down the row the apples will be so abundant that they will bend the boughs nearly to the ground. Now that

Paul (who is the infant son of Laird and his wife, Sara, and who was born six months after Laird finished a cell biology Ph.D.) is on the verge of walking, the thought of sharing this experience soon with our first grandchild reminds us to leave the fruit on the lower branches where other little children can reach it. Although the pickings will be best at the far end, as we pass down the row the fruit looks so tempting we snatch the most succulent apples, and our bags are full before we're halfway along.

Should we stop when we have enough for foreseeable pies, tarts, apple-sauce, and sharing with our students during long seminars? Or do we get more bags and pick apples that we know we'll have to give away, just for the pleasure of the picking? Whatever we decide, we're always done in a half hour, forty-five minutes tops if we stop at the barn to buy free-range eggs—brown and white are the same price; spreadable fruit preserves—strawberry, black-berry, apricot, black cherry, and blueberry; pale, crumbly Vermont cheddar; or late vegetables—beets, green peppers, surprising fall rhubarb. We could get a rainbow of squashes—small acorn, indeed a dark green acorn shape; the larger buttercup, dark green with orange rays; pink banana, a smooth oval the size of a small watermelon; or blue hubbard, large, warty, and cratered like the moon. They make me wish I liked squash. Each holding a handle, we carry the brimming bag between us to the car.

Seven years after our sudden arrival in Connecticut, we're still surprised to be here. We had lived for a decade in postcard-pretty Williamsburg, Virginia, where the "inner city" consists of Colonial Williamsburg and the College of William and Mary. Our house, in a woods near the college lake, was made of mellowed, white-frosted rosy bricks recycled from the oldest insane asylum in the country; we'd wake up in the mornings to the sound of our neighbor's son's fife and dodge colonial-garbed cyclists on their way to work. We had good jobs, good friends. Our two sons had enjoyed their high school years at Lafayette High, whose history included Bruce Hornsby and Lawrence Taylor, and taking math at William and Mary, which made history with George Washington and Thomas Jefferson. But we could never have picked blueberries in Williamsburg; that steamy summer climate would have turned them into cobblers on the bush.

Before moving to Williamsburg, we had changed jobs and geography sev-eral times in the process of negotiating two academic careers. We thought we'd settled in Williamsburg for life until Martin announced, over dinner one night, "I'm ready to move. I've had the same job for ten years and it's too predictable." In the twinkling of an eye, we, who can deliberate for weeks over buying new towels, had changed jobs and moved to Connecticut. The very week our furniture was unloaded we picked two quarts of the summer's last berries at Crooke's and knew we were home. Ever since, I have kept in the freezer a year's supply, including a special reserve hoarded for blueberry pancakes during the Christmas holidays, the other time besides summer when our children and those dear to them can be counted on to convene in Connecticut.

This August everyone is coming late on Friday night, Bard's thirty-second birthday. How can he be slated for a tenure review at Cornell this year when Martin and I feel like novices in our own jobs? He has already convinced us he won't make it, and we have decided that it's all right to discuss survival strategy but not to utter even a syllable on the question much closer to our hearts—will Vicki go with him when he leaves? And will she marry him if she does? We can count on Sara, a lawyer from whom no clue escapes, to be our silent ally in searching for implied answers to the questions we can't ask. But we have no formal agenda for this gathering, we never do; that's not the point. In anticipation of the family's arrival, I pick two brimming bowlfuls of blueberries. Everyone knows they can count on a pie.

Martin and I always do the pies together. He makes the shell, and I heap it with the fleshy fruits of summer's abundance—strawberries, apricots, peaches, nectarines, or, of course, blueberries. Cherries are too much trouble to pit, and raspberries too intense, though we throw in a few for color. If the fruit is going to sit long enough for the juice to run, I coat the inside of the baked pie shell with a mixture of four tablespoons of cream cheese thinned to spreading consistency with a little milk. If the pie will be eaten soon, I don't bother. Then I fill the pie shell with fresh fruit. The recipe calls for two cups, but I always add a third, even a fourth, until the fruit starts to spill over the sides. I pour over it a sauce made of two cups of the same fruit as the pie filling, or different fruit, it doesn't matter, cooked with a quarter cup of water, three quarters of a cup of sugar, and two tablespoons of cornstarch mixed with a little cold water. When the sauce—blueberry this time—has thickened, I turn off the heat, add a tablespoon of butter and another of Grand Marnier or triple sec or even crème de cassis and let it cool. (You will find the recipe on page 160.) Tonight Martin crowns the glistening berries with an extra-high lattice, an airy turban made by weaving raw strips of dough over the outside of a large pie plate and baking them briefly.

The welcoming pie is still warm when Laird and Sara arrive from Boston. They put Paul to bed as Bard and Vicki come in, yawning and stretching from the six-hour drive from Ithaca. Bard's hair is too long and bushy, and his beard is shaggy; could that affect his status at Cornell? I don't ask. We gather to devour this cooling cobalt, served on plates to match and washed down with tea from Bard's handmade mugs, azure to indigo. We're talking so vigorously we forget to sing "Happy Birthday" until it's time for second helpings. The remaining slivers disappear fast during our leisurely break-fast, so there is no choice but to pick more berries. "Let's make jam," says Vicki, "low sugar," and we're off, except for Martin, who elects to stay home with Paul, the earliest riser of us all, now ready for a nap. Next year they'll come too.

Crooke's summer helper, a college student who can be counted on to slip some extra berries into my pail while she's weighing them, assigns us to a row of highbush berries, both sides. We drop the smaller denim and the plump navy globes nearly bursting their skin into pint containers and empty these into two plastic laundry pails. It is an unspoken point of family honor not to eat fruit plucked from the bushes—well, not more than a taste. If caught in the act I will argue for a broad interpretation of "a taste," and besides, the drops that the birds would get anyway don't count. In an hour our pails weigh in at twenty-eight and a half pounds, full almost to the brim.

Blackberries

The summer I was nine and fat, I went blackberry picking every evening with my father. He said that bending from the waist would help me to reduce. So after dinner we would smear our faces and arms with mosquito repellent, acrid and oily, that my father invented when he was teaching freshman chemistry during the war, after all of his chemical engineering students were drafted. Every night was a test to see whether the new batch would work better than its predecessor. Every night we returned with more bites.

We'd walk silently through the woods in back of our house and cross the railroad tracks; I would scramble up the embankment, expecting the Boston and Maine to bear down on us any second. Then my father would clutch the wires together so we could climb over the six-strand barbed-wire fence to reach the pasture where the University of New Hampshire dairy herd grazed. Sometimes Burke, my younger brother, came with us, but he didn't have the patience to pull and twist the tough brambles in search of this dubious fruit. I did. After picking for an hour, we seldom took home more than two cups of berries, which I do not recall ever eating, although Burke devoured all the ripe ones right off the canes. The rest were hard and small and sour, and the seeds got wedged in our teeth. Nevertheless, when cleaning cupboards during one college vacation, I discovered a jelly jar of agate crystals, labeled "Blackberry 1944" in my mother's schoolteacher script.

To be near my father, I would endure cow manure, sometimes so fresh it stuck to my shoes, the briar scratches that still sting in memory, the sticky heat that emanated from the fields, and the clouds of mosquitoes that thickened at dusk and eventually drove us home. Even if he didn't say much except to urge me on our walks to "straighten up," he had asked me to go with him.

I had stopped explaining why I hunched over when I walked. The night before Halloween I had been curled up reading on the floor of my brother's room when Burke decided to test his new Superman costume by leaping from the top bunk of his double-decker bed. He had landed on my spine, red rubber boots first, and it still hurt to stand erect. "The cape was too small," he said. If I ignored the pain, my father admonished, it would go away.

It was good to get away from the house. Every day that summer, after my father went to work, my mother would put my baby sister, Linda, into her crib in their bedroom, already crammed to the rafters with two dressers, his and hers, a sagging, unmade double bed from their grad school years, and a bulbous-footed cedar chest. The crib, jammed against the wall, left only a narrow way out.

Then she assembled what she needed for the morning—three oranges, two detective-story magazines, an ashtray, and a pack of rationed cigarettes. She invaded my bed and disappeared. On the days she wore her diagonally striped rayon blouse and faded gray slacks—her daring alternative to the starched cotton housedresses favored by both her mother on a hand-to-mouth farm in Independence, Indiana, and her mother-in-law in urban Detroit—there was a possibility she'd emerge before noon. But the pink chenille bathrobe whose shards caught in my sheets signaled a long stay. I would hang around the doorway, feeling even uglier than usual, waiting for her to braid my hair. When I tried to do it myself, I couldn't get the rubber bands on tight enough, and the loosely plaited hair would come undone by lunchtime; my mother's braiding lasted through the night before straggling wisps emerged. Otherwise I tried to keep out of her way, even though this meant staying out of my own room.

I did not want her to find my secret diary. Or my private manuscripts of work in progress; I was going to be a novelist like Dr. Seuss. Or the cigar box I had padded with milkweed fluff and covered with scraps of electric blue moiré that unraveled when I tried to sew them together. There I kept all of my Detroit grandma's letters, my school report cards ("Lynn is doing satisfactory work"), and two notes from a boy in my class who once kissed me when he caught me during the daily recess game of "Boys Chase the Girls" before I was fat. He would never do it again, I knew, for that summer I couldn't stop eating second, even third helpings of mashed potatoes, even though I feared I would become as bloated as my mother's second sister, Aunt Evelyn, from whose doughy bulk, twice Mom's size, emerged my mother's sharply etched profile, still pretty.

I especially did not want my mother to discover the plasticine piggy bank that held the money I had been saving since first grade to buy a typewriter, even though at the moment it was nearly empty. I had lent her the contents

($37.42) for a train ticket to her mother's funeral in Indiana, when her mother, Stella Alice Kisling, died on Memorial Day weekend after a gall-bladder operation. The bank was closed, and Mom had to leave in a hurry. Although she promised to pay me back, I felt utterly bereft as the train pulled out of Durham's small station in the gray dawn, empty except for the ranks of giant metal milk cans standing sentinel for delivery in Boston. I was already sore at heart—not for the loss of the grandmother I had seen only three times, swathed to her chins in costume jewelry—but for my mother's absence, abetted by my typewriter funds.

She returned two weeks later with a suitcase full of rage that she continued to unpack until her own death nearly sixty years later. The venomous letters from family members who perpetuated the feud that until they died off, one by one, remained sharp in her mind even amidst the dull detritus of her last months. She could quote verbatim from the cache of correspondence over Stella's legacy—one hundred ten acres of Indiana farmland—Linda and Martin and I discovered when sorting through her lifetime lode of cancelled checks, tax papers, stock certificates from bankrupt companies, children's locks of hair and report cards, blotchy curled-up prints from my father's photography experiments, and studio photographs of Edwardian dandies and belles so glamorous they must have belonged to a different family altogether.

Charity and the benefit of the doubt were alien to my mother's family. Exchanges, bitter and biting, whether in schoolmarm copperplate on scented floral paper or in pencil on lined notebook paper, comprised the correspondence between her father, her two sisters—Marjorie, the petite eldest, Mom's double; and Evelyn, whose lissome teenage blondness had made her the designated family beauty—and various weaselly conniving cousins. After twenty-seven years and the taxes, lawyers, and real estate agents had been paid, each surviving combatant netted a cool thousand dollars. Nevertheless, suspicion continued to cling to the documents like the hint of an alien perfume—what of the oil rights? The mineral rights?

Those two weeks in Indiana had been a time not to mourn but to revisit the contentious Kisling history and continue the arguments. Some grievances were older than Mom was. Mildred had been born last, a replacement child for Archie, the only son, who died at two and a half from eating medicine he'd pried from a forbidden cupboard. I had found his picture, the only one her family ever took, hidden in our earliest family album under one of Evelyn as a tiny child; half smiling as if dreaming, eyes closed, Archie lay in a white sailor suit in his padded satin coffin. Mildred should have been a boy.

There were grievances Mom couldn't help. She saw herself as the family Cinderella, made hideous by freckled face and arms, though these are

18

invisible in pictures. She should have been as pretty as Marjorie (who also had freckles) and Evelyn, and would have been if she hadn't had to wear their hand-me-downs. Other grievances she provoked. She should have stayed on the homestead in Independence instead of eloping with an engineering student from Detroit who wore a white, Palm Beach summer suit and white bucks for his visit to the farm, who wouldn't touch her mother's batter-fried chicken or creamed okra, who laughed at the way they said *greazy* instead of *greasy*, and put his dainty flapper wife through the University of Michigan with a bachelor's degree in biology while he got his Ph.D. If she thought she was too good for her family, she had another think coming. They did not attend her graduation. I could not have imagined then that the disputatious Kisling tradition would be carried on for decades of my own life history, but as I've explained in "Living to Tell the Tale" (which appears later in this book), it did.

I was afraid my mother was angry at me. Shortly after she had returned from Indiana, I had gotten up early and put on my favorite dress, a red pinafore with white flowers, to wear to the third-grade picnic on the last day of school. The house was unnaturally quiet. "Everybody's still sleeping," I thought, and went out into the bright, birdsong morning to feed the cat. It was the last moment of sheer happiness I remember of that summer. For as I sat in the sunshine, our Studebaker appeared suddenly in the driveway, and my parents got out. Where had they been? "Your mother tried to run away and I'm bringing her back." My father did not look at me but clutched my mother tightly by the arm and marched her up the peeling back steps of our rented house and into the kitchen. The screen door slammed. Later when I asked, "Why did she do that?" my parents replied, "You've been dreaming." They had given the same answer two Christmases earlier when I walked into their last-minute present wrapping: "You've been dreaming. Santa Claus brought the tree and these presents. We're just rearranging them." And again, the day after that: "It never happened. Why do you keep insisting? You know we never lie to you." So I never again uttered the question that I woke up with every morning for months, "Would this be the day she would run away for good?"

If I was perfect, maybe my mother would stay. When she wasn't in bed she was out in the garden, watering, chopping weeds furiously, lugging rocks. We were trying to grow our own food to help the war effort, though I couldn't see what my father's anemic cotton and tobacco plants had to do with victory. The scraggly cotton bolls got waterlogged and mildewed; the tobacco leaves drying in the garage grew brittle with dust and crumbled when he tried to roll them into cigars. I hated to garden. It was hot and sweaty and the dirt dammed up under my fingernails and clogged my sneakers. I wasn't strong enough to do much good except to help pick the profusion of tomatoes and green beans. Burke liked to crunch up the potato bugs and squash the tomato worms, green inside and out, but spent most of the day in the foxhole he'd dug in the backyard, throwing pine cone grenades at Linda and pretending to shoot his toy rifle at me and anything else that moved.

I would do the housework, though I'd rather read books. My goal was to finish every book in the children's room of the Hamilton Smith Library by the time I graduated from eighth grade. The fiction section ended at the right of the door; I began there and went counterclockwise, Mark Twain and Robert Louis Stevenson—*Kidnapped* with wonderful N. C. Wyeth illustrations—straight around to Lewis Carroll and to the ultimate reward, Louisa May Alcott, in the far corner. I loved *Little Women* and *Jo's Boys* and *Rose in Bloom* so much that I rarely crossed past the big windows to get to the science section; I'd just reverse direction and reread *Little Women* one more time. After two perusals I skipped *Heidi*, whose mother had died, for the same reason that I avoided *Bambi* altogether after sobbing nonstop through the second half of the movie.

Outdoors was best, full of crickets and ladybugs and ants and bees, whose similar habits I understood from both observation and books. The air was sweet with pine and spruce sap, cut at intervals with faint whiffs of the skunks who shared the woods and meadows behind the house with foxes, black-snakes, box turtles, opossums, porcupines, raccoons, and rabbits—to name only those animals that regularly showed up in our yard. I especially liked to hang out the laundry the way my Detroit grandma had taught me, each item shaken with a snap to get out the wrinkles, all the diapers together in a row, sharing clothespins; socks paired; pajama tops next to pajama bottoms. I tried to hang the clothes as soon as my father squeezed them through the wringer, flattened into fish shapes. He had learned to do the laundry when my mother went to Indiana for the funeral, but the clothes had remained in their wicker baskets until she returned to unwad the stiffened lumps that still smelled of mildew. By midsummer the navy blue stains from a UNH sweat-shirt that had splotched all the underwear in those moldering baskets had begun to bleach out, and the clothesline, clean, sweet smelling, and orderly, became a work of art except for the sheets, which buried me when I tried to hang them with precision.

Indoors, however, defied order. To dust and run the carpet sweeper (the rocket-shaped Electrolux was too heavy for me to lug around), it was neces-sary to organize the stray carpentry and garden tools, old newspapers, unan-swered mail, toys, laundry, wet rags, dirty dishes, spent pipe cleaners, bottles of curdling formula, and my mother's art supplies—clay dug from the garden, drying weeds, beach rocks and glass worn down by the tides, shells, driftwood—abandoned at random on the kitchen counter, dining table, end tables, under the couch, and up the stairway. There was no place to put anything except the dishes, so I washed those, emptied the ashtrays, and piled in separate heaps everything that seemed to belong together. I earned typewriter money for dishwashing (ten cents) and setting the table (five cents), making the coffee (one cent), peeling potatoes (five cents)—I always peeled extras. My parents had not docked my pay while I was figuring out how to do things right, though it seemed logical at the time to wash the celery with Ivory soap (guaranteed 99 and $^{44}/_{100}$ percent pure, what could be better?) and to scrub the kitchen floor by emptying pails of soapy water on it before tackling it with a mop. My father swept the excess right out the back door when he came home from the lab, but not before gallons of suds cascaded down the stairs to the already dank basement. Sometimes I could get Burke to dry dishes, if I invented word games that he had a chance of winning ("I'm thinking of a president whose initials are F.D.R.") and offered him a subcontractor's fee. Linda I played with for free; she was better than any doll.

Around noon my mother would come downstairs to feed Linda, who had spent much of the morning rocking back and forth in her crib, banging her head. We could hear her jouncing rhythm all over the house, and if the crib had been banged to block the door we had to find the screwdriver and take it off the hinges to get her out. I soon learned to fix lunch—diluted Campbell's soup, vegetable beef or chicken noodle, and white-bread sandwiches. I ate everybody's leftovers, and Burke, who virtually stopped eating that summer, left a lot. Peanut butter, baloney, when we had enough ration coupons for it, drenched with ketchup, or my favorite that nobody else liked—open-faced sandwiches of cold potatoes and leftover green beans embedded in mayonnaise, decorated with mosaic designs of pinched-off bits of American cheese and raw onion rings. If I'd had a bike, I could have pedaled to swim at the UNH pool, but it was too far to walk, and my parents wouldn't get us victory bikes—"No good," they said. So even when my mother was up, I was stuck at home.

The house, too small to start with and made smaller with everything in sight, looked the same when we'd finished lunch as it had before I tried to clean up. When my mother went out to the garden, I braved the stale smoke and orange peels in my room to make the bed and sneak in as much reading as possible before Linda needed attention after her nap. Along with the library books, I devoured *National Geographic, Life* (although my father thought it had too many pictures and not enough words), *Time,* and the

Saturday Evening Post, which made Wednesdays special with cartoons and good stories and Norman Rockwell covers, but why was it titled *Saturday Evening* when it always came on Wednesday? And I wrote, mostly letters that summer. To make sure I got real letters, I answered junk mail: "No, Burke cannot sell subscriptions to *Country Gentleman.* He is only seven years old." I wrote twice a month to Barbara Grover, a pen pal in Ishpeming, Michigan, until she started using words I didn't understand and couldn't find in the dictionary: *schmuck, fuck.* And every week I answered my Detroit grandma's letters that always began, "Dear Lynn Marie." She was the only one who called me Marie, but that was her name too, so using it was like sharing a secret. The letters always ended "Love Grandma"—she seldom used punctuation— and oh I did. And when my father came home from work, we would go berry picking.

Finally summer was over and school started again. The following May, while I was still recuperating from three weeks of red measles, we moved across the street to a much larger house where I had a room of my own with a built-in desk, cubbyholes, and two closets that stretched far under the eaves. The house had a small greenhouse, where Mom could start plants, and space for her potter's wheel. The war's end meant we could buy an automatic clothes washer. We could have a puppy, a border collie named Shag so we could tell shaggy dog stories. I trained him to sleep at the foot of my bed, but when his head appeared next to mine on the pillow, adrool with breathy saliva, he was banished downstairs.

That summer I got so many ear infections and high fevers that my parents had my eardrums lanced and lanced again, and finally had my tonsils and adenoids removed. Still the mysterious fevers continued, and the fear they would lead to mastoid, meningitis, even polio meant that I had to stay in-doors all summer, mostly in bed, even when the rest of the family went for walks after dinner to train the dog. Mom made me two pretty bathrobes of congenial fabrics, not chenille, changed my sweaty sheets every day, and began again to make from scratch the chicken soup and crusty bread and Dutch apple pie that the whole family loved, Burke especially.

This is the only time I have ever been a baseball fan; I listened to every Red Sox game, knew all the stats. I learned the language: *rhubarb, pepper, raspberry.* Along with Eleanor Roosevelt, Ted Williams was my hero, even though I suspected the authenticity of the signature on his glossy photo; the ink wouldn't run when I moistened it with spit. During the measles, I had read the *Complete Works of Sherlock Holmes,* and Mom followed this up with armloads of fiction from the library—her current favorite, Booth Tarkington, an Indiana author whose hero swore by saying "job jab it," though beyond the Penrod books I found them pretty dull; and exciting mysteries by Ellery

Queen and Agatha Christie. The librarian disapproved of Nancy Drew, girl sleuth, as well as the Bobbsey twins, whom I myself had already dismissed doubly boring compendia of cliches. And I began to write detective stories of my own, in longhand on lined school paper, illustrated with drawings in vivid pencil paint colors, in which clever, urbane female detectives outwitted combinations of Mata Hari and Tokyo Rose.

My period started a week before my eleventh birthday. When I asked my mother to interpret the evidence—I thought I'd somehow cut myself—she looked very sad and said, "Now you'll understand why they call it 'the curse.' You can expect to spend three days a month in bed like I do, the cramps will be so bad, and you won't be able to swim for a week." I did not argue with her; I had decided never to argue with her. But I vowed, silently, "I'll *never* have cramps. I won't stay in bed. I'll wear Tampax"—which she forbade, I think now, because she equated their insertion with having sex—"and go swimming anyway." I would exercise every day; I would never be fat. A few minutes later, she gave me a sanitary belt and a white sundress trimmed in red braid with a matching bolero jacket that I suspected she'd made for my birthday. "Why white," I wondered, "when the stain is red?" "Be sure to hide the pads," she said. "And don't breathe a word of this to your brother." Later that summer, I asked her when I could start wearing a training bra. When she snapped, "Training for what?" I decided to buy a bra myself, even if it meant using some of the typewriter money she had paid back. By the time I went back to school, with braids cut off and a Toni home permanent, I had grown six inches, only an inch and a half shorter now than Mom, and lost all the weight I had gained during the summer that never happened.

Blueberries

As cooks, we invent and improvise. Now that Laird is on summer paternity leave from his lab at MIT, he grills everything outdoors from their backyard garden—corn; green and yellow peppers; tomatoes; okra, which he alone likes amidst the family rejection of mucilaginous vegetables. I wouldn't be surprised if he tried to grill brussels sprouts. Vicki, who works in a food development lab, is the only one who's made low-sugar jam before and preserved it in sterile jars, so we follow her lead in the kitchen. She has providentially suggested the purchase at Crooke's of a package of Pomona's Universal Pectin ($2.95 an ounce), "a low methoxyl type of pectin derived from citrus peels and pulp, its jelling power activated by the calcium naturally present in most fruits," rather than by "the 55–85% sugar required by ordinary jams." One package is guaranteed to make "approx. 20 Cups of Jam with rich, full flavor undiluted by large amounts of added sugar." Vicki, Bard, and I drive to the hardware store, an eleven-mile round-trip, to get the right kind of jars. I have never seen so many different kinds, my mother canned tomatoes and bread-and-butter pickles at night after we'd gone to bed for fear we'd get scalded, and I've never canned anything for fear of botulism. We settle on the simplest—two dozen Ball number 60 Mason jars that will hold six ounces apiece, and jar lids whose metal inserts are decorated with fruits that match those embossed on the glass.

Home again, Vicki begins by making calcium water. "What's that?" Sara asks, and Vicki explains that it's a half teaspoon monocalcium phosphate (the small packet from Pomona Pectin) mixed with a half cup of water. While Laird, Sara, and I wash and stem the berries, Bard and Vicki sterilize the jars, rings, and lids and line the jars up on white towels in expectant rows. As Bard mashes the berries, Vicki calls out instructions: "For every four cups of mashed berries, add a quarter cup of lemon juice and a cup of sugar." I add the juice to the berries in the stainless steel stockpot Bard and Vicki gave us two years ago, for our anniversary. Sara measures the sugar. "Mix every cup of sugar with two tablespoons of pectin," intones Vicki, "but don't put it in the pot until the berries have come to a rolling boil." Martin joins us to begin dinner preparations, and we realign our positions at the counter.

We are dancing a barefoot ballet in the kitchen now to avoid the floor-level jet of air conditioning, spilled berries, and bubbling syrup. Instead of tutus, we wear T-shirts, variations in blue and white, my Escher doves in flight and Sara's Adirondack porch chair facing an island complemented by Martin's Cat in the Hat. Laird, holding Paul erect by both hands, wobbly but eager, bops in and is gone again. To the blueberries bubbling in the kettle Sara adds the calcium water while Bard stirs. Vicki fills the jars, screws on the lids, and boils them in another kettle for five minutes. Martin and I chop parsley and mint and oregano from our herb garden in preparation for the tabouli that will let everyone taste the tomatoes, the only food we can grow predictably besides the herbs and spring onions. We will eat it with grilled salmon.

With tongs, Bard lifts the jars out. They will cool on the counter during dinner and our evening walk and the conversation that will last until we start falling asleep, one by one. Martin and I decide to wait and write to Bard about getting his hair cut during this crucial year ("If you get tenure you can dress the way you want"), and the message comes back on e-mail, "I went to a barber the day before your letter came. Tee hee." There's an abundance of berries left. Everyone will get a bowlful to take home tomorrow, along with five jars of jam. We'll save a jar to use on blueberry pancakes when we gather to celebrate Paul's first birthday, after Thanksgiving, during the holidays.

Soon it will be time to pick apples again.

Once More to Writing *Blue Berries*

I'm forever telling my students, as John Ciardi advises, "Write hot, edit cold." But two years after I wrote the blackberry section—last of all—this essay is still so close to the bone, the heart, that I can't be objective about it. Have I avoided sentimentality? self-pity? special pleading? As a writer I want my readers to feel sympathetic toward that ten-year-old and toward her mother, temporarily defeated by being so vulnerable to her remorseless family history and the incessant minutiae of housewifery. Writing this essay, and reworking it extensively after its initial publication, still trying to make sense of things that don't make sense, has enabled me to understand the essence of these lives, inextricably interwoven, in my heart if not in my mind. But no excesses; in this case, the literary decorum should reflect a New England sensibility. I want my readers to gain an understanding too, born of New England and the book of Job, of the fragile ephemerality of happiness, earned from life's passage through the valley of the shadows of suffering and death. Exile and ostracism are still beyond the scenes here; a single essay can't contain it all. I want my readers to care not about my family as people, but about the way I have portrayed them. I want even city folk to become enamored of the apple orchard and the blueberry patch. I want to pay tribute to the Crookes and the integrity, aesthetic as well as agricultural, of their family farm. So I run the risk of all essayists—suppose readers sink it with "so what?"

But I like this essay, and I take heart from Peter Elbow's sensible observation, "What really happens when people learn to write better is this: We write something. We read it over and we say, 'This is terrible.... But I like it. Damn it, I'm going to get it good enough so that others will like it too.' And this time . . . we actually work hard on it. And we try it out on other people too—not just to get feedback and advice but, perhaps more important, to find someone else who will like it" ("Ranking, Evaluating, and Liking," 199–200). Could I expect my students to write in a single semester essays analogous in depth and difficulty to this piece that took forty years to live, eighteen years to write? No—and yes.

I have decided that even though the semester does not provide world enough and time to enable students to write an essay in such a protracted manner, or to revise it the twenty-five or so times I've done with this, the attempt is worth the effort. There is no other way to learn to write what matters—to the writer and to prospective readers—than to pick a subject one cares enough about to be worth the effort of transforming the work of life into a work of art. I have realized anew from the writing of "Blue Berries," most painful, most joyful, the following principles, in addition to those identified at the beginning.

1. Writers have an immense personal stake in their personal writing, more profound than they expect or realize.

2. Personal writing is much harder than it looks, in subject, in technique.

3. However, writers, as Elbow says, will work much harder on writing they care about than on writing to which they're indifferent.

4. Powerful writing elicits powerful reactions—from the writer, from the reader.

5. Because the personal writer's presence looms large in class, and in the text, an objective response is impossible, and consequently, so is objective grading.

Each of these principles has implications, somewhat different for freshmen than for MFA students in creative nonfiction, for teaching the writing of personal essays—too numerous and complicated to tack onto an essay that is, after all, about picking blueberries. And remember, if the sauce for your blueberry pie won't thicken, mix up another tablespoon of cornstarch in two tablespoons of cold water and stir to get the lumps out, add some of the boiling hot blueberry liquid and mix rapidly; then pour it into the blueberries still bubbling on the stove and stir as if your life depended on it.

Coming Clean

Confession as a Lying Art

Personal Confession, Take 1

Who, Me?

This is a personal confession. I am an honest woman. I am telling you the truth here; indeed my knee-jerk reaction is to tell the truth.

Already you begin to suspect that I am lying. Why should this be so?

Personal Confession, Take 2

The Eternal Sunshine of the Spotless Mind

I am a happy person. I have led a very happy life, which, to the extent that this is possible, grows even happier with the passage of time. My husband of forty-eight years is smart, successful, sexy; we go to the gym every day, have a rich cultural life, and travel all over the world. The lives of our two sons and their wives are happy for comparable reasons; their children are on the same trajectory.

By this point you're either reading me as insufferably smug, incredibly dull, an incorrigible liar, or all three. Experience tells me that Twain's observation "Always do right. This will gratify some people and astonish the rest" could be modified to "Always tell the truth," with the same predicate. If I've just told you a fairy tale, the autobiographical version of the American Dream, why don't I simply cut to the chase—"They all lived happily ever after"—and get it over with? But give me a break, a chance to convince you that I'm telling the truth, even if you don't trust what you hear. For as one of my friends observed during the antiwar sixties when my phone was being tapped by the FBI, "If they ever question you in person, not only will you answer all their questions, you'll volunteer, 'But I've also done the following things you didn't even know about.' And then you'll come clean all over again."

As you may infer, my happiness is high maintenance, not—as befits an academic—in material ways, but in support for reading, writing, and research. As a consequence of the overarching principle of our egalitarian marriage, Martin saw to it that, even in the sexist fifties and early sixties, I got a Ph.D. (as did he) and had time to begin the writing that now fills four yards of shelf space, much of it supported in recent years by fellowships and the perks of an endowed chair, the first in the country in my field. (Pride of authorship makes me want to add more yardage, but I just measured the bookshelves and have even shaved off a few inches in the interest of efficient sentence flow.) Our high-tech sons sailed through Michigan, Washington U, MIT with straight As and prestigious fellowships; from the age of eighteen through postdocs and beyond, they haven't cost us a cent. We live near enough to celebrate holidays and family birthdays with marathons of good cooking, bad puns, and tramping in the nearby woods, with a ritual stop for dropped-stick racing at the "Pooh-stick bridge." Next summer as a family we'll tackle the Alps, after I finish a five-week teaching stint in Florence.

Basta! How could the four yards of publications, the bad puns, and the Pooh-stick bridge fail to convince you that I'm telling the truth in these and all the other details? Yet I surmise that what I've just confessed represents a set of truths that, even if you share such abundant good fortune, you will reject as autobiography. Is my story really, as Twain observes, "stranger than fiction"? Does happiness automatically deserve distrust? derision? Perhaps you even hate me, an innocent you've never met—not for having such a happy life, but for acknowledging it. Admit it—what you'd really like to hear more about is the eavesdropping of the FBI snoops—what I did to warrant this, and if I got into hot water, how deep.

Pressures to Lie: Media vs. Moral Imperatives

Good news rarely grabs the four-inch headlines. Tales of goodness, beauty, and righteousness get the small type, while the desolate Ds—Drinking, Drugs, Disease, Dysfunction, Disability, Devastation, Disaster, Death, and, oh by the way, D-I-V-O-R-C-E—are writ large. These themes are also prominent in contemporary autobiography, where secular confession (where is Augustine now that we need him?) commands enormous interest, often at the expense of more moderate tales. Sympathetic readers expect authors admitting to these Ds to spill the beans along with the tears; in misery do we trust.

In earlier eras, such topics were properly the subjects of confessional fiction, such as Defoe's *The Fortunes and Misfortunes of the Famous Moll Flanders* (1722), whose notorious heroine, "twelve times a Whore, five times a Wife," zestfully reaped rich rewards from prostitution and thievery until her mandatory repentance in exile at the book's end. This is a plot whose contours, salacious and sensual, readers love—a pattern so appealing that it is repeated today in many confessional autobiographies, such as those of alcoholics. Typical are autobiographical confessions such as Pete Hamill's *A Drinking Life* (1994) and Caroline Knapp's *Drinking: A Love Story* (1996), in which lengthy rounds of pleasurable, then desperate, drinking are recounted in tantalizing detail before the obligatory sober ending. As Ana Kosok, reviewing Hamill, summarizes, "I was born in a Brooklyn tenement, I drank all my life and then I stopped." Nowadays, as Holly Brubach explains, it is only in fiction, where "it's always the cocktail hour," full of "the anesthetic sense of well-being, the bonhomie, the ignominious exploits that alcohol inspires," that the protagonist comes to no good end (90).

In "The Autobiographical Pact," Philippe Lejeune explains the fundamental relation between author and reader: the author purports that the work is true; consequently readers can trust the writer and accept the author's claims, and confessions, as the truth (19–21). Because readers place such high value on credibility, from Defoe's time to the present, confessional works are often marketed as nonfiction to encourage larger sales, and "true" confessions run the gamut from the fictive Moll Flanders to her twenty-first-century counterpart, James Frey. For economic reasons Random House made a calculated decision to publish Frey's confessional *A Million Little Pieces*—a lurid account of drug abuse, cruel and inhuman imprisonment, and amazing rehabilitation—as memoir rather as a novel. In allowing this to happen, Frey committed major violations of the Autobiographical Pact. He scammed his literary agent and his careless—or indifferent—editor, Doubleday's respected Nan Talese. He scammed his readers. And, for a while, he scammed Oprah, his erstwhile champion who became an avenger for truth and justice, chastising Frey at length in front of a righteous audience of millions. Although he apologized, and Random House offered refunds to those who bought the book under the belief it was an autobiography, after the exposé the work nevertheless lingered on the best-seller lists.

The presence of works such as *A Million Little Pieces* continues to accentuate troubling questions for writers, teachers, editors, marketers, and readers of autobiography, for these deceptive confessional autobiographies erode public trust in the genre. Indeed, the issues of truth, veracity, reliability, and honor that have always underlain and complicated the autobiographer's art have been exacerbated in the present time. As Richard Sinklos observes in "I Cannot Tell a Lie (From an Amplification)," "It is already an old saw that the barriers between reality and fakery have all but dissolved in the age of Google search results that rank information roughly according to popularity:

lip-synching pop stars; scripted 'reality' and 'fake news' TV programs that draw big audiences; and the latest biopic or 'inspired by true events' block-buster." Sinklos concludes, "Mr. Frey has tried to argue that his fabrications, such as chunks of his life story devoted to imaginary prison stays, were merely intended to amplify the spirit of his tale of recovery and redemption. There is no doubt that he abused the innate desire by people to relate to something real. But if he had it to do all over again, would he really take it back? Or was he playing the information game by scary new rules of the Internet age" (3), which seem to call for "truthiness" rather than truth? (See also the special issue of *Creative Nonfiction,* number 29 [2006].)

Space does not permit amplification here of all the outlets for auto-biographical lies on the Internet, a million little pieces of unverifiable self-portraits and confessional accounts. Many are, of course, posted for the usual autobiographical reasons, as George Orwell says in "Why I Write": "Sheer egoism." "Aesthetic enthusiasm." "Historical impulse. Desire to see things as they are, to find out true facts and store them up for the use of posterity." And "Political Purpose. . . . Desire to push the world in a certain direction, to alter other people's idea of the kind of society that they should strive after" (1082–83). Moreover, many alleged autobiographies are also posted on social sites such as MySpace, Facebook, and LiveJournal, which are, as Kathrine Aydelott, University of New Hampshire information librarian, notes, "especially created for self-promotion, which of course, also implies especially made for exaggeration, experimentation, and obfuscation" (e-mail to author, October 31, 2006), as well as for much scarier reasons, among them financial scams, extortion, pornography, and stalking.

As Orwell has observed, "No book is genuinely free from political bias" (1083)—or biases of all sorts. He himself has been accused of inventing some of the most memorable details in his personal essays, such as the incident in "A Hanging" where "the victim turns aside to avoid splashing his feet in a puddle a few yards from the rope" (Crick, 85), and of emulating "'Dickens' habit of telling small lies in order to emphasize what he regards as a big truth'" (Orwell on *Martin Chuzzlewit,* in Crick, 113). Every autobiographer, every author, provides managed news, as I am doing here, through, as Orwell notes, "selecting" (Crick, 112), structuring, shaping, editing. It's impossible to tell everything, so—eager to keep our readers engaged and coming back for more—we tell the best stories we can. But are the best stories, the most trusted, tales told and retold, necessarily on the worst subjects? Do the bad stories inevitably drive out the good? Must I confess to Major Misery as a consequence of one—or preferably more—of the devastating Ds to compel your trust? to ensure your good will? to impel you to keep reading?

The Gold Standard of American Autobiography

An autobiographical gold standard prevailed in America from the Founding Fathers' time until confessional works erupted in the last quarter of the twentieth century, boils on the face of probity. Until recently, failures—life's losers and major transgressors—did not, as a rule, write their autobiographies. Great Men presented their lives as fully functional: rational, well-organized, goal-directed compendia of public accomplishments and success, righteous role models for readers to emulate. Benjamin Franklin's exemplary *Autobiography* (published posthumously in 1793) and Frederick Douglass's equally exemplary *Narrative* (1845) established the prevailing mode. Franklin, in his famous list of thirteen virtues, is explicit about the qualities that in combination "make a man healthy, wealthy, and wise": temperance, silence, order, resolution, frugality, industry, sincerity, justice, moderation, cleanliness, tranquility, chastity, and humility (149–50). Although humility, "Imitate Jesus and Socrates," may be an oxymoronic characteristic for any American autobiographer, these prototypical works are recipes for success, showing how poverty, hardship, social marginality can be overcome through hard work, perseverance, honesty, and idealism to attain—you guessed it—the American Dream. Franklin's self-acknowledged "errata," particularly breaking his engagement to Deborah, the woman he later married, are but humanizing elements in an otherwise exemplary record. D. H. Lawrence's critique of Franklin as "this dry, moral, utilitarian little democrat [who] has done more to ruin the old Europe than any Russian nihilist" (21) notwithstanding, American autobiographies were for two centuries declarations of independence, embodiments of individual as well as national self-reliance and success, admired and emulated. The two autobiographical fragments with which I began this essay are right on the money as illustrations of the gold-standard model.

Today, however, autobiography has gone off the gold standard. The confessional mode, particularly since the advent of popular TV shows that encourage confession—true or false, such as Oprah and her seamier competitors (think Geraldo, Jerry Springer)—has lowered readers' expectations of the genre, now remote from its noble beginnings in the *Confessions* of Saint Augustine (A.D. 397). Celebrity culture, never known for understatement, continues to up the ante for personal disclosures ever more intimate and lurid, promoted indiscriminately by publicists, publishers, talk-show hosts, Web sites, and bloggers. The sensational trumps the truth so often that readers of all types of autobiographies—primed for revelations of prurient pseudoinformation—distrust lives of principle, discretion, probity, and righteousness unless they are marred by the miseries catalogued earlier under the dreadful Ds. So, in the absence of a thousand little pieces of scandal, I'll start with small transgressions and escalate the misery quotient of my confession until it compels your belief.

Personal Confession, Take 3

Meaning Lies in the Reader

Readers' distrust of happiness reminds me of my mother's perpetual distrust of innocence. I never lied to her, though she often accused me of prevarication. Once, when I was twelve, she was out when my father called from the only camping trip he ever took to New Hampshire's north woods without her. "All's well," he said. Using long distance was a major event in those days, reserved in our parsimonious family for the announcement of Significant News, usually bad, usually death: "Come right away." So I should have relayed this momentous message immediately on her return. But I forgot, and when I finally remembered several hours later, she lit into me, "You deliberately did this to upset me." "Nope, I just forgot." "You're lying. How could you do this? You wanted me to worry." "Did not." The debate and others like it dragged on for years. Once Mom accused me of stealing her current issue of the *New Yorker,* by which time I'd had a subscription of my own for thirty years. "But even if I didn't," I said in high dudgeon (I have never heard of low dudgeon), "I wouldn't have taken your magazine without asking you." "How do I know that?" she snapped. "You'll just have to trust me." "Why should I?" she said. "Why shouldn't you?" I replied, "I gave you that subscription." And we were off again.

I never could convince Mom of my innocence, but it was through such incidents that I learned—not to lie, just not to tell the whole truth. What my mother didn't know wouldn't hurt me. I didn't smoke, although our house reeked of my mother's cigarette smoke and my father's dead cigars; nothing to discuss there. I didn't drink; ditto. But I did learn in secret to drive on my boyfriend's ancient Model A Ford, a simple crate that wouldn't go over twenty-five miles an hour flat out, and tooled on home after school one day sporting my brand new driver's license. There were other conspicuous omissions in the edited narrative of my relationship with this youth who hunted, fished, built dories, and read no books with his blazing blue eyes, but I could not at the time acknowledge the nature of his appeal. Yet my mother could hardly complain about the driving, having defied my father's prohibition against women drivers ("You might have an accident and hurt the children") by teaching herself to drive on back roads with my preschool brother and me in the backseat, too innocent to spill the beans to our unsuspecting father.

Do you believe this, Dear Readers? Although the sex life Mom imagined for me, as a teenager, then college student, then solo traveler around Europe the summer I graduated from college, was far more risqué than the sex life I actually led, if you think I am going to tell you more here you are asking for a confession that I am not prepared to make. Bland stories may be too unremarkable for confession, but must their very innocence encourage distrust, disbelief?

Personal Confession, Take 4

Spilling the Family Secrets

Right from the start I was a fearful child, and I quickly learned which fears I could admit to my parents. Photographs reveal that I was terrified of Duke, the family bulldog, whose exuberance threatened to knock me over every time he stood up with his paws on my shoulders, covering my face with sloppy saliva kisses. Family legends reiterate that on weekend drives, long or short, I worried that we would run out of gas—a fear that persists to this day. Before I began first grade, I feared I would be booted out if I misspelled a word; my mother sent me off on the first day of school armed with the talismanic "a-n-t-i-c-i-p-a-t-e."

But there were truths that I understood in my bones I could not tell anyone, especially my parents. I knew my parents loved my cuddly baby brother better than me. After my parents suppressed my subtle attempts at pinching him to make him cry ("See, he wants to go back to the hospital"), I knew I could not tell them I was throwing blocks as hard as I could at the baby in the playpen rather than gentle pitches to give him toys to play with. I could not tell them that when I actually hit him and was sent to bed that I was gouging out patterned pockmarks in the soft plaster walls with my fingernails, behind the bed frame where they wouldn't show. By the time I was six I could not tell them that I had decided to be perfect so they would love me best, because even then I knew I could never attain that goal. I could not live without making messes, tearing my clothes, or disobeying my parents. I would in defiance play with a girl whose parents, it was rumored, had been divorced, even Lydia Church, though she was a year younger; and with Rosie LaRue as well, who smelled of what I now understand to be poverty— kerosene with a hint of urine. I also felt, though I did not have the words for this at the time, that love should be freely given, not earned. Yet I hid the plates and glasses I accidentally chipped or broke as I was doing dishes and mended the socks in which I'd worn holes with large lumpy threads that hurt when I walked.

Sometimes my parents insisted on silence. In "Blue Berries," I have anatomized my mother's clinical depression during my ninth year that weighed heavily on my ballooning body and unquiet mind. As with many other family matters (as an adult I once casually inquired of Mom, "Do you have a joint checking account?" "Don't ask personal questions," she snapped), this

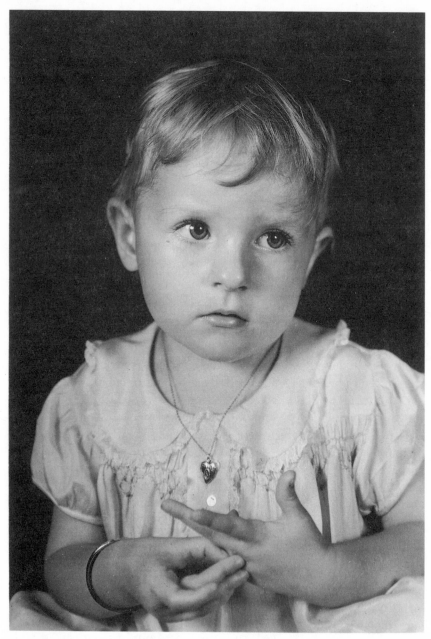

Lynn Marie Zimmerman at age two and a half, Grand Forks, North Dakota, 1936

was a secret not to tell anyone, not to discuss *en famille,* not to talk about at all. If my parents didn't acknowledge Mom's morning-long sojourns in my bed, her long silences punctuated by angry diatribes against her absent family, her cursory attention to her own children, these didn't happen. If they weren't happening, I couldn't talk to anyone else about them either—not to anyone at school, teacher or playmate; not to relatives, a thousand miles away; not to my brother (my baby sister could herself barely talk); and certainly not to my gruff father, who would simply clam up if I ventured into this no-man's-land.

Thus they also insisted on lies, erasures, rewritten as family history, and presented as the truth a version that expunged the sins of the great-uncles and great-grandfathers, rumors I heard much later of murder (the reason the noncom Prussian soldier fled the country, for "striking a superior officer"), child molestation (possibly), and alcoholism (certainly). Perhaps every family does this, but we were Zimmermans, morally superior went the rhetoric, and strong, invulnerable, invincible—a difficult party line to maintain, I thought, during World War II when we lived near the seacoast where rumors of German U-boats were always bobbing up. And full of lies as well, I understood, about my puny self. I did not know then, as "Living to Tell the Tale" explains, that I was a twin, that my sister had been born dead.

I did understand, however, that Zimmermans were supposed to be supersmart. Common sense told me that none of us were geniuses, especially myself, parental claims notwithstanding. It's not surprising that my parents loved William Steig's emblematic *New Yorker* cartoon in which a chastened youth looks up at a report card held with distaste by a man in a suit looming bulbously from his armchair, captioned "A B+ isn't good enough for a Zimmerman." No lie, that was the actual name in the cartoon. My parents made dozens of copies of "the B+ joke," which would arrive, anonymously, through the generations, at midterm and final exam times. They referred often to their own superior academic records; my father proudly wore his Tau Beta Pi key and served as faculty adviser to Sigma Xi at UNH. The implications of the fact that all of his many books and periodicals were self-published dawned on me only gradually, as I myself became an academic. And it was a surprise to discover, when sorting family papers as my mother was dying, her final transcript from the University of Michigan, 1933, her cumulative GPA barely a B, with a C in freshman English.

Truth and Consequences

There. I've come clean; every word I've said is true. I've confessed to you—complete strangers—childhood fears, family secrets, taboo topics great and small. And, paradox of paradoxes, I've acknowledged great and abiding happiness; do you interpret this as confession, boasting, or simple statement of fact? Yet the ethos of our time is calculated to engender cynical suspicion of the good, the true, and the beautiful; big, bad confessional lies drive out simple truth. So do you really think I'm lying, that life can never really be this good? (I myself wonder if to admit to joy in print isn't tempting fate, that the gods will surely punish this disclosure.)

Zap! Last night, rushing to reach the Shaboo Jazz Festival, where a friend was playing bass, I tripped over a spike sticking out of an unfamiliar sidewalk and fell full on my face, wrenching my shoulder in addition to banging up hands, knees, elbows, nose, and chin. I have arisen, bloody and swollen and shaking, from long hours in the emergency room to tackle this copyedited manuscript. And four months later I am correcting page proofs with my arm in a sling, the aftermath of rotator cuff surgery. I try to sleep sitting up, for I have not been able to lie down for twenty-seven days and counting. The gods are indeed on the job.

All along, as you've been reading, I've expected you to respond, to test your beliefs against my claims, to bring your knowledge of the ways of the world and the deviousness of authors of fiction and nonfiction to bear on my writing, substance and style. As free agents—but just how liberated are you from the conventions of culture, taste, context?—you will choose what to believe, what to trust. Just as you will choose what to reject, what to love, and, I hope, what to remember.

2

Becoming a Writer in a Dis/Orderly Discipline

The Seven Deadly Virtues

Everywhere I go I'm asked if I think the university stifles writers. My opinion is that they don't stifle enough of them. There's many a bestseller that could have been prevented by a good teacher.

Flannery O'Connor, *Mystery and Manners*

Leavis did to Blackadder what he did to serious students: he showed him the terrible, the magnificent importance and urgency of English literature and simultaneously deprived him of any confidence in his own capacity to contribute to or change it. The young Blackadder wrote poems, imagined Dr Leavis's comments on them, and burned them. He devised an essay style of Spartan brevity, equivocation and impenetrability.

A. S. Byatt, *Possession*

Cry Me a River: Academic Virtue in Action

It is my first quarter of doctoral work at Ohio State, and as a Michigan snob I am taking the hardest courses on the books from professors known as the denizens of Murderers' Row. These are truly killer courses. The seminars meet every day, five unremitting days a week for two hours, and every night each course (I am taking two) requires three to five hours' preparation. It is also my first quarter of teaching. The only advice proffered in 1958 on how to teach freshman composition is "Have the students"—there are twenty-five in each of my two sections—"write something every class period." What they write, I have to comment on. Accustomed to the more generous rhythm of the semester system, afraid of flunking out, I struggle to keep on schedule. One misstep and I will fall into the abyss of no return.

And then, halfway through the ten-week quarter, I realize I have an unworkable term paper topic in one course and have to begin anew. In the other seminar, we have a critical paper due every week; I can stay on keel if I have a one-day extension on one of these. "More time," I plead with the instructor, a savant who publishes a book a year, on our way to class, "just this once?" "No!" he says, elaborating emphatically, "Punctiliousness is a virtue, and in graduate school you must turn your work in on time. No exceptions." We enter the seminar room, the professor, seven male students, and myself, seated in my usual spot to the professor's left. Tears start to slide out from under my eyelids, whether from rage, fear, or frustration I do not know. I try to squeeze my eyes shut to hold them in, but to no avail. Splotches begin to appear on my notebook as I take notes. Soon the page buckles. I use up all my Kleenex, then the handkerchief a classmate smuggles me, but I cannot stop. I cry for the entire two hours; the instructor never looks at me. I turn in his paper on time, get an extension on the other one, and that night the lender of the handkerchief takes me for a long walk around campus and teaches me an entire lexicon of swear words I have never heard before, many of them anatomical impossibilities.

The Emperor of Ice Cream:
The Primrose Path vs. the Straight and Narrow

Flannery O'Connor was more right than she realized. The university stifles most creative writers except the most intrepid, even reckless, the good along with the bad, in the process of teaching them to write according to the conventions of the academy in general, and their specific disciplines in particular. That is the thesis of this essay. The more advanced the degree (except for the small percentage of English majors who land in graduate creative writing programs), the more firmly embedded does the student become in the literary conventions of the discipline of the major, anchored by the seven deadly virtues of academic life. These are, as I will explain below, duty, rationality, conformity/conventionality, efficiency, order, economy. And, oh yes, punctuality. In fact, the academy, like any other bureaucracy or large organizational system, can't run without these virtues. All are the hallmarks of the conventional degrees in English literature that concentrate on literary criticism—the only game in town when I was in grad school.

But these very characteristics that make one a good academic (or a good bureaucrat or a good citizen) promise to stifle the creativity necessary to write novels, poetry, drama, and creative nonfiction of quality, the primary texts that give critics something to write about. The writing of a critical article or book chapter generally proceeds according to logical, rational means (allowing for the occasional but necessary Aha! insight) and yields a fairly prescriptive argumentative format. Whereas the critic starts with the subject text at hand (often buttressed by other theoretical and critical texts), the creative writer starts with the blank sheet of paper, which John Updike sees "as radiant, the sun rising in the morning," moving by fits and starts through experimental combinations of mind and heart, insight and association, sound and rhythm and sense to produce writing that is both novel and valuable (see Flaherty, sec. B, 6–7). Innovation is a risky, unruly, passionate, and uncertain process, accommodating the disorder and inefficiency of randomness and the necessary time-out for reflection and revision. Though we could call these antitheses to the deadly virtues the "seven lively sins," the count would be inexact.

It should be clear that for most people, literary criticism is intellectually much easier than creative writing. Whereas creative writing sprawls over space and time, literary criticism is more compact, its process less variable, its outcome more predictable. Thus, as a more efficient, more manageable enterprise, criticism becomes the default choice of all but the boldest, most independent students. Indeed, if students are as timid as I was, even in graduate school (I finished my doctorate in English at Michigan, starting again from scratch after the year's exile at Ohio State, and I always turned my papers in on time, no extensions, no incompletes) and long afterward, they will be brainwashed to collaborate with the very suppressors of their attempts at creative risk taking. They can't help it.

I use myself as a case in point, representative of all students who majored in English because they loved to write, aspired to become Famous Authors, and who wimped out, ending up instead as English professors. We have met these people as caricatures in Garrison Keillor's Professional Organization of English Majors, the overly polite, grammatically correct nerds who write vapid couplets, jejune stories, and end up isolated and impecunious, working at McDonald's and hoping in vain for a publisher, any publisher, to recognize their uncertain talent. Like many, I had hopes of publishing novels or poetry, though what I was actually writing would today have been called creative nonfiction—at the time, a genre without a name, despite the work of distinguished essayists such as E. B. White, James Baldwin, and Virginia Woolf. Like Molière's Bourgeois Gentleman, who was surprised to learn that he'd been speaking prose all his life, a label would have helped to legitimate what I considered a suspect, if not outlaw, activity.

I went to college to become a Great Writer. Of course there were other reasons; I wanted to get away from home and a boring boyfriend, in particular. I had the tools—a brand new Smith Corona portable typewriter and a dictionary. As a chronic reader and writer from an early age, I had the will. And I had the affirmation, for throughout twelve years of New Hampshire public schooling there was plenty of corroboration that I was a good writer—teachers' accolades, editorship of the school literary magazine and paper (*The School Spirit*, what else?), and a plethora of writing prizes. I fully expected to emerge in four years with a B.A., well on my way to greatness, even though I didn't know what that meant or how to get there. That was what college would teach me.

So I enrolled in a creative writing course every semester—fiction, essays, drama—all from senior faculty with distinguished reputations, though they never read us what they wrote, as I have since begun to do with my own students, in judicious snatches. I expected them to be the hardest courses I was taking (eschewing slogans and gimmicks, I soon dropped the advertising course as too easy and insubstantial), and they were indeed tough and exhilarating. There were no rules, formulas, or formats, just the messy process of experimentation—does it sound better this way? Or that? Is this character convincing? Does the setting suit the subject? Even more important, is it a good story? If so, why? Or why not? Toughest of all, why would readers care about this? So what?

In creative writing courses, and only in these courses and in Philosophy of Ethics, was my understanding of the world as I was coming to know it validated, through writing written (and read) as much from the heart as from the head. For creative writing courses honored the expressions of feeling, intuition, imagination, experimentation, the associative leaps and bounds. All other courses, irrespective of their disciplines—English, history, biology, geology, statistics, economics, political science—proceeded by "logos, linearity, conjunction, formulation" (Root, 18), thereby offering a rational understanding even of the essence of an irrational universe. Understanding the logic was easy. So was translating it into the conventional, usually argumentative, academic paper in which I deliberately took issue with the conventional wisdom (including the teacher's), marching through Georgia with the thesis up front followed by several major points, each buttressed by evidence that led inevitably to a conclusion, reasonable, appropriate, and certain. It was a lot more fun to follow the meandering path of creative writing, and exhilarating to do the hard work of listening at the "deep heart's core" that reading Yeats was helping me to understand.

As we read our works in progress (how grand that sounded) in class, I was also paying careful, elaborately casual, attention to the other students. Was their writing better than mine? worse? Those with distinctive and unusual talent, such as Marge Piercy and Anne Stevenson, frightened me; they were so good and so original and I knew I was neither. Dressed in black turtlenecks and long flowing skirts, in contrast to my preppy plaids and Peter Pan collars, they looked like real writers. They behaved like real writers, too; I suspected them of taking lovers instead of dating boys. They must have lived on cigarettes and black coffee. Their very presence kept the class on knife edge for fear of comparisons that would wither inept manuscripts to ash. That I wrote better than the rest of our ultimately forgettable classmates didn't matter; I was looking at world class.

I was also looking for hints from my professors. Could I make it as a writer? I never dared to ask outright. Although I earned As in every course, the only faculty member who explicitly urged me as an undergraduate to become a writer was my violin teacher—and he had never seen a syllable I wrote. Only my freshman English teacher encouraged me to enter the Hopwood contest, Michigan's prestigious writing competition endowed by the author of the Broadway smash hit of 1921, *Getting Gertie's Garter,* and open to students at all levels. Some sophisticates enrolled in the master's program just so they could compete for the thousands of dollars in Hopwood prizes, but having lost at the freshman level with a sophomoric satire on my hometown, I never dared to submit any other work. The acerbic voice of my Inner Critic continually overrode the External Critics' esteem. For a number of those A grades were actually A pluses. The teachers' pencilled comments, "publish this," implied that I knew how to go about doing so. But in fact I hadn't a clue.

Moreover, in my junior year I won cash prizes in the *Mademoiselle* College Board Contest for both fiction and nonfiction—the only double prizewinner in this prestigious national contest immortalized by Sylvia Plath (herself a double prizewinner two years earlier) in delicious send-up in *The Bell Jar.* I paid more attention, however, to the fact that, despite these awards, I and I alone among the prizewinners was not invited to go to New York to serve as a guest editor. Gail Greene, another student in my fiction class, whose name morphed that semester to Gayle and then quickly to Gael, went instead, thereby filling what I surmised was Michigan's quota. As a stringer for the *Detroit Free Press,* she was surely more sophisticated than I, though I did not believe she was a better writer. Still smarting from the news of her win and my loss that had arrived in a cute pink envelope the hour before our class met, I offered congratulations, hoping she wouldn't notice the catch in my throat. "Yeah," she replied, looking out the window where the sun rose and set in the direction of the Hudson River, rather than the Huron, "Well, thanks"—the only three words she cast in my direction during the entire semester. My opinion notwithstanding, Greene clearly had the right stuff, serving thirty-four years as *New York Magazine's* restaurant critic, her celebrity abetted by the titillating *Blue Skies, No Candy* (1976). Would a stint as *Mademoiselle* guest editor have provided the validation I sought as a writer and changed my life, as it may have done for Greene? It's impossible to know.

Ode to Duty: Academic Writing and the Seven Deadly Virtues

When I close my eyes I can see the Steinberg cartoon in vivid colors, a sprightly little girl speaking in bright lines, arabesques, and curlicues that form flowers and butterflies floating over her head. The bulky man to whom she sends these expressions of joy replies, straight black lines slashing through the dancing colors. That man could be my father, Oswald Theodore Wilhelm Zimmerman (nickname of "Odd"), ever and always reminding me to do my duty: "If there is a conflict between what you want to do and what you ought to do, you *must* do what you ought to do!" When as a sophomore I first encountered Wordsworth's "Ode to Duty"—beginning "Stern Daughter of the Voice of God!"—I automatically substituted "Odd" for the deity, immediately recognizing that it was my father who would apply "the rod/To check the erring, and reprove," just as he had always done, in sarcasm and in scorn.

So here I will do my duty to my readers, just as I promised, and anatomize the characteristics of the seven deadly virtues and their influence on writers in the academy. Make no mistake. In bureaucratic contexts, these qualities are genuine virtues, necessary to the efficient and economical running of the academy or any other budget- or calendar-driven organization. What establishment, including the family, is immune to these concerns? Nevertheless these seven deadly virtues can combine to derail if not to kill off entirely the uncertain or duty-bound writer's creativity, especially when confronted with the juggernaut of academic writing coming down and always coming down the track.

Duty. *Duty* is the umbrella deadly virtue, for it encompasses a moral obligation to practice several other deadly virtues in the course of meeting one's responsibilities and the deadlines signaled by *punctuality.* Among these significant aspects of duty are the exercise of *rationality; conformity* to middleclass morality; and *conventionality,* adherence to the norms of one's academic discipline—the latter two characteristics intertwined in academic writing. I am surprised to note, in the *American Heritage Dictionary* definition of duty, meanings 6a, "The work performed by a machine under specified conditions," and 6b, "A measure of efficiency expressed as the amount of work done per unit of energy used." In fact, if one construes the writer as a word-producing machine the definition fits very well, and *efficiency,* along with *economy,* its corollary, may be regarded as other duties of the writer.

Rationality. The academy purports to be nothing if not rational. The writer is supposed to sound rational, not emotional, and maintain professional distance from the subject, not allowing love, hate, enthusiasm, or other emotional reactions to the topic to bleed into the discussion. Thus the dutiful academic writer, whether student or faculty researcher, is constrained to write rationally. This work is usually construed as argumentative writing, critical or otherwise. It is organized according to a logical plan and proceeds by a series of logical steps to a logical conclusion. As a consequence, even when talking about others' creative writing, it is rare for the critic to incorporate creative segments—say narrative, dialogue, or poetry—in a critical piece, let alone to write the entire piece in a creative mode. To do so might, *quelle horreur,* signal the operation of a host of nonrational elements, including the imagination, passion, and play of the creative writer instead of the dead seriousness that dominates academic discourse, as A. S. Byatt's Blackadder learned to his detriment (see epigraph).

Some editorial policies expressly forbid creative writing in critical dissertations or journals; others discourage it. A few journals, such as *College English* and *College Composition and Communication,* in the past decade have, on rare occasions, allowed authors such as Nancy Sommers, Wendy Bishop, and myself to tell true stories or to write hybrids of creative nonfiction and analytic writing. As a formal acknowledgment that there are valid ways beyond the rational of making, understanding, and transmitting knowledge, in 1993 *JAEPL,* the *Journal for the Assembly for Expanded Perspectives on Learning,* was established to provide a forum that—through encouraging explorations of "aesthetic, emotional, and moral intelligence; archetypes; body wisdom . . . silence; spirituality; and visualization"—would extend "the frontiers of teaching and learning beyond traditional disciplines and methodologies" based on rationality and order (volume 9, inside cover). This journal, sponsored by the National Council of Teachers of English, manifests a number of the values and ideals validated by current research in positive psychology and discussed in recent issues (January 2000, March 2001) of the *American Psychologist* devoted to "happiness, excellence, and optimal human functioning" (theme of volume 55, number 1).

This is not to say that creative writing is neither rational nor analytic, or that the creative writer lacks intellectual seriousness, severity, rigor, or commitment to the subject at hand. I am only arguing (yes!) that these qualities are cloaked in the freedom of invention and form and suppleness of voice that characterize creative writing. William H. Gass contends that critical writing is far less rational than it purports to be, that it is in fact a "veritable Michelin of misdirection; for the article pretends that everything is clear, that its argument is unassailable, that there are no soggy patches, no illicit inferences, no illegitimate connections; it furnishes seals of approval and underwriters' guarantees" ("Emerson and the Essay," 25). But to pursue this line of thought is, alas, beyond the scope of this essay.

CONFORMITY, CONVENTIONALITY, and their consequent predictability—though anathema to creative works except the most formulaic westerns, detective stories, or bodice rippers—are the necessary hallmarks of respectable academic writing. Academic readers expect academic writing to exhibit decorum and propriety appropriate to their discipline. When they are reading for substance they cannot afford to be distracted by departures from conventional form and style, what my agriculture colleagues object to as "flowery writing." To violate the conventions of the discipline in which one is writing is to mark the writer as either highly naive* or very unprofessional. Or so the academy believes. Arabesques and pirouettes, however graceful, are not encouraged.

Nor is the author's individual, human voice generally welcome, particularly in papers written by teams of authors, as in the hard sciences. Gass observes that such writing must appear voiceless, faceless, "complete and straightforward and footnoted and useful and certain" even when it is not, its polish "like that of the scrubbed step" ("Emerson," 25). This suppression of the self, which might otherwise be manifested in the individual writer's voice and distinctive features of syntax and vocabulary, has the effect of making a given piece of academic writing sound like every other piece in the same field. For a single writer's voice to speak out would be to speak out of turn and thus be regarded as intemperate, immoderate—calling attention to the speaker rather than where it properly belongs, on the subject.

Again the same journals that allow for affective presentations also allow their contributors, instead of writing exclusively in critical jargon, to use their own, identifiable voices, for which such authors as Peter Elbow in composition studies and Nancy K. Miller in autobiography criticism have become recognized. In general, the author's untenured status dictates conformity to disciplinary conventions. Although the safety of tenure might encourage authors to come out as human beings, the decade or more of forced compliance in graduate school and on the job is much more likely to instill future adherence to the rules than to encourage romantic rebellion, especially when other academic rewards depend on continuing to play by those very conventions. My colleague, geologist Bob Thorson, has explained to me that his award-winning *Stone by Stone: The Magnificent History in New England's Stone Walls*, though 287 pages including notes and bibliography,

---

*An example must suffice, though in true essayistic spirit I apologize for using an footnote and the necessary citations as well. Now for the peroration. In general, to claim in a critical paper on Shakespeare that "Shakespeare was a great writer," though true, is considered a mark of critical naïveté, for everyone (however that is determined) knows this. Nevertheless if a noted critic, say Stanley Fish, were to make that claim, the cognoscenti would attribute this to extreme sophistication—since he couldn't possibly be that naive—and try to puzzle out what arcane meaning he intended by making such an obvious statement.

"counts as much as one article" in merit-raise calculations because it's written for a general audience rather than specialist peers.

EFFICIENCY, ECONOMY. Prudent academic writers squander neither time ("time is money") nor words. *"Omit needless words,"* emphasize Strunk and White, in the enduring *Elements of Style;* "A sentence should contain no unnecessary words, a paragraph no unnecessary sentences" (23). In *A Writer's Companion,* Richard Marius reiterates, "Professional writers are efficient. They use as few words as possible to say what they want to say. They use short words rather than long ones when the short words express their meaning just as well. They get to the point quickly" (663). This advice appears geared more to a svelte body of Word Watchers in, say, advertising or the sciences than to the more zaftig corpus of creative writers who must flesh out their skeletal texts in order to please themselves and attract readers.

By this criterion, the writer's ideal composing process would be equally efficient. I question how often the ideal is actually met, for it is antithetical to the unruly, wasteful, disorderly means by which creation usually occurs.[†] Thus although Lunsford and Connors in *The St. Martin's Handbook,* for example, accurately explain that writing process is "repetitive, erratic," recursive, "and often messy," rather than proceeding "in nice, neat steps," they hold out the hope that "writing can be a little like riding a bicycle: with practice the process becomes more and more automatic" (3–4). To the extent that process follows format, this may be true. It may be possible to write on automatic pilot if writers are working with predetermined forms of academic and professional writing, such as research reports, business memos, literature reviews, lab reports, and are writing against deadlines where time is truly money.

But, as any poet would attest, there is nothing automatic about either the practice or the process of writing within the conventional forms of poetry. Couplets, sonnets, villanelles, odes do not come trippingly off the pen any more easily than the less circumscribed genres of essays and novels. Even allowing for the occasional product of divine inspiration that arrives full

---

[†]Neurologist Alice Flaherty's research reveals the consensus "that drive is surprisingly more important than talent in producing creative work." As Thomas Edison noted, "Genius is 1 percent inspiration and 99 percent perspiration," but the 1 percent "sliver that separates the workaholic genius from the merely workaholic" is crucial. "Generating reams of text without some talent is not enough. As Eyler Coates put it, 'We've all heard that a million monkeys banging on a million typewriters will eventually produce a masterpiece. Now, thanks to the Internet, we know this is not true'" (quoted in Flaherty, "Writing Like Crazy," sec. B, 7).

blown from the head of Zeus, to insist on or to expect efficiency in the creation of poetry or any other creative work would be to substitute a deadly virtue for a lively art.

ORDER. Order itself can be a deadly sin or a lively virtue. It's a sin if it interferes with the act of creation itself. Creation is an inefficient process in part because it is disorderly, proceeding often by free association, randomness, or the state commonly referred to as "the deep well of unconscious cerebration." If writers try too early in the work's gestation to impose order on thoughts-in-process, this attempt may cut them off prematurely. PowerPoint presentations caricature the deadly version of order, arrangement made explicit in a series of short sentences or sentence fragments, limited, limiting. Five-paragraph themes likewise become their own caricature. In fact, any written construction where the organizational scaffolding obscures or interferes with either the substance or the style becomes victim to the very mechanism intended to sustain it.

Yet writing that looks disorganized is as disreputable as disorderly conduct in the realms of both the academy and belles lettres, for disorder implies mental laxity and shows disrespect for one's readers. Order here is a virtue, and a lively one. In the best of all writing, what looks casual, as if it were the product of chance and circumstance, simply is not. Even the appearance of disorder, the stray curl escaping from the tight bun of hair, must be carefully calculated and aesthetically justified. Strunk and White acknowledge this in their realistic analysis that accommodates both the necessity of good design and the vagaries of the procedures by which it may be attained: "A basic structural design underlies every kind of writing. Writers will in part follow this design, in part deviate from it, according to their skills, their needs, and *the unexpected events that accompany the act of composition*" [italics mine]. Writing, they say, "to be effective, must follow closely the thoughts of the writer, but not necessarily the order in which those thoughts occur. This calls for a scheme of procedure." However, they add, "In some cases, the best design is no design, as with a love letter, which is simply an outpouring" (not so, I contend, among great letter writers, who leave nothing they can control to chance, including Cupid), "or with a casual essay, which is a ramble" (15). This is disingenuous of White, among America's supreme essayists, who leaves a most careful path of footprints in returning "Once More to the Lake."

PUNCTUALITY, like order, is another virtue that can be deadly or lively. As my Ohio State professor made all too clear, the academic and business worlds must run like clockwork in order to function well. If the writing produced against their deadlines is simply good enough to do the job but no better, that's all right for most people, most institutions, most of the time. When the Muse must report for duty on time, at least the work gets written.

Only selected creative writers and major thinkers—Proust and James Joyce come to mind—are expected to meet Matthew Arnold's criterion of "the best that has been known and thought in the world" and allowed by the workaday world (to which they can remain sublimely indifferent) to take their sweet time about attaining this standard of excellence—and even then, not at all times or under all circumstances. What is premature closure on a work in progress must be decided by individual authors (perhaps nudged by editors with deadlines of their own) on a case-by-case basis, a balance between production and procrastination. Space limitations prevent me from demonstrating the deterioration in quality that too often occurs when authors are rushed into producing hasty sequels to their earlier works, novels, say, or serial autobiographies that had been written with world enough and time.‡

Ain't Misbehavin': The Virtue-Laden Personality

Even if I hadn't been the dutiful daughter, I'd have flunked the *Mademoiselle* College Board anyway. I lacked the personality of the hard-boiled journalist embodied in Dashiell Hammett; my good cheer and habitual courtesy negated a possible seat at the Algonquin Round Table, even if I'd written well enough to warrant one. I have been persevering but not pushy, intellectually innovative but not reckless—though as my position has become more secure I have been taking bigger and bigger risks, in subject, style, and technique. From my student days to this, my writing has proceeded deliberately. I've never been able to write fast, or against daily deadlines, or first drafts that are final drafts. Some portions of what you are reading are in their fourteenth, fifteenth, no, twentieth incarnations. In short I have been by temperament, and ultimately by training, far better suited for life in the academy than in the newsroom or a garret. I have wanted to live a life of the mind, but—until my recent, more damn-the-torpedoes incarnation—not to die for my art.

Whether or not I possessed the talent, I lacked the ego. If all artists regard their work as painter John Currin does his own, "I always thought I was the best, even when I wasn't the best. Every artist worth his salt thinks he is the best" (Solomon, 44), then I was not a true artist, for I always thought the

---

‡However there are significant qualitative differences between Maya Angelou's *I Know Why the Caged Bird Sings* (1969) and *Gather Together in My Name* (1974), and between Frank McCourt's *Angela's Ashes* (1996) and its sequel, *'Tis* (1999)—generally assessed as "tisn't." Nevertheless the spiral is not invariably downward; both authors have written even later works that are more highly esteemed than their second volumes.

Lynn Bloom in her office at the University of Connecticut, Storrs, 1996. Photograph by Peter Morenus, University Relations, University of Connecticut

canonical writers were the best. So I had been taught throughout college, and so I believed in the talent of at least the Major Writers, those who had two powerful names, like Virginia Woolf and Ernest Hemingway and Robert Frost, and reputations to match. Novice creative writers in search of exemplary models learn to compare their efforts not with the formative works of writers they admire, but with their mature, benchmark writings; alas, poor Blackadder. Novices seldom study major authors' works in progress to notice Emily Dickinson's fly, perhaps, stretching its wings rather than buzzing, or Thoreau's underbrush that only over time spruced up into Walden's immortal woods. As a rule they dissect, only and always, the finished, polished writings from which the detritus of the creative process has been swept clean. Beginners can't match these, or even come close. Only the strongest or the most naive egos, perhaps coupled with awards and early publication, can sustain aspiring authors at this stage.

The rest, always judging their work against the Masters, who are invariably "better than me," can never measure up. Such judgments are always self-defeating and ultimately drive many to take the more conservative route: the moderately talented and those very talented who irrationally consider themselves mediocre, the unsure, as well as those who need the assurance of regular paychecks.§ Until the job crises of the past twenty-five years, teaching appeared to be the path of greater professional certainty, and this dictated a degree in English, rather than in creative writing. Today neither alternative is certain; jobs listed in hope on the MLA's fall Job List melt like snow in spring, particularly those in creative writing. By not taking the Big Risk, I,

---

§ Sylvia Plath was an accomplished and well-rewarded writer of twenty-six, married to poet Ted Hughes, when she addressed these issues in her journal: "What if our work isn't good enough? We get rejections. Isn't this the world's telling us we shouldn't bother to be writers? How can we *know* if we work hard now and develop ourselves we will be more than mediocre? Isn't this the world's revenge on us for sticking our neck out? We can never know until we've worked, written. We have no guarantee we'll get a Writer's Degree. Weren't the mothers and businessmen right after all? Shouldn't we have avoided these disquieting questions and taken steady jobs and secured a good future for the kiddies?"

Whereas the more faint of heart would have taken the steady job, this determined poet asserts the creed of courage and commitment that even the most talented writers need: "Not unless we want to be bitter all our lives. Not unless we want to feel wistfully: What a writer I might have been, if only. If only I'd had the guts to try and work and shoulder the insecurity all that trial and work implied" (entry for December 12, 1958, Sylvia Plath, *The Journals of Sylvia Plath*, 270). Plath's sense of insecurity is justified, even though at the time she wrote she had been publishing her poetry regularly, and in respected places.

like most of my 1960s peers, sealed my fate, heading full tilt down the critical track buttressed by the seven deadly virtues, particularly after I entered graduate school, where the union card was a doctorate, which had to be in literary criticism, or philology, or linguistics; there was no creative writing alternative at the time.

Although I believed at the outset of my doctoral study, and continue to believe, that criticism is a parasitic activity, for even those who proudly proclaim the death of the author sustain their own reputations on other people's creative works, I nevertheless spent seven intensive graduate years learning how to do just that. Having chosen an academic career, professional survival required me to publish early, often, and in academic journals, and to turn out clean, well-lighted papers that followed their convention—and I liked it. (I thought of comparing the pleasure at seeing the stack of resulting publications to the joy of encountering a pile of crisp starched and ironed shirts, but since ironing ranks second only to washing floors on my scale of detested household tasks, I eschew that simile.) Little did I realize how inimical duty and its somber handmaidens would be to the creativity I also craved. Nor could I have known how long it would take to escape from their stultifying influence, although this devotion to duty did earn me tenure at several different schools, onetwothreefour just like that (see "The Two-Thousand-Mile Commute").

And All That Jazz:
One Foot on the Tightrope, the Other in Midair . . .

Tenure, for the timid, cannot be overrated. This safety net offers the security to venture out on the tightrope of creativity; of risk; of labor-intensive innovative projects, short- or long-term, with the assurance that if all else fails, if no one loves the new work as its proud creator does, the job will still be there. Even after I am safely tenured and understand this intellectually, I don't feel confident in my writer's heart and continue to crank out the conventional academic papers—partly as a way to demonstrate to my colleagues (I am department chair for a while and have to set an example) that composition studies is a serious, tough-minded discipline and not for intellectual wimps. Then, in 1987, an existential crisis impels me to take the dangerous step of coming out as a human being in my writing. Terror makes me reckless.

My husband, Martin, a professor of social work, cheerfully healthy for the three decades of our marriage, has begun waking up with headaches that within a short time keep him (and soon me) up throughout the night. Their escalation takes him from the dentist to the internist to the local ENT specialist and finally, as his vision dims, to an ophthalmological surgeon at the state's major medical center. By this time I am chauffeuring him everywhere he needs to go, for he cannot see well enough to drive, though with blind faith he continues to teach. On the long journeys to and from the hospital, to another far distant hospital where the emergency CAT scan is performed, and back again, we are listening to *Barchester Towers*, on tape. I cannot now remember anything about the plot, or even the characters, but I remember hanging onto every syllable of every sentence, sensuous and sinuous and spellbinding, as if our lives depend on not missing a thing. We even rewind the tape to recapture the glory of the best lines, again and again. And when we see the films of the scan, the clenched-fist white spot under Martin's right eye, bigger than a golf ball, pressing against his brain and diagnosed as a malignant brain tumor, I know that I have to write about what means most to me at this moment, and to write in the tall pronoun so skinny that there's no place to hide.

Weighed in the balance of life and death, there is little to lose if this new work, fully human but incorporating just as precisely the controlled support and sense as any of my formal academic writing, doesn't get published. But it does, all of it, and in better and better places. I complicate the intellectual and aesthetic demands of every task at hand, cutting back and forth between narrative and analysis, illustration and argument, just for the delight of being out there on the tightrope. In the grave act of writing I defy gravity, ever experimenting. I forget about the safety net; I just need to cling to the sounds and the sentences.

Oh, I still write academic documents, keeping the arabesques and pirouettes, the jokes and puns and perorations out of the innumerable reports, memos, reviews, grant applications, letters of recommendation necessary to make the academic wheels go round. These days it sounds to me as if I am ventriloquizing these works, trying to subdue though never to suppress my human voice that might distract the readers from the necessary work at hand. A little razzle, but no dazzle.

But as you will see, creative nonfiction, free-form essays, on academic topics and well beyond, are where my heart is now. Why did it take so long to start to play, to work so hard, to have so much fun? This is a rhetorical question, answered by the book you are reading now. Yet aspiring writers, in as well as out of academia, should not feel obliged to wait half a lifetime to write their heart's desire. They should not need the compulsion of a major crisis, or perhaps even the security of tenure, to lay their lives on that taut line. Chill the devotion to academic Duty, and if the writing is good enough, the rest will follow.

"If the writing is good enough," there's the rub, exacerbated by the salt-in-the-wound of George Bernard Shaw's sage observation, "He who can, does. He who cannot, teaches." We who teach fear that we "cannot." Yet if creative writing is important to us—and it is, or we wouldn't be English teachers—we should at least give ourselves the chance to write in the genres that attracted us to the profession in the first place. This means getting in touch with our Inner Writer, turning off the nay-saying voices (at least for awhile), and allowing enough high-quality time to develop our work. In a life full of demands and distractions—and whose isn't?—we may have to carve out the time in half-hour or hour-long chunks when we can be isolated, alert, productive. No excuses, no postponements. If we keep this appointment with our writing even three times a week, over time the writing will add up, a collection of manuscripts born to be read and validated by competent, critical readers. Easy to say, hard to do, exhilarating to have done. Without persistence the work will not be written, and without rigor the writing will not be revised and re-revised until it attains professional luster. This compressed discussion makes the process sound too easy, the results inevitable, though the qualities identified here—commitment, concentration, perseverance, and rigor—could readily be construed as the virtuous foundation of a productive life of any sort.

Some authors find sustenance, support, and solace for this long, often-solitary process in writing groups, such as the celebrated one formed at Duke in the 1980s by Cathy Davidson, Jane Tompkins, Alice Kaplan, and Marianna Torgovnick. An informal jury of one's peers, these meet on a regular basis and thus provide deadlines as well as critical feedback, at whatever stages of the process the writer desires. I personally have found comparable groups either too argumentative or lacking in rigor, so I write alone and wait for a critique until the penultimate draft of any piece is done; commentary too soon, before I'm sure where I'm going, could derail the project. At that stage, with trepidation that has diminished only marginally over the years, I count on my husband, a prolific author and journal editor, and a couple of other reliable readers to read with meticulous acuity and stringent suggestions for improvement. Then I rework the piece again, perhaps several times, with more critical readings—still too easy a description.

Then it's time to submit the work, and wait. Our initial attempts, whether creative or critical, run a high risk of rejection. Acculturated to the demands of the seven deadly virtues, we are likely to interpret the rejections (even of our juvenilia) as proof that we lack talent, that our "writing is bad, conventional, sloppy, dull, dumb, offensive"—the first reason for rejection offered by Dave Smith when he was coeditor of the *Southern Review*. Indeed, Smith estimated that in an average year the journal received "in excess of twenty thousand poems," of which he published the works of some forty-eight poets, many of which he solicited from frequent contributors: thus the odds of rejection were 400:1, probably higher for poets unknown to the editor. Yet that rejection may actually mean a number of possibilities other than bad writing, which Smith also identified: "Writing is average; we have no time to teach improvement"; acceptable writing, wrong subject; "writing is good but spotty: subject undiscovered, unfocused, incomplete"; good writing, but wrong genre or wrong timing or too long; or—what we might fear most if we but knew it—"Writing is good but John Updike's, already in consideration, is better" (14–17).

Even if we were told any or all of these reasons, and they made us feel better, what should we do when the tenure clock is running? Should we continue to send our work to literary magazines, or turn to academic writing in hopes of better odds for publication? These are individual judgments, gambles. As we all know, there is an abundance of little magazines far less selective than the *Southern Review,* just as there are second-, third-, fourth-tier academic journals whose acceptance rates are published annually in *PMLA's Directory of Periodicals.* We can continue to write, continue to submit our work to the most hospitable publications if we choose not to start at the top and work down, keep a lot in circulation, persevere, and hope for the best. Unless we have been tone-deafened by deconstructionist or other critical jargon, if we write with intelligence, enjoyment, and rigor for, as Gertrude Stein says, "myself and strangers," it is likely that our work will be published. I am tempted to add the real-world reminder, "even if we have to do it ourselves," but of course that doesn't count.

Upon publication of one's creative writing, the writer gains stature, authority, a certain cachet. A new audience will appear, strangers drawn to become friends. These days, in addition to citations, I get personal mail, which I always answer. See for yourself; just write me at Lynn.Bloom@UConn.edu. In engaging my readers I am never disengaged. I care about this writing as much as, well, life itself. This writing is so exhilarating I would die if I could not do it.

Readers also want to tell me their stories, and to know about my life. Did this really happen? Whatever it is, you bet it did. And what happened then? Who would ever ask about the life of the writer behind a strictly academic essay? Who would care? So, did my husband survive? If you've read this far you already know. Martin's just fine, thank you. Surgery removed the tumor. The biopsy, which took six complicated weeks, revealed it to be a cyst composed of the same cells that form teeth, the most rare, and the most benign, of possibilities. With his new life, he has enabled mine as well, replete with a superabundance of lively sins.

Coming of Age in the
Field That Had No Name

I wake to sleep, and take my waking slow.
I feel my fate in what I cannot fear.
I learn by going where I have to go.

Theodore Roethke, from "The Waking"

The Call of Stories

From the moment I heard the call of stories, even before I could read, I wanted to tell stories of my own. I would become a Great Writer. So I turned, naturally, to their biographies. If I could figure out how great writers wrote, I could learn to do it myself.

I longed to get locked into the local library—a gracious, white-columned, Georgian edifice shared by the town of Durham and the University of New Hampshire—where my ambition was to read all the books. If I could be surrounded by the works of Great Writers twenty-four hours a day, maybe their strategies, as well as their substance, would seep in. To this end, I plotted. I would smuggle in my battered, blue school lunch box (eating in the library was strictly forbidden), secreting among the peanut butter sandwiches saved from lunch a flashlight instead of a thermos; I could survive on water from the drinking fountain. I planned to hide in Biology at closing time, a remote section of the stacks whose illustrated volumes I had often consulted in identifying specimens for the Girl Scout "Wild Flower Finder" and "Bird Finder" badges. But that was where the man in the long raincoat lurked, I had seen him, so after everyone left I intended to move straight to the Fiction and Biography section and stay there all night. Surrounded by books, I could "take my waking slow."

What if a lingering librarian came after me? I knew the tread of her sensible shoes and could elude her. What if I were pursued, even caught, by the man in the raincoat? or the night watchman, with a flashlight of his own? or even the police? I would have to improvise.

Day after day I would run the three snowy blocks from school to the library's welcoming warmth. Day after day I would await my chance. But invariably as the librarians turned out the lights at closing time, I would pull on my woollen snowsuit, wrestle to the door a stack of books I could barely see over, and wait in the icy darkness for my father to pick me up on the way home from his lab. I would have to learn the secrets of the Great Writers some other way.

Learning to Walk the Walk

My undergraduate intention to become a Great Writer was expanded in grad school by a desire to become a college professor, a Great Writing Teacher, as well. It's easy to say now, forty years later, "Oh, I've always been in composition studies, as well as in literature." But in the 1950s and '60s the field now so vast and so protean was, simply, inconceivable. There was no field, let alone discipline, that one could name, and there were no specifically labeled composition studies courses, no research models or literature, no mentors either at Michigan or anywhere else. There were, however, ways to learn how to read literature and to write and to study writing. I would "learn by going where I had to go," for at Michigan there was the latitude, through invention and improvisation, to put what I would study together in ways neither I nor anyone else had previously imagined.

The available intellectual context at Michigan at midcentury for what would coalesce as composition studies thirty years later consisted of such courses as Old and Middle English, historical and structural (pre-Chomsky) linguistics, philosophy of aesthetics, and creative writing. For a doctoral candidate in English to enroll in these courses in addition to the requisite doctoral seminars that in fact did march from Beowulf to Virginia Woolf (thereby replicating the undergraduate honors curriculum) was tolerated as bizarre eclecticism; my adviser even let me sign up for an advanced biology course in genetics. Why I expected to understand writers' biology from a course that began with fruit flies and sweet peas I cannot now remember, but my math gave out as the huge, humming jar of F16 generation fruit flies, red-eyed and white-eyed, was passed up and down the aisles. I switched to an American literature course just in time to walk in on "I heard a fly buzz when I died"—music to my ears.

The usual route to Michigan's doctorate in English, modeled after Harvard's, bypassed the act of belletristic writing altogether and followed the traditional path through the literary canon. Of the many hundred works on the understated eleven-page reading list—one line reads "William Shake-speare, *Complete Works* (Including poems)"—the only ones that occasionally appear in contemporary composition studies are I. A. Richards's *Principles of Literary Criticism* and Kenneth Burke's *The Philosophy of Literary Form.* Yet Michigan faculty cared a great deal about what their students were reading and how they wrote; such teachers as Sheridan Baker, Donald Hall, and Arthur Eastman (with seven other Michigan colleagues) were leaders in the writing and editing of such highly influential textbooks of the 1950s through the '80s as *The Practical Stylist, A Writer's Reader,* and *The Norton Reader.* At Michigan throughout my graduate as well as undergraduate years, I took a writing course every semester—exposition, fiction, play writing, but no poetry. I would stick to prose. Primarily from these writing courses I came to understand firsthand what I continue to learn and relearn with everything I write and what I now teach to every student in every course, the princi-ples and practices I articulate at the beginning of this book, in "Blue Berries."

Counterplotting the Masterplot

I did not, however, learn from these courses what stories to tell. If anything, a decade of subjecting the Great Writers' great books to New Critical analy-sis was as intimidating as the jar of fruit flies had been. For the subtext of critical analysis that I came to understand in literature course after literature course was that, as a young American woman with a small-town orientation, my own stories didn't count. And neither did my style, always precariously close to the personal.

What stories, after all, did I have to tell? I who hadn't dared to spend a stolen night in the library did not dare to spend stolen nights anywhere else either. I had not roamed the high seas, fought at the front, or hit the road, the stuff of men's stories from here to eternity. I had not contemplated pat-ricide or suicide, the '50s woman writer's road to immortality. I was sleep deprived from *gemütlichkeit,* not *weltschmerz,* pushing the 10:30 social cur-few every night, then writing course papers until dawn. Lacking shades, leather, or a Harley, I couldn't even fake a literary persona. Ann Arbor had, at the time, no coffeehouses, no cafes, only Drake's Sandwich Shoppe and the Old German restaurant; a single beer led invariably to sleep, not pro-fundity. If there was a salon, I wasn't invited. I regret sounding so conven-tional, but take heart from Eudora Welty's observation that "All serious daring starts from within."

My roommate used to say that I hadn't suffered enough to be a Great Writer. That in my mind I lived life on the margin as the principal actress in a series of improvisatory roles in the guerrilla theater of life didn't seem to count. That I was heading for a Ph.D. ("taking a man's seat," my adviser sneered) in an era when PHT women teachers were largely confined to K–12 was the norm hardly seemed the stuff of fiction. That I wanted to do research in an area that didn't exist seemed to me perfectly natural; as long I could figure out how to do the work, labels didn't matter. Nor did my parents' label for the man I would marry, "That Jew."

My parents had never approved of anyone I dated in either high school or college. They mocked the youth who invited me to the junior prom, "He's Catholic, and besides, he's too fat." They spoke with elaborate condescension to my high school boyfriend, a voc-ed hunk with awesome pecs, who built me an Adirondack chair in carpentry class and dyed his suede shoes bright blue to match the pair his mother got for me from the shoe factory where she worked. By the time I got to college, I had learned it was futile to explain or to argue about any of my decisions, professional or personal. "What good is literary criticism?" jeered my father the scientist, and when I'd try to answer he'd shoot back, "Prove it!" So I remained silent as they condemned one undergrad du jour ("His grades aren't good enough"—"for a Zimmerman," he might as well have added) and froze out the parents of another whose Hungarian neighborhood was squeezed among the railroad tracks of downtown Detroit, not far from my German father's own birthplace. So it was not surprising that my parents treated Martin like a Cold War enemy when I brought him to meet them, as I explain in "Living to Tell the Tale."

That spring I accepted Michigan's offer of a teaching assistantship, but because rumor said they'd take it away if they learned I was married, I did not tell the doctoral adviser of my impending wedding in England. In an era when marriage was EverySingleWoman's ultimate goal, the big bang before a life of duty and self-sacrifice kicked in, mine was a secret I was dying to tell. My one-way ticket to England took all the money I had, except a $50 rainy-day fund. Martin, I trusted, would pay for the wedding and our summer of European travel. The Adirondack chair, however, impervious to the ravages of weather and insects, sat in my parents' yard until they died.

How could I dare to tell these stories, and the stories within them, that I myself scarcely understood? How could I find the right language to write about what burned at the bone? In a culture that celebrated the family cohesiveness I myself held as an ideal, who would listen? So when Martin and I returned to Michigan, I excised the first person from my repertoire and concentrated on critical papers, academic exercises that I believed I had no right to publish either. Who was I in comparison with all those well-known literary critics?

It took years to finally believe in my heart what I knew in my mind from analyzing the stories of others, that to write autobiography is a way to make sense of things that don't make sense. It took that long to acknowledge to myself that, true to the American tradition, I too had the right to sing the song of myself—or at least, to try. And it took twenty-five years of encouragement, indeed urging, from Martin, who trusted my storytelling long before I trusted myself, for me to write those stories down.

My Doctoral Dissertation,
a Composition Study before There Were Composition Studies

In a pioneering seminar on literary biography, I had become intrigued by three interrelated questions, existential and epistemological: "What is the truth, the meaning of a life?" "What is the creative process of Great Writers?" "How do you know?" In the early 1960s, these questions were asked by philosophers, by novelists, and by individual biographers, not by critics. Except for book reviews and Leon Edel's slender volume on why he was a Freudian literary biographer, there was hardly any criticism of either biography or autobiography. In that course, the students had to work in primary sources, the biographies and autobiographies themselves, and in the biographers' source materials—letters, diaries, documents, manuscripts. Everything we investigated was original, and the possibilities were endless. Everything we discussed leapt or ignored the boundaries—between literature and history, philosophy and psychology, fact and fiction, belletristic writing and criticism. The literary landscape, grim and drab from critical strip mining, with deep pits around the Major Literary Figures, became instantly reconfigured as a glimmering Garden of Eden, with a myriad of possible new avenues of access to familiar literary figures.

In quest of how the Great Writers wrote, I decided to write my doctoral dissertation on literary biography, *How Literary Biographers Use Their Subjects' Works: A Study of Biographical Method, 1865–1962*. This was a study of reading and writing texts about the writing of texts—the biographies of writers of four centuries: a poet (George Herbert), a prose satirist (Jonathan Swift), a novelist (Charles Dickens), and a playwright (George Bernard Shaw). I'd have included women writers, too, had there been enough good biographies for my study. However, I needed at least six for each subject, and the major biographers, women and men alike, wrote mostly on men.

Composition studies today provides the language (italicized in what follows) for me to explain what I was doing thirty-five years ago. I wanted to understand how the two dozen biographers in my study worked—in other words, *constructed their subjects and constructed their texts*. In order to do this, I had to read the bulk of their sources: all of the authors' primary works and significant criticism of these, the authors' published correspondence, and other biographies of the primary authors as well as others by the biographers in my study. I had to read as much critical material on biography as I could locate, biographies of figures prominently associated with my subject (Hester Thrale, John Forster, Ellen Ternan, Beatrice and Sidney Webb, among others), and criticism of writers often compared with my subjects (Donne, Pope, Thackeray, Wilde, among others). Thus my dissertation on *textual construction* involved a host of interrelated topics common to composition studies.

In part, my dissertation was a study of *reading:* in this case, how literary critics and historians read their source materials, primary and secondary; the subjects' works and correspondence; earlier (often rival) biographies; criticism; and a host of other documents. Thus my dissertation became, perforce, a study of *the nature of evidence,* and of the *methodology* and *rhetoric* employed in using that evidence. I was especially hoping to see how biographers accounted for and understood their subjects' creative processes (read *writing processes*) in the diverse genres. But except for one who included a painting of Herbert being inspired by an angel in a garden—as good an explanation as I would ever get—every biographer throughout the entire century of biographies I studied read every author's works in every genre as "personal equations," straightforward or thinly veiled autobiography. Characteristically, Carl Van Doren asserted, "Gulliver's travels were Swift's travels. . . . Among the Houyhnhnms [in Book IV] Gulliver was almost undisguisedly Swift" (307, 191).

When the biographers weren't reading their subjects' works as direct transference of personal experience into poetry, fiction, even nonfiction, they read the works as emotional analogues and psychological projections of the authors' lives. For instance, Dickens's biographers claimed that the more vivid and intense Dickens's novels were, the more closely they resembled his life. Characters whose initials were D. C. and C. D., such as David Copperfield and Charles Darnay, were scrutinized for particular resemblances to the author. Thus Edgar Johnson's *Charles Dickens: His Tragedy and Triumph,* well received in 1952 (and reissued to equal acclaim in 1977), found both David Copperfield and Pip in *Great Expectations* "deeply revealing" of "the wounds that were still unhealed after a quarter of a century" (678; see also 982–83). These biographers read as historians about persuasions literary, cultural, ecclesiastical, social, political; as critics, they read as Anglicans, Marxists, Freudian, or Jungian analysts. The women biographers read as men (see *How Literary,* 93). No matter what their stance, even the biographers writing when New Criticism was the academically sanctioned way to read primary texts always read creative works as virtually unmediated autobiography.

Thus my dissertation was also a study of the *rhetorical conventions and parameters of a scarcely examined genre of nonfiction prose.* It was a study of *rhetorical arrangement*—including the selection, nature, and organization of evidence—and of emphases and omissions (aha—gaps!). It was a study of *personae*, of both the primary authors and the biographers, and thus a study of *style*—particularly syntax, vocabulary, and tone. It was a study of *reader response* to the authors' primary texts over four centuries.

Nevertheless, and here's the caveat, because this was also a *quantitative study* as well as a *qualitative study*, it was highly unusual for a literature dissertation at that time or at any time. In it I examined how often biographers used each subject's works in particular ways. I presented the results in tables, to the astonishment of my committee. The tables, in fact, signaled an affinity with the *scientific method*, an *inductive process* common in those composition studies from the 1960s to the present that deal with numbers of things (students, papers, errors, words in T-units), including the twenty-thousand-item database of essays in textbooks I am currently assembling to study "the essay canon." I had unwittingly prepared to do this during a brief—yes, sophomoric—period when I decided that I would be an even Greater Writer if I learned about people through a double major in psychology as well as English. I plunged in by taking statistics, where I learned how to do another kind of reading—formulas, charts, tables, graphs, scores, percentages; how to do and interpret statistical surveys; and the grammar of number crunching. Although this requirement was so alien to the literature I loved that I never took another psych course, in my dissertation I was able to use what I'd learned, and am using it again in *The Essay Canon* and a host of related articles.

In response to my *basic research question,* "How do literary biographers use their subjects' works?" I *identified the* sixteen *most common ways,* among them: "life contributes to works" (e.g., Dickens's claim, "The Brothers Cheeryble live"); "works differ from life"; "works reveal information"—coded or uncoded—"about life" (such as a description of Dickens's childhood home from "Dullborough Town" in *The Uncommercial Traveler* ("How Literary Biographers Use Their Subjects' Writings," 146); and the most prevalent of all, "autobiographical interpretations of works." Then I *collected the data* (how many times each biographer used one of the identified ways), *tabulated it* ("let me count the ways"), and *interpreted it.* Interpretation added a number of *whys* to the *how* question, in particular, why do literary biographers through the centuries persist in reading poetry, satire, fiction, and drama as unadulterated autobiography? (I did not, however, anticipate that critics would soon be reading autobiography as fiction.) Why do even careful scholars and psychoanalysts ignore the creative process? From these interpretations of the evidence I *drew my inductive conclusion.*

Although this configuration of concerns may have been unique in literary dissertations of the time, its individual methodological features (except for the tables) have been the staples of twentieth-century literary criticism, as they are now in composition studies. That *composition studies* now provides many of the labels I have employed here should signal a closing of the gap between literature and composition rather than a demarcation of separate and unrelated concerns.

"Trust yourself. You know more than you think you do."

However, in the early 1960s, the fact that my dissertation was remote from the community of literary scholars and that I was fascinated by the writing processes of real writers cemented my status in exile. Compared to the expulsion from my family, this ostracism seemed remote and unreal. The first Christmas after our marriage, I had written to my parents, "We're driving"— part of Martin's dowry was a baby blue Nash Rambler—"to New Hampshire for the holidays." "You can come," my mother's letter said, "but not Martin." We sent them, that year, a present we couldn't afford, a sleek, satiny, pewter pitcher from Amsterdam, and we stayed at Michigan and studied for exams.

We would have the ideal family of our own, we promised each other then and often, and we would become the best parents we could. This meant a parenthood of continual improvisation. We'd invent our own roles and learn them, babies in arms, rather than following either our parents' rule-bound scripts or the ethos of the time. For our own mothers, and for most of our peers, biology determined the destiny of a woman's lifelong servitude to spouse and children. A 1960s variation allowed the Good (middle-class) Mother to work outside the home until the sixth month of her first pregnancy, then to put professional work on hold until her youngest of—preferably four—children had graduated from high school.

But Martin and I never regarded work and family as antithetical, and I expected to devote ample time to both. I had written the bulk of my dissertation while I was pregnant and finished it after we moved to Cleveland, with Bard (named for you know who) on my lap or in a playpen nearby. I was accustomed to working with a child in the room; I always commandeered the biggest room in the house, so we'd have plenty of space. And I kept right on after Laird (named for you know where) was born, for it was vitally important to me that our children would always feel secure and welcome at home. It took the entire salary I earned from part-time teaching at Western Reserve to pay a sitter eighteen hours a week, so I was glad that the intellectual passions of my life, reading and writing about reading and writing, could be largely pursued at home rather than in a lab or in an office. I learned to work during the only times available—the interstices of the carpool and nursery school schedules, housework and hospitality; and at night after everyone else was in bed.

When Martin wasn't at his research job, he was being a 2000s daddy, thirty years ahead of his time. Thus even while we were encouraged by Dr. Spock's cardinal dictum, "Trust yourself," we were defying the division of the sexes that pervaded the earlier editions of *Baby and Child Care*. Our two sons, like Konrad Lorenz's ducklings, imprinted themselves on whichever parent they saw first in the morning.

I still couldn't tell my own stories, but I now felt free—indeed, obliged—to tell someone else's, for analyzing other peoples' literary biographies mandated that I write one. It would be, like my dissertation, a hybrid of literary and what we now call composition studies. In 1985 Robert Scholes articulated in *Textual Power* the philosophy implicit in all my teaching and research ever since I earned my Ph.D. The best way to understand a text, says Scholes, is to create a text in response to it. We can and should introduce our students to "the codes upon which all textual production depends" and then encourage them to write their own texts in response to the literature they read (25–26).

Indeed, even as in Scholesean innocence I was finishing my dissertation, I had decided that the best way to understand biographical method was to write a biography myself. What could I learn from the creation of a primary work that wasn't apparent when I analyzed other people's literary biographies? What kinds of connections would *I* make between the subject's works and the life? Could one ever be understood in isolation from the other? This was a totally taboo critical question in the 1960s, but vital to my way of thinking about the subject. Did biography as a genre necessarily misrepresent the creative process, or did the particular biographers I'd studied fail to understand how creative writers wrote because they themselves did not write creatively? I still wanted to find out how a Major Writer actually wrote books —what I might have called research on the *composing process* (a term Janet Emig had yet to invent), big time. It never occurred to me to begin with something small and manageable, say, an article. I would leap straightaway into what I can see now is the researcher's black hole—a full-length biography, where one can never know too much about one's subject. The biography I wanted to write would *amplify my dissertation research*, rather than replicate it, a *direct means to tease out and test out its methodological implications* (again italics identify composition studies language).

I decided to write the biography of a significant American writer, embedded in the context of the times. Because I wanted to be free to test out my own theories and to avoid excessive dependence on secondary sources, the biography—a *single case study*—would have to be written mainly from *primary sources*, a mixture of *literary, social, cultural, and political history* and *creative nonfiction* (another term waiting to be invented). I would have to be the subject's first biographer. That I never conceived of discovering and resurrecting a neglected, safely dead woman writer or her work, such as Harriet Jacobs, Harriet Beecher Stowe, Louisa May Alcott, or Kate Chopin, was another phenomenon of the time; these subjects would await later distinguished feminist research.

Characteristically I chose to do research the hard way, but to me the most exciting. I decided to write about a living subject, to whose life, milieu, and primary documents I would have unrestricted access, without other interpreters (say, biographers, historians, critics, or journalists) as intermediaries. Thus I would have to be a more unobtrusive *participant-observer* than, say, James Boswell. I would have to like this as-yet-undetermined subject; why expend all the effort this would take on an uncongenial figure? To ensure my intellectual independence, that person would have to agree in advance to cooperate but not to interfere with my writing. That these sound biographical principles embedded equal mixtures of intellectual arrogance (read *chutzpah*) and naïveté is apparent only in retrospect. How I, a novice researcher, with no publication, no reputation, no status, no institutional support, and no funding, could expect a prominent author to agree to these conditions was a Boswellian act of faith, hope, and innocence.

Coming of Age with Doctor Spock

Geography, maternity, economics, and the middle-class mores of the mid-1960s were as influential (some might say restrictive) as passion in my choice of subject. My two children were infants; I couldn't go very far away from Cleveland for very long. So I would have to write about the most significant author living in Cleveland, at a time when that riot-torn city was labeled "the Mistake on the Lake." In fact I decided to write about the most popular, most influential author in America at the time, Western Reserve colleague and Cleveland Heights neighbor Benjamin Spock, M.D., whose *Baby and Child Care* had for twenty years been selling a steady million copies annually, ever since its publication in 1946, its sales surpassed only by the Bible. I knew at the outset that I would have to penetrate the myths, public and private, surrounding this person, even with the considerable affinity toward the subject that is requisite for investing oneself in research of any kind.

But I did not know a subtle way to approach the national hero he was at the time. So I simply called him up and got right to the point, "I've recently finished my Michigan doctoral dissertation on literary biography . . . and now I'd like to write a real biography—of you." At sixty-four, on the verge of retirement from his pediatric professorship, Spock was as unaware of celebrity protocol as I was. Within an hour of our first meeting, he granted me unrestricted and exclusive access to a lifetime accumulation of primary

Lynn Bloom and Dr. Benjamin Spock at Butler University, 1972. Photograph by Bob Stalcup, Butler University

sources: professional papers, manuscripts, correspondence (including some ten thousand letters from readers of his book), "royalty statements, tax returns, newspaper clippings beginning with his undergraduate days at Yale, his Olympic gold medal (Yale crew, 1929)," and magnificent family photographs. Trusting me more than I trusted myself, he provided weekly interviews; letters of introduction to friends and enemies—no one was indifferent; the opportunity to follow him around the hospital, attend classes, and sit in on his pediatric practicum. No strings. He even lent me a white coat so I'd blend into the hospital milieu, and I hired his former secretary, herself at home with her own baby, who knew his voice and how to spell all the proper names, to transcribe so many hours of interview tapes that we wore out two recorders (Bloom, "Growing Up With Doctor Spock," 278).

During the five years of writing and rewriting *Doctor Spock: Biography of a Conservative Radical* (1972), I became an ad-lib researcher, continually improvising my research methods beyond the boundaries of even the unconventional literary scholarship I'd used in my dissertation. What had begun as a study of a significant writer's *composing process* (which Spock reenacted, pacing the floor and, amidst long silences, showing how he dictated the first draft to his wife, who typed it) and *publishing history* was becoming, in part, an *ethnographic case study* that incorporated *cultural* as well as *literary criticism*. So, perforce, I learned to draw on the methods of *ethnography* and *cultural anthropology, history of medicine, intellectual* and *cultural history*. These coalesced in addressing such questions as "What were the origins of Spock's pediatric advice? the innovations? the influences?" as they pertained to what was in part a study of the *making of knowledge* not in pediatrics, but in the *advice manuals of popular culture*.

To understand the book in context required as well the methods of *investigative journalism* and *participant observation*, particularly because Spock soon retired to devote most of his efforts to opposing the Vietnam War. As the scope of the biography itself continually expanded, I had to locate the source and context of each bit of information and then figure out how to get it and how to corroborate it. My sources included not only highly politicized documents, but also—in this *microcosmic ethnographic study* (a comfortable concept, alien term)—a plethora of peace activists, politicians, lawyers, gossipy neighbors in Cleveland Heights (we lived about a mile from the Spocks before they retired to Manhattan), in addition to the likely subjects—family members, doctors, editors, publishers, parents of "Spock babies" (including Margaret Mead), and the very babies themselves, my own children among them. I went on peace marches, pushing my children in their stroller, trailed by FBI snoops. I spent two summer vacations in New England and upstate New York, corroborating the details of Spock's life while Martin took the boys to beaches and playgrounds. Our disarming entourage gained access to people guarding their privacy along with the family secrets—Sally Spock's swimming pool, Marjorie Spock's organic farm ("You'll never have a sick chicken if you feed it earthworms"); no one denied hospitality to parents with small children in tow on a hot summer afternoon.

To determine Spock's influence, I read all his rivals. To determine Spock's effectiveness, I checked out everything he said against my own children's growth, health, and behavior, a research procedure that had escaped my graduate professors' notice. What serendipity—as we named our border collie. Spock's recommended mixture of consistent firmness and love was indeed producing children of good will and good cheer. Although I couldn't cure anything, Spock's precise descriptions enabled me to become an expert diagnostician, able to spot chicken pox at a thousand paces. I also became a connoisseur of tone, as a parent and as a writer. For Spock's reassuring voice emanated from his ability to imagine concurrently the perspectives of a frightened parent and a sick baby, and calm everybody down: "A convulsion is a frightening thing to see in a child, but in most cases it is not dangerous in itself." Contrast this with a competitor's "A convulsion is terrifying to parents, but a baby rarely, if ever, dies because of one" (*Doctor Spock,* 125).

Thus the biography became a far more complicated *rhetorical study* than I had initially imagined and far more than a rhetorical study. As Spock's politics and pediatrics became inseparable, what I had conceived of as a *textual analysis* of the rhetoric of Spock's advice to parents became intertwined with an *analysis of the rhetoric of the peace movement* and of its critics. As one of the "nattering nabobs of negativism," Spock and the "Spock-marked generation" drew the wrath not only of Vice President Agnew's speechwriter, William Safire, but of the Department of Justice, which indicted "The Boston Five" for conspiracy to encourage draft resistance. I had to learn enough law, in principle and in language, to write accurately about the trial, in which it became clear that the FBI (which also tapped my phone during the entire research period—"Hello, spies") had no sense of metaphor; a casual remark of irritation—a hostess's "Oh, I could kill him, he's so late for dinner!"—would be interpreted as a threat of murder. Attending and writing about the trial, which raised complex issues of ethics, human rights, and the law, and complex and contradictory ways of interpreting these, affirmed my own sense of the biographer's *professional and personal ethics*—including the importance of scrupulous accuracy, fairness to one's subject, the need to ground what one says in facts (John McPhee calls this "the literature of fact") even in the course of imaginative recreation of scenes and characters.

Writing the biography of *Doctor Spock* reaffirmed the major lesson I'd learned from writing my dissertation, the importance of inventing flexible research methods to suit the demands of a protean subject, unpredictable and ever evolving. And from Doctor Spock himself, the Strunk and White of baby book authors, I learned to write with clarity and absolute precision, as if a life depended on it. His friendly, accessible style knocked the dissertationese clean out of my own writing as I learned to translate technical language into nonspecialized terms, to break up long sentences and paragraphs to please the ear and the eye. From Spock's oral composing, I learned to listen to the words, the music, the sounds of silence. I resolved never again to write in language that I wouldn't speak, a decision that over time enabled me to create my own, human literary voice and eventually to write creative nonfiction, so thoroughly dependent on voice and the character of that speaker.

I wanted to change the world with my first hopeful volume, just as Spock had done with his. I did not. I wanted *Doctor Spock,* published in 1972, the year the pediatrician ran for president as the People's Party candidate, to help end the Vietnam War. No luck. Having written about a popular figure, rather than a high-culture author, I had no illusions that *Doctor Spock* would be my entrée into the world of literary scholarship, as it might well have done today, when literary studies often encompass cultural studies. Though canonical, *Baby and Child Care* belonged to the wrong canon, and its author as well. I hoped, of course, that the book would receive critical acclaim (it did); that it would make some money (not a chance); and that I would instantly become everyperson's biographer of choice (alas, no). Above all, I hoped that with *Doctor Spock* I would write myself back into my parents' proud hearts, but that was not to be.

"I learn by going where I have to go."

To light out for the territory ahead is, in the American tradition, to learn by going where one has to go. With no boundaries, the only constraints are those of the imagination; the journey itself becomes the goal. Each of us who arrived in composition studies before that destination was labeled has traveled a different path, mapped a territory whose specific contours have taken shape in the course of the quest. That my particular passport to this new world, fraught with perilous promise as the unknown always is, had as its bona fides a dissertation on biographical method and a biography of the author of a revolutionary American book makes it a travel document like none other.

That many of us in composition studies have taken parallel pilgrimages along other lonesome roads makes it a pleasure to sit around the campfire at professional meetings and reminisce about how we improvised our work, our lives. In my case, the risks of rejection, exile, and ostracism have been a fair trade-off for the exhilaration of working in the field we were inadvertently inventing. Some who grant *composition studies* the status of "a field" argue that it is still too haphazard, too undisciplined to be a discipline. That this—shall we say rowdy?—field is still in the process of acquiring shape, coherence, form—a culture, and consequently a name of its own—is a continual source of promise and of pleasure to those of us still on the journey, still learning where we have to go. What fun.

Living to Tell the Tale

The Complicated Ethics of Creative Nonfiction

I alone have lived to tell the tale.

Ishmael, *Moby-Dick*

How it felt to me: that is getting closer to the truth about a notebook.
. . . I imagine, in other words, that the notebook is about other people.
But of course it is not. . . . Remember what it was to be me: that is
always the point.

Joan Didion, "On Keeping a Notebook"

Getting the Record Straight

It's 5 A.M. when I arrive at the university hospital. I mean to go to the emergency room but instead find myself lurching toward the main registration desk with nausea so profound that every few yards I have to sit on the floor of the long, glistening corridor to keep from fainting again. I must have hit my head when I fainted in the dorm room. My hair is matted and sticky and beginning to stiffen where the blood is drying, and I am here because I understand, in the lucid intervals between violent stomach cramps, that my head needs stitches.

I finally reach the desk and croak my name to the attendant, "Lynn Marie Zimmerman." "Were you ever in this hospital before?" she asks. This is my fifth year at Michigan, where I am now a master's student in English and an RA in charge of a hundred first-year women who all need help with their papers on "The Waste Land." "Yes," I say and cling to the counter as another wave of food poisoning threatens to engulf us both. "I was born here." "Then you must have an ID number," she says. "What's your birth date?" I tell her.

"I'll be right back." "Oh please hurry before I die," I pray, and surprisingly, in this B.C.E. (before-computer era), she returns in minutes. "I have the numbers. Were you born first or second?" she asks. "I don't know," I whisper. In my agony I can barely process this authentication of family rumors. Throughout my childhood, my aunts and uncles casually alluded to my twinhood as if I knew for a fact what my parents had never told me. "Well," she continues, "you were probably born first. The other baby was born dead; she didn't get enough nourishment in the womb. Usually in a multiple birth the firstborn survives." She adds kindly, "Your sister's name was Linda Kay." "LynnandLinda," I have heard my relatives say. If Linda had lived, would we be identical, like my father's twin cousins WayneandWarren, as lithe as tap dancers, whom only their wives could tell apart? But children who know the family secrets also understand the family taboos. I know that I cannot now or ever ask my parents about this Linda I have never met.

When I reach the surgery, I vomit again, writhing in pain, and pass out cold. I have always thought I succumbed to the powerful ether fumes saturating that small space. But as I write this I am not so sure, with "Lynnand-Linda," irrefutable confirmation of my twinhood, buzzing in and out of my brain. The doctors hospitalize me for three days for observation, and when I begin to feel better I flirt with my orderly, a dental student with a dimple in his chin. The intern who releases me writes on my record that I have a "history of fainting spells and convulsions." I insist that he add "when suffering from food poisoning." It is important to get the record straight, although I do not know whether he actually provides this crucial correction. I date the orderly for nine months afterward, and we never discuss "The Waste Land." But that is a different story.

The Ethical Standard: "How it felt to me"

Every writer of creative nonfiction is an Ishmael who alone has lived to tell the tale—the true story that only he or she can tell. I write for the usual reasons writers write about anything important: to get at the truth; to make sense of things that don't make sense; to set the record straight; to tell a good story. I have begun to tell you here the story of my birth records, and as I tell you more pieces of this true story, and the stories embedded in that story, I will be telling other people's stories as well—whether they like it or not, whether they know it or not. Whether my true stories are the same as theirs, or different, they are the stories that as a writer of creative nonfiction I am obliged to tell. From the moment of my birth, my parents revised the truth of significant aspects of their lives, and mine. Although they came to accept these erasures and additions as true, their revisions are problematic—at times damaging—to me, to my husband and sons, even to their wives and children. Now it's my turn to tell the stories. In these stories from real life, I aim to write what Philip Gerard, in *Creative Nonfiction,* defines as the essence of the genre, "stories that carry both literal truthfulness and a larger Truth, told in a clear voice, with grace, and out of a passionate curiosity about the world" (208).

Writers of creative nonfiction live—and die—by a single ethical standard, to render faithfully, as Joan Didion says in "On Keeping a Notebook," "*how it felt to me*" (134), their understanding of both the literal and the larger Truth. That standard, and that alone, is the writer's ethic of creative nonfiction. In contrast to the official story, creative nonfiction presents the unauthorized version, tales of personal and public life that are very likely subversive of the records and thus of the authority of the sanctioned tellers. Although one might ask, "Is it ethical to do so?" the only viable answer is, as it has always been for all writers, "It would be unethical *not* to do so." Because writers of creative nonfiction are dealing with versions of the truth, they—perhaps more consistently than writers in fictive genres—have a perennial ethical obligation to question authority, to look deeply beneath the surface, and an aesthetic obligation to render their versions of reality with sufficient power to compel readers' belief.

Writers giving advice on how to write creative nonfiction uniformly take this stance. As a rule, their advice books conflate ethics with evading legal issues. Their major concern is to tell the truth, and in the process to avoid lawsuits—a matter of prudence and jurisprudence, but not strictly an ethical issue. Robin Hemley, in *Turning Life Into Fiction,* says that for writers of nonfiction, "the only absolute defense . . . is that the facts stated must be *provably* true" (177). Lee Gutkind, founding editor of *Creative Nonfiction,* regards name changes—whether to protect the innocent or the guilty—as the slippery slope to fiction: "Once you change a name, what else have you changed?" If I do it, he says, "then my reader has a right to doubt my credibility" (quoted in Gerard, *Creative Nonfiction,* 201–2). Philip Gerard's discussion of "Law and Ethics" is based on "the governing ethic of the creative nonfiction writer . . . You don't make it up": no composite characters, no tinkering "to make the story turn out the way it *ought* to have rather than the way it *did* turn out in real life," no fudging the facts or quoting dialogue out of context. "Truth," he says, "lives in precise, right words" (201–5).

Yet other ethical questions arise, particularly when writers are delineating family relationships. Do the same conventions of civility, courtesy, familial obligation—including tolerance and forbearance—apply in the writing of creative nonfiction as they do in real life? Or is there a double standard, one for art, one for life? Writers in general urge the single standard. In *Writing Life Stories,* advice on *How to Make . . . Life into Literature,* Bill Roorbach says, "My vote is to tell whatever story you have to tell exactly and truly," though unlike Gutkind, he would change names. "If you have half a conscience, there will be the urge to protect people in your life. They never asked to be put on the page. You're not a journalist, exploiting others for their stories. But listen: *It's your story, too.* If, like Scott Russell Sanders, you had a parent who drank, *that drinking happened to you.* . . . Do you have a famous grandfather? *That fame happened to you.*" Roorbach identifies quite a few relationships: "Was your father crazy? Your mother a master of guilt? . . . Your old lover manipulative?" He continues, "Negative emotions and traits, such as jealousy, greed, misery, and meanness, are all part of the story—your story—and shouldn't be left out any more than the good stuff should be left out: generosity, love, happiness, health. The truth is the whole story" (or, I personally would add, many stories), "never half." Consequently, Roorbach cautions, "When the voice in your head . . . says, 'Don't tell anyone,'" that voice, driven by "some sense of propriety, or revenge," is taking away your story that is, after all, "your life" (79–80).

But writers of creative nonfiction have to tell, as Didion says, "what some would call lies. 'That's simply not true,' the members of my family frequently tell me when they come up against my memory of a shared event. 'The party was *not* for you, the spider was *not* a black widow, *it wasn't that way at all.*' Very likely they are right," Didion continues, "for not only have I always had trouble distinguishing between what happened and what merely might have happened, but I remain unconvinced that the distinction, for my purposes, matters. . . . Our notebooks give us away," she explains, "for however dutifully we record what we see around us, the common denominator of all we see is always, transparently, shamelessly, the implacable 'I'" (*On Keeping*, 134–36).

If "the implacable I" means that the author will insist on her own perspective in contrast, even in opposition, to others' interpretations, so be it. In its presentation of truth, creative nonfiction—like an artist's rendering of any kind of person, event, or place, in any medium—doesn't have to be fair, just faithful to the vision, understanding of "the implacable *I.*" No matter what their subjects think, creative nonfiction writers defending the integrity of their work should not, I contend, expose their material either to censorship or consensus. This position, adherence to a single truth, represents the Kantian moral imperative. Nevertheless, this principle can be abused; where living people are concerned, there can be virtue in protecting the innocent, the vulnerable, the voiceless, private people who would be destroyed if their inmost secrets were betrayed, as Eakin argues (see below). This is an ethical issue that I suspect all scrupulous writers of creative nonfiction and biographers of living people contend with routinely—and resolve differentially, on a case-by-case basis.*

However, Annie Dillard, a Benthamite insisting on the greatest good for the greatest number, carries her censorship to an extreme. In writing her autobiography, *An American Childhood,* she explains in "To Fashion a Text," "I tried to leave out anything that might trouble my family" and gave them the right of censorship: "I've promised to take out anything that anyone objects to—anything at all." While Dillard's autobiography has, as she claims, "nothing but good to say about all named people" (69–70), experience tells me that such an operative philosophy would inevitably result in an untrustworthy presentation of both the author's state of mind and the characters of her family members. Whose life is so bland, whose family is so harmonious, that such a saccharine rendering would be true? Or credible? Moreover, such familial courtesy might, intentionally or otherwise, serve to protect more than the family secrets. As an operative principle of the text, such self-censorship could easily become a mandate to affirm the goodness and normative character of one's own household, its class- and status-bound values, and thus a way to critique, if not condemn, the "others," outsiders, the not-us.

Birth Certificate: Creating the Blanks

I am never haunted by my dead twin sister's ghost, either before or after the hospital verification. We were intimates for a scant nine months, but I never knew her in this world. Although at seven and eight I read the Bobbsey Twins books—imagine, two sets of twins in one family!—I never identify with any of that fatuous lot, considering them clones of the Campbell's soup kids. The Linda Kay Zimmerman I do know is my actual sister, seven years younger than I and very much alive. What haunts are the blanks in my birth certificate and the shadowy motives of the parents who put them there.

To spend the summer after college graduation wandering about Europe, land of my English major's dreams, I need a passport, and to get this I need

---

*That there is no single, invariable resolution of this issue I have explored at length in the foreword to my biography, *Doctor Spock,* which addresses the implications of Lawrence Durrell's observation that "our lives are made up of selected fictions" (xv–xxii). As a biographer I made the ethically defensible decision to protect the privacy of some vulnerable, noncelebrity Spock family members; as a writer of creative nonfiction I have made comparable decisions in the piece you are reading. Both works are verifiably true.

a birth certificate. "Where is it, Mom?" I ask during Christmas break. "Oh, we lost it," she replies, "I'll get you another one." In my preoccupation with a troublesome senior honors thesis, it doesn't register that my parents never lose anything; after my father's death in 1982, forty-four years of canceled checks appear among his papers.

As I write this, I am holding the replacement, "Michigan Department of Health, Division of Vital Statistics, Certificate of Birth," No. 96. My birth date is given correctly, July 11, 1934. (Vanity makes me want to shave a few years off this, but I am, after all, telling a true story.) Luella M. Smith, clerk of the circuit court for Washtenaw County, has signed and sealed a "true copy of the record" of my birth, "now remaining in my office," on "the First day of March 1956"—twenty-one years after the fact. And Luella M. Smith has committed perjury, for she swears that this is a "true copy . . . of the whole thereof." But on the line where it says "Sex of child," *Female,* and "Legitimate?" *Yes,* two spaces are left blank: "Twin, Triplet, or Other?" Nada. "Number in order of Birth." Nada. What the hospital knew, the Department of Health must have known. I surmise that Ms. Smith omitted these most vital of statistics at my mother's request, for on another birth certificate I have at hand, that of Bard, our eldest son, born on August 12, 1962, in the same hospital, also recorded by Luella M. Smith, the birth space is carefully checked "single," and "How many other children were born alive but are now dead?" is marked "0."

Why do my parents, a chemical engineering professor and a biologist who firmly believe in genetics as destiny, take pains to conceal this very vital statistic? Why don't they discuss the circumstances of this pregnancy and birth with me, the single person on earth to whom these have the greatest bearing? If they wish to spare my feelings as a child, why not come clean when I'm an adult and pregnant with children of my own? If they remain devastated by the death of Linda Kay, why do they give their next daughter a memento mori incarnate, the same name? With a self-effacing sense of honor, I decide that my parents should be the ones to initiate the discussion of these issues so vital to me; if they don't volunteer the information, I will never ask. And they never do. Thus these questions appear in fragments I shore against my ruins; there are no rational answers to fill in these blanks. There are no answers at all.

There is no rational explanation either, for why two years after my parents create blanks in my birth certificate, they choose to excise me from their lives entirely. "Break it off," they hiss, their lukewarm Christianity at the boil when Martin, en route to graduate study in Edinburgh, arrives as a prospective son-in-law. Treating him like vapor, my father speaks only to me

Lynn and Martin Bloom on their wedding day at the registry office in Epsom, Surrey, England, July 11, 1958. Inside, the Wedgwood bowl–like room was filled with summer garden flowers. A sign on the outer door admonished, "No Confetti."

throughout the entire visit. "Martin," several inches taller than my five-foot-seven father (he'd have insisted on another half-inch) and more robust, "is a wimp. How can he support you with a bacherlor's in philosophy?" He adds, "if you get married you won't finish your Ph.D." The cacophony continues for months, "Take off your ring," "We'll boycott your wedding," until the real reason erupts as I am stuffing everything I own into a suitcase to leave, again for Europe on that fateful passport, to marry Martin in exile. "As Martin's wife you'll be the victim of anti-Semitism for the rest of your life. If you marry him"—they proceed to prove their claim—"we will have nothing to do with you, or your husband, or any children you may have." If they could efface their names from my birth certificate, they would do so.

The Ethical Standard: "The right to an inviolate personality"

Literary critics who do not themselves write creative nonfiction take the opposite tack, siding not with writers but with the point of view in an 1890 article by Samuel D. Warren and Supreme Court justice Louis Brandeis,

"The Right to Privacy." Here they argue for "a general right to privacy for thoughts, emotions, and sensations . . . whether expressed in writing, or in conduct, in conversation, in attitudes, or in facial expression. . . . the right to an inviolate personality" (82, 85; quoted in Eakin, "Unseemly Profession," 162). Some critics distrust autobiographers categorically, in their presentation of themselves and others around them. In a surly diatribe, "The Art of Self: Autobiography in an Age of Narcissism," William H. Gass asserts that autobiographers, from St. Augustine to Willie Morris to Holocaust narrators, are a self-indulgent, self-serving gaggle of "monsters," revisionist liars absorbed with trivial personal details: "Autobiographers flush before examining their stools. Are there any motives for the enterprise that aren't tainted with conceit or a desire for revenge or a wish for justification? To halo a sinner's head? To puff an ego already inflated past safety?" (45). In contrast, says this novelist, "Fiction is always honest and does not intend to deceive" (50). By the logic of Gass's tirade, since autobiographers won't label their work *fiction* and post appropriate warnings, the only ethical thing to do is to stop writing altogether.

In contrast is Paul John Eakin's measured and cautionary "'The Unseemly Profession': Privacy, Inviolate Personality, and the Ethics of Life Writing." This skeptical critic focuses his inquiry on "the moral consequences of the act of writing itself"—the writer's selecting of intimate details, discussing "hitherto unspeakable things,'" "'merchandising pain,'" ventriloquizing—"making the other talk" and "making someone else into 'episodes'" in one's own narrative (143, 180–81). "What," he asks, "is right and fair for me to write about someone else? What is right and fair for someone else to write about me?" Do we "own" the facts of our own lives, or don't we? (160, 171)

Eakin maintains that in the wrong hands—and often, even in the right ones—the standard of telling the truth is inadequate to protect the privacy of people whose life stories are intimately and necessarily intertwined with the author's. His sophisticated, wide-ranging discussion includes works by adult children who unmask their parents (Kathryn Harrison's *The Kiss,* Philip Roth's *Patrimony*); relations between ethnographers and their subjects (*Black Elk Speaks*); and collaborative autobiographies (John Edgar Wideman's *Brothers and Keepers*). He disparages the "imperative of the creative imagination," the writer's claim that "an artistic 'necessity'" overrides any other considerations" (152–53), giving the impression throughout that he sides with "the ethicist who would draw the circle within which the individual is sacrosanct and may not be touched" (186). Nevertheless, at the very end of his long and largely negative analyses of autobiographical practices that breach this sacred circle, Eakin concludes that "existing models of privacy, personhood, and ethics may have to be revised" to attain an ethical balance between "the rights of individual subjects" and "the moral responsibilities of those who write about them" (186).

I think Eakin, who has evidently never written autobiography (personal conversations with the author, July 2000), is too cautious. If he were as astute an autobiographer as he is a critic, Eakin would come to understand that when critics begin to write creative nonfiction about their families and deal with the problems—human and technical—that such writing presents, they change their tune. Nancy K. Miller, long a distinguished critic of autobiography, has for over a decade been blending criticism with autobiography (see *Getting Personal*); her most thoroughly autobiographical work is *Bequest and Betrayal*. In a characteristic passage, sandwiched between two autobiographical vignettes of her mother's death and dying, she explains:

> Leaving home has always been a condition, often a metaphorical one,
> for writing autobiography. For women this departure does not go
> easily, even at the end of the twentieth century. . . . The daughter's
> story reads something like this: You need to separate from your mother.
> You leave home, cut yourself off (there is always . . . a cut, a wounding).
> You write about this. What you left is your material. You make repara-
> tion for your leaving by writing, and by this act you return home, only
> as author, not authored. You've written the story, rewritten the story
> that wrote you. Earned and betrayed the bequest. (94)

Miller could have been writing about what you are reading here.

Beyond the Birth Certificate: Paying the Price

To supplement that enigmatic birth certificate, my parents tell me only one additional fact, and only once, in response to my persistent questioning as a child, "Why do I have such a big scar on my knee?" "When you were born you were so tiny"—there is no blank for "weight" on the birth certificate—"that they put you in an incubator. The heating element burned your knee."

In the years since I have become a parent, and now a grandparent, I can imagine the complexities of that birth day. My parents are expecting two babies—a double celebration for my father's double doctorate in chemistry and chemical engineering and for his first teaching job, at the University of North Dakota. At $1,500 a year, that will be a way up and out of the Depression. They expect perfect children; after all, the attending physician is head of OB-GYN at the University of Michigan. But even he cannot prevent medical error, let alone control fate. Instead, they bring home a single infant with a brand more livid than a birthmark, a daughter who from the outset will never be perfect.

Although I'd like to see this as a story with redeeming joy—pleasure in the bassinet half full—I am not convinced that is my parents' story. "You hated to be held," says my mother, "You'd stiffen when we picked you up. Burke was the cuddly baby." Burke, blue-eyed, red-haired, favorite son, is two years younger, born on the fourth of July. (That's true, check the record at Deaconess Hospital, Grand Forks, North Dakota. Would I make up such a hokey detail?) In all the baby pictures Burke is smiling; I am not.

My father is not smiling much either; his blinding, disabling migraines have begun. This dapper dandy, lithe and elegant in an ice cream flannel suit, who had Charlestoned his way through the Roaring Twenties, is falling into ever-deepening spirals of depression, with cynical interpretations of the world and everyone in it. Once the life of the party that continues to emanate, nonstop, from his large, genial German family in Detroit, he says goodbye to all that and moves us again, this time to New Hampshire, to get away from all the good will. Surely his change of temperament is not due entirely to the circumstances of my birth, though it begins at this time. Might toxic chemicals in the lab be transforming his personality, even as they mottle his skin cordovan, purple, green?

Only Burke and I are exempt from his corrosive cynicism (Linda II hasn't been born yet), and then only when we are young. Our best times are spent listening to my father's nightly stories, high-calorie adventures of a boy and a girl whose misjudgments keep them on the knife edge of disaster until—just before lights out—the Churl-Churls, a band of gruff, sententious little men, come to the rescue. I vow to become a writer; to delight readers with words, my own and others', is the most exciting life I can imagine. In junior high I establish a literary magazine; in high school I edit the paper. I win essay contests, losing only once, by writing—at my father's insistence—"Why I Am Proud to Be an American" in the style he teaches his chemical engineering students.

My father has begun to drink every night, muscatel from green gallon jugs, while poring over stacks of blue books or page proofs of the technical compilations he edits and publishes. He is never drunk, but he is withdrawn, morose; the postwar world is going to hell, and no one will listen to his brilliant solutions. Much later, reading Scott Russell Sanders's clear-eyed, compassionate "Under the Influence: Paying the Price of My Father's Booze," I recognize myself in Sanders's words: I lie in bed at night, loving my father, "fearing him, knowing I have failed him. I tell myself he drinks to ease the ache that gnaws at his belly, an ache I must have caused by disappointing him somehow, a murderous ache I should be able to relieve by doing all my chores, earning A's in school" (5).

*Lynn's father, O[swald].
T. Zimmerman, 1963*

I too do the chores, earn the As, the scholarships, the degrees, the publications, the positions, the elected offices, and the fancy titles. But to no avail. The only letter my father ever writes to me in his twenty-four years of life after I marry Martin is to acknowledge the gift of my first postdissertation book, *Doctor Spock: Biography of a Conservative Radical,* published to enthusiastic reviews: "How subtly you cut Dr. Spock down to size with your penetrating satire. Congratulations on your marvelous hatchet-job." He has profoundly misread my ethics as well as my work. Like Cordelia in *King Lear,* I can say nothing.

The Ethos of Creative Nonfiction: Ways to Tell the Truth

To be credible, the writer of creative nonfiction has to play fair. This is a statement of both ethics and aesthetics. The presentation of the truth the writer tells, however partisan, cannot seem vindictive or polemical. Annie Dillard rightly cautions against using personal writing to air grievances: "While literature is an art, it's not a martial art" and should not be used, she says, "to launch an attack" or defend yourself against one, "real or imagined" (69). If my writing has been successful up to this point, most—even better, all—readers, like the readers of any creative nonfiction, will be on my side, whatever side that is, however many changing facets of the subject may appear during the course of the piece. (However, if they see it as attack literature, I have failed.)

Such reader-writer collaboration is a subtle partisanship, elicited by the narrative elements of the work such as character, point of view, tone/voice, and selection of details rather than by frontal assault. In creative nonfiction, the author-as-character is either the central figure in the piece (no matter what that person's significance in the real-life events being narrated) or the central consciousness, or both. To reinforce that perspective, and to compel belief in the point as well as the point of view, the author's tone and selection of details are crucial. Here's how these elements work together to create the writer-reader alliance on which the ethical judgments of the work's content and message ultimately rest.

CHARACTER. By subordinating others who were actually on the scene in more prominent ways, or writing them out of the narrative entirely, the author becomes the hero or victim, or plays some other central role, and thus lends weight to the story through participation and witness. Often the writer simply eliminates potential rivals for attention altogether. The aesthetic ethic of storytelling does not demand equal representation for all characters; it requires heroes, villains, and a supporting cast. For instance—and here I am making a categorical statement to encourage readers to think of exceptions—the only sibling who figures prominently in contemporary autobiographies of American childhoods is Russell Baker's feisty sister whatshername, ah, Doris. Barely limned are the siblings of such canonical autobiographers as Maxine Hong Kingston (*Woman Warrior*), Richard Rodriguez (*Hunger of Memory*), Mary McCarthy (*Memories of a Catholic Girlhood*), Paul Monette (*Becoming a Man*), and Annie Dillard herself. When siblings get more space, as does Frank McCourt's miserable entourage in *Angela's Ashes,* they are largely treated as a group, enhancing both the author's individuality and prominence.

POINT OF VIEW. The author, or the character who is the author surrogate, alone has lived to tell the tale, from his or her own perspective, suffused with her own values. The storyteller attributes motives to herself and other characters, selects the events and details to emphasize or subdue, and interprets the context and the events. These interpretations, even when they signal an unreliable narrator (Mark Twain's tall tales,

Hunter Thompson's gonzo journalism) or are conveyed in the wild styles of Tom Wolfe (*Mau-Mauing the Flak Catchers*) or David Foster Wallace (*A Supposedly Fun Thing I'll Never Do Again*), are compelling. In "Why I Write," Joan Didion articulates what all writers do: "Writing is the act of saying *I*, of imposing oneself upon other people, of saying *listen to me, see it my way, change your mind*" (30).

TONE/VOICE. In all writing, the author controls the tone, the voice that helps to determine how readers will respond to the events, characters, and other details that drive home the author's point of view and message. In "About Voice and Writing," Peter Elbow explains that "although it may seem peculiar to say that we can sense the fit between the voice in a text and the unknown writer behind it (especially in the light of much post-structural literary theory), in truth people have an ingrained habit of doing just that: listening not only *to* each others' words but also listening *for* the relationship between the words and the speaker behind the words. . . . We habitually listen to see whether we can trust the speaker" (xxxix). I make the same claim here as with point of view: in creative nonfiction, tone and voice are clear, conspicuous, unmistakable—and therefore an ethical expression of the author's attitude toward the subject. Stories that are written from the heart must be understood from the heart, and tone is a powerful index of that understanding.

SELECTION OF DETAILS. The author, of course, chooses details to reinforce the characterizations, the point. Yet in an era whose aesthetic dictates understatement rather than overstatement, the subtle rather than the obvious, the interpretation is left to the reader. Every detail calls forth a judgment from the reader, no matter how neutral the presentation, as the narrative sections of this essay demonstrate.

In well-written creative nonfiction, there is no mistaking the author's point of view; everything—characters, actions, revealing details—is saturated with values that the author can count on readers to recognize and, ideally, to share. Thus I would argue that creative nonfiction, because the author's stance is so clear and ultimately so powerful, has the potential for being a more ethical expression of the author's ideas than seemingly objective academic articles might be, for the latter are actually withering arguments in wolves' clothing, as characterized by Olivia Frey in "Beyond Literary Darwinism." Basing her analysis on all the articles in *PMLA* from 1975 to 1988, Frey concludes that virtually all employ "the adversary method," ranging from "the very mild adversarial stance . . . to outright hostility," invariably intended "to establish cognitive authority not only by demonstrating the value of one's own idea but also by demonstrating the weakness or error in the ideas of others" (512). Because in creative nonfiction the author's point of view and process of exploring the subject are identifiable, up close, and personal rather than buried in academic anonymity and jargon, this mode of writing is more honest and therefore more ethical than writing that purports to be balanced and objective but in fact is not.

There is no question about whose truth gets told in creative nonfiction. It has to be the author's, with all other truths filtered through the authorial rendering, a narrative argument that Didion labels "an aggressive, even a hostile act" ("Why I Write," 30). What truth to tell, however, is more problematic. For the writer's vision varies over time and intervening circumstances, inevitably influenced by the protean personalities and complex motives of the people one is writing about. What is true for writers is true for readers as well; as we experience more of life ourselves, learn more, and as the world itself changes, we come to understand events and people differently. Thus although the facts of the story, any story, remain the same, its truth—like the impressions in time-lapse photography—can change. And does.

Rereading My Father

My difficult birth day has yet another outcome, unforeseen and unpredictable —another touchy subject, another family taboo. From the moment of my birth, my father, believer in the power of science, in better living through chemistry, in his ability to attain perfection through rational action, and in his own infallibility, vows never to seek medical help for the rest of his life. And, except in his seventies to have a badly broken arm set, he never does. He will do the rest himself. That he also advocates a spartan upbringing for his children, with minimal reliance on doctors, embeds another set of stories that bleed beyond the borders of this essay.

As my father ages, the effects of his do-it-yourself repairs become conspicuous. Odd (an enduring childhood nickname for "Oswald") never admits that he is blind in one eye from a teenage industrial accident. He wears two pairs of dime-store glasses, one protruding at curious angles from beneath the other, except when he drives. Then he takes them off. Later still, he resurrects the gold-rimmed spectacles of his college days, now held together with random bits of wire and a paper-clip hinge. His teeth, crooked and crowded, turn mottled ivory from the cigars—dead and alive—clenched in his mouth, and then green and black from decay. Over time, they exfoliate the blobs of white epoxy, bright against their background, with which he has filled the pits and craters. He learns to smile with his mouth closed, or not to smile at all. His breath smells bad; none of the seventy-five or so splayed toothbrushes I find when cleaning my parents' basement after he dies can do the job.

Three years after my marriage, when we have pasted together a fragile truce, he has a heart attack while cutting down a Christmas tree—Martin and I are with him—but he insists on carrying the tree home all by himself. (Mom intimates that he has attacks in subsequent years, but he never tells.) A decade later, while skating with his grandchildren—figure skating was his youthful passion, and at seventy he can still do daredevil spins and jumps—he has a concussion, but revives in time to reject the 911 ambulance. Thereafter he has no sense of smell. Pans burn on the stove when his back is turned. The savor of his cigar is lost, and he quits smoking, cold turkey. But it is too late. His throat and mouth have become ulcerated, swollen; finally, in constant pain, he cannot swallow. Linda Kay and I are allies on family matters.[†] For three years, we plead with him at long distance, on visits, in vain, to see a doctor. My mother, long since resigned to his intractability, helps him administer a host of palliatives he concocts with futile alchemy, some caustic, some toxic. He dies in her arms. March is the cruelest month.

The Ethics of Creative Nonfiction: Measuring the Odds

Despite Roorbach's reassurance that "the story is *you*, baby. It's your life" (79), ethical concerns mount as I tell these stories. What, as a writer, do I owe Oswald T. Zimmerman (aka "Dr. Zimmerman" to his students, "Pop" to his children, and "Odd" to everyone else) as a character in my creative nonfiction? Must I honor him as a daughter, even though disowned? Does he deserve special respect because he's dead and can't issue alternative interpretations or denials from the grave? Must I accommodate the views of my mother, who at ninety-three will disown me again if she finds out I am telling family secrets? Should I consult my sister? Or my brother? Suppose, surprise, a producer loves my family stories and turns them into a Major Motion Picture. Do I owe my relatives a chunk of the profits? No. I owe my family, like everyone else in my life and in my writing, the literal and larger Truth, as Gerard says, told with clarity, grace, and passion. Exactly what I owe my readers.

[†] If my twin had lived, it is impossible to know whether we would have collaborated on this or on anything, though in my imagination we would have had an ideal relationship, like the sisters in *Little Women*. And she would have looked like all the women on my father's side of the family—small boned, straight brown hair, fair skin—in contrast to the actual Linda's larger bone structure, flaming red hair, and freckles.

It should be clear by now that the ultimate attribute of the ethics of creative nonfiction is the shared ethos of writer and readers. Readers expect the writer to tell the truth. Writers, in turn, trust their readers to understand and respect that truth, and the larger Truths their work implies, even though readers may not share the values embedded in it. This ethical principle dictates an aesthetic fulfillment—that the meaning will be conveyed through character and story that will provide their own clear-eyed witness to the truth, that witness untainted by vindictiveness or special pleading.

The creative nonfiction I've offered here permits a variety of interpretations from A-mbiguity to Z-immermanesque, some complimentary, others not. I have tried to represent the facts fairly, relatively unadorned, though my choice of details and of language is hardly neutral. My writing will elicit readers' judgments, as much from the reservoir of their own values and experiences as from the work they're reading. To concentrate on the story at hand, I have pruned the underbrush of other stories; to maintain an appropriate tone, I have resisted the jokes and satire that pepper our family dialogue.

To write with understatement rather than overkill, again a measure of trust in my readers, I have included minimal evidence for many incidents, characters, dialogue. In truth I could not have provided much more corroboration of my twinhood except to tell a brief story that would have been distracting in the beginning of this narrative. Just before our younger son begins his freshman year at the University of Michigan, we attend a Zimmerman reunion at a lake outside Detroit. There are aunts and uncles and cousins (four with nice, new Jewish spouses) we haven't seen for nearly a quarter century, since the big surprise wedding shower my Grandmother Zimmerman threw in defiance of my parents to welcome Martin as a new family member. No one mentions the fact that I'm a twin, so unremarkable that I've forgotten it myself. Then WayneandWarren appear, energetic septuagenarians dressed identically in boaters, blue oxford shirts, ice cream flannels, and white bucks, their tans setting off blazing blue eyes and Ipana smiles. They see my name tag, "Hello! I'm Lynn Marie . . ." and break into grins of delight. "Twins forever," they exclaim in unison, enveloping me in giant hugs, and sweep me up again and again into the family.

Throughout this writing I have fought my impulse, doubtless born of writing so many academic papers, to analyze, interpret, and explain, and particularly to justify my own behavior. "Love me," I want to say, "Love these people, this story," even while suppressing the impulse to do so, for ultimately love is not the issue. If I have told the story well and true, the story that I alone have lived to tell, readers will understand it in their own ways and will enrich their understanding of the world we share. With grace, and good fortune, they will come to see what through the process of time and writing I myself have come to understand, as T. S. Eliot explains in "Little Gidding" (*Four Quartets*):

> ... to make an end is to make a beginning.
> The end is where we start from. And every phrase
> And sentence that is right (where every word is at home,
> Taking its place to support the others,
> The word neither diffident nor ostentatious ...)
> Every phrase and every sentence is an end and a beginning,
> Every poem an epitaph. ...

Academic Essays and the Vertical Pronoun

Welcome

A bunch of us were sitting around on the porch of the House of Theory, enjoying the cool breeze, a glass of pinot grigio, and swapping stories in actual words—neither langue nor parole—of the good old, bad old days. Cathy and Jane and Marianna and Alice. Phyllis, Nancy, Sandra, Susan . . . Carolyn would've come but she was busy being Amanda. And many more, men too, coming out from the shadows now, into the sun. We had been laboring for long years in that stuffy house, trying to untangle miles of syntax, to define complex abstractions with other abstractions, tired of defending ourselves against interpellation, hegemony, erasure. We were missing Julia; hoping Gayatri, and Judith too, would come out, but they remained inside. After our eyes, accustomed to the interior darkness, got used to the light that flooded the porch, we realized—*quelle horreur*—that every last one of us was wearing black. As we tore off the turtlenecks, replacing them with pastels, prints, even plaids, in a swirl of fabrics (vive la difference!), we began to talk of the novels, poetry, nonfiction, not texts, we would read, the essays we would write. I could swear that Virginia, a mote in the middle distance, was proffering a platter of raspberries and angel food cake, sweetness and light.

On Academic Essays of the Future

"Welcome" illustrates what I predict will be the ethos for scholarly writing in the early twenty-first century. It depicts some of the reasons for the movement that is already under way in academia, as more and more people turn to writing essays with persona, voice, wit, panache, intelligence, and grace. In so doing, they move away from writing conventional academic articles, particularly those bearing a heavy burden of esoteric theoretical language, their "dry dull voice . . . born," as William H. Gass says, for "immediate burial in a

Journal" ("Emerson," 26), to more lively works. These may be published in academic journals, to be sure, but because they are accessible and interesting to a potentially wide readership, they may and do appear in a host of magazines little and big, niche and more general, newspaper op-ed pages as well.

This essay will explain why, in addition to sheer theory fatigue, personal-sounding academic essays are coming into the light. Today's essays—I am referring here primarily to short works of literary criticism—reflect a literary climate in which changes beginning in the late 1970s to early '80s have converged in the early twenty-first century. These include: the disappearance of the New Critical ethos, whose views on the depersonalization of the author reinforced deconstruction's death of the author; the blurring of literary genres in various fields; the stylistic influences of the New Journalism; the powerful presence of the personal in the mass media, including the Internet that, coupled with an argument for clarity, has carried over into the personal presence of either superstar critics or personal publication in prestigious journals. If the tastemakers can come out in the first person, so can everyone else. But, make no mistake, the vertical pronoun is not a foolproof guarantee of quality any more than a plethora of footnotes; writers whose tin ears can't hear the jazz of language, its sounds and rhythms, need to listen up.

Vicki, Bard, and Rhys Bloom, 2003. © Ridgefield Studio, Paul F. Korker, photographer

Disappearance of the New Critical Ethos

Modernist aesthetic dominated critical taste from post–World War I to well after World War II. In "Tradition and the Individual Talent," T. S. Eliot presented the manifesto of Modernism, including the principle of authorial self-effacement and detachment from the completed work: "The progress of an artist is a continual self-sacrifice, a continual extinction of personality," a process that operates much like that of a catalyst, in which "the mind of the poet is the shred of platinum. . . . The more perfect the artist, the more completely separate in him will be the man who suffers and the mind which creates; the more perfectly will the mind digest and transmute the passions which are its material" (499–500). That this stance misleadingly presents knowledge (whether critical, historical, or scientific) as an objective phenomenon, independent of its human origin, is a deception so ingrained in the habits of writers and readers that they forget the fact that all knowledge is generated, interpreted, filtered, and shaped by personal agency, personal agenda as it is transmitted. Nevertheless, this concept of ordered, highly structured, depersonalized writing provided the critical aesthetic for many strands of the critical movements in the 1970s through the '90s, epitomized in Gerald Graff's 1985 summary of the complaints against the 10 percent of academic professionals who constituted the overpoweringly influential "vanguard" literary critics in the 1980s and '90s:

> Today one hears the complaint that literary theory has taken over the literature departments and is distracting students and professors from literature itself. It is said that the traditional study of literature as a humanistic enterprise is in jeopardy. Instead of advancing humanistic values, literature professors are cultivating opaque jargon and pseudoscientific systems. Hiding behind smoke screens of esoteric terminology, theorists turn their backs on outsiders, including most students, and carry on endless private conversations with other theorists. Literary works have been demoted to secondary importance, serving as mere occasions for displays of theoretical agility. (62)

But the critical landscape has changed in the twenty-first century, with the defrocking of de Man for his Nazi sympathies, irritation with Lacan, the death of Derrida, and, some argue, the death of theory itself. Faculty and students alike are eager to return to passionate readings of the literature they were once enamored of, rather than to approach beloved works through a thicket of theory (see Phyllis Rose, "The Coming of the French," passim). As we shall see, their own writing now seems decidedly Romantic in self-expression and sensibility, the Wordsworthian "spontaneous overflow of powerful feelings," with the twist that the emotion is recollected not necessarily in tranquility, but in the heat of the moment.

Blurred Genres

Academics should be receptive to blurred genres; they invented them in the latter twentieth century. In "Blurred Genres" Clifford Geertz observed the "enormous amount of genre mixing in intellectual life": "philosophical inquiries looking like literary criticism (think of . . . Sartre on Flaubert), scientific discussions looking like belles lettres *morceaux* (Lewis Thomas, Loren Eiseley) . . . documentaries that read like true confessions (Mailer) . . . theoretical treatises set out as travelogues (Lévi-Strauss) . . . methodological polemics got up as personal memoirs (James Watson)" (19–20). To which we could add the crossover experiments of Barthes's *Mythologies* and *S/Z,* and Federman's *Critifiction.* As Geertz implied, no single set of literary features (persona, form, style, and a host of narrative techniques) remained the exclusive property of a particular genre; contemporary authors could pick and choose among genres as they wished. In *The Vulnerable Observer,* Ruth Behar explains Geertz's analysis in *Works and Lives,* of the ways that memorable anthropologists of the twentieth century—Lévi-Strauss, Evans-Pritchard, Malinowski, and Benedict—so individually and distinctively "transfigure their observations of other people and places into such persuasive rhetoric" that afterward the subjects are "unimaginable except through the texts of their authors" (7). So powerful is the effect of the anthropologist's writing on the subject that, says Geertz, "One can go look at Azande again, but if the complex theory of passion, knowledge, and causation that Evans-Pritchard said he discovered there isn't found, we are more likely to doubt our own powers than we are to doubt his—or perhaps simply to conclude that the Zande are no longer themselves" (*Works and Lives,* 5). Do not such powerful readings of other cultures strive for the same effect that critics aim for in their "strong readings"?

The New Journalism

A number of the literary features apparent in what Tom Wolfe labeled as "The New Journalism" are conspicuous in these blurred genres. What made journalism "new" from the 1960s onward was, says Wolfe, "not simply the discovery that it was possible to write accurate non-fiction with techniques usually associated with novels and short stories" (21), but the opportunity to use these techniques in dramatic and radically new combinations to make the writing intensely realistic and superlatively exciting. These devices include whole scenes and "scene-by-scene construction," extended dialogue, shifting "point-of-view, and interior monologue." Wolfe's conspicuous contribution, in addition to a mannered style that includes "the lavish use of dots, dashes, exclamation points, italics . . . interjections, shouts, onomatopoeia" and more (21), is to provide a superabundance of details symbolic "of people's *status life*" (32), thereby recording "everyday gestures, habits, manners, customs, styles of furniture, clothing, decoration, styles of traveling, eating, keeping house, modes of behavior toward children, servants, superiors, inferiors, peers" (32), what Geertz would call "thick description." By reminding readers of the distinctive, ubiquitous, ever-alert authorial presence in and behind the writing, these techniques in combination give contemporary nonfiction a human angle of vision, a human voice, however demure or outrageous its register, whatever its subject.

The devices of New Journalism, particularly writing from a distinctive, identifiable personal point of view that pays excruciating attention to status life minutiae that earlier writers had previously ignored, make the writing sound extremely intimate; the writer appears to be confiding private (and not necessarily flattering) observations and telling secrets, his own or another's, to a privileged audience. Wolfe has identified multiple voices in which the characters, or the narrator, speak: dialogic, polyphonic, cacophonic, all distinctive, individual, and sounding personal even though they are carefully constructed personae revealing neither more, nor less, than the author wants the readers to know. Truman Capote, Wolfe notes with approval, employed these literary techniques throughout *In Cold Blood* (1965), his "nonfiction novel," and Wolfe exploited them with deliberate excess in *The Electric Kool-Aid Acid Test* (1968) and other nonfiction of the 1970s. Other belletristic nonfiction writers, including many essayists, have continued to use them, with varying degrees of moderation and exuberance, from that day to this. These authors range from the relatively restrained Annie Dillard (who is not above an occasional "Yikes!" in *Pilgrim at Tinker Creek*) to David Foster Wallace's strobe-lit essays on virtually everything, such as "A Supposedly Fun Thing I'll Never Do Again."

In "Getting Away from Already Being Pretty Much Away from It All," Wallace's account of ten days at the Illinois State Fair in 1993, his reportage about attending the Open Poultry Judging is characteristically Wolfean:

> now my nerve totally goes. I can't go in there. Listen to the untold
> thousands of sharp squawking beaks in there, I say. . . . It's 93 and
> I have pygmy-goat shit on my shoe and am almost weeping with fear
> and embarrassment. . . . I've never before realized that "cacophony"
> was onomatopoeic: the noise of the Poultry Bldg. [*sic*] is cacophonous
> and I think it's what insanity must sound like. No wonder madmen
> clutch their heads and scream. There's also a thin stink, and lots of

bits of feather are floating all over. And this is *outside* the Poultry Bldg. ... When I was eight, at the Champaign County Fair, I was pecked without provocation, flown at and pecked by a renegade fowl, savagely, just under the right eye, the scar of which looks like a permanent zit. (109)

Wallace's sharply detailed rendering of the Poultry Building as Grand Guignol, where the insane noise of "untold thousands of sharp squawking beaks" and noxious smells strike fear not into the narrator's cowardly heart but his scrotum, is a reminder of his "savage" victimization by "a renegade fowl" when he was eight. Why is the author, whose trust and authority readers expect to esteem, presenting himself not as an antihero but as a wimp? Why does he tell us these humiliating details? Certainly not as a warning to stay away from domestic poultry; in fact, the very specificity of the account recreates the scene so exactly that the readers are cheek-by-fowl with Wallace as tour guide through State Fair hell and must perforce take his side, sharing his values for the moment, if not for all time.

The Powerful Presence of the Personal in the Mass Media

Nonfiction of all sorts, including many straight news pieces even in the formerly staid *New York Times,* incorporates many of the New Journalistic techniques, though they are often more subdued than in David Foster Wallace's work. There are cultural reasons why personal sounding nonfiction—whether exaggerated, as is Wallace's, or more subdued—is so pervasive and so popular. Nonfiction is being written today from a human perspective with a sense of human presence; such writing, including academic writing, appears both more informal and more personal than ever. As in dress, essays have moved from modernist three-piece suits with matching hats and handkerchiefs to jeans and T-shirts; from "trousers rolled" by one who dares to "walk along the beach" to bikinis and bare feet. Contemporary essays leave a trail of footprints rather than footnotes. The essay, the most informal, always, of genres has become, in some ways, even more informal in its contemporary presentation of the authorial persona as the reader's intimate friend and confidante. Of comparable influence to the pervasiveness of New Journalistic techniques in print media is the personal orientation of television and many Internet sites.

We live in an age of media intimacy; personal exposure is now the normative mode because of the invasive influences of television and the Internet. The private has become public, as attested by the sad but inspiring autobiographies on "Oprah," confessions of televangelical sin, real-time paternity tests, Judge Judy's no-nonsense interpretations of individual guilt and innocence, "extreme makeovers," "reality" television that captures people at their weakest and worst. When played out on the Internet, the individual's fifteen minutes of fame can extend indefinitely, through webcams that allow voyeuristic viewers access to a formerly private person, twenty-four hours a day for months at a time. Anybody and everybody can write their electronic autobiography, and millions do. Personal Web sites and blogs allow their authors to present themselves any way they want, in text, music, photographs, and video—looking for love in all the right, or wrong, places; becoming pregnant (or not) or parents; playing games; hating (rarely loving) their jobs; experiencing spirituality, disability, disaster, war; undergoing sex changes or other sea changes—divorce, homelessness, bereavement. Chat rooms extend the intimacy. That there is a sufficient amount of fiction amidst the nominal facts to keep viewers continually on their guard does not diminish the ever-increasing attraction of the media. No longer do intimate photographs appear primarily in *People* magazine and the supermarket tabloids; larger-than-life images pulsate up close and personal on the sixty-four-inch plasma screens in our very bedrooms.

Cinema, television, and the Internet have had major influences on print media, particularly in the past decade. They have influenced visual dimensions that appear in the printed text: photographs, paintings, drawings, color, white space, layout, and design. In this supercharged environment, it would be hard for essayists (like all other writers), even authors of academic articles, *not* to sound more personal and informal in the twenty-first century than they did in the twentieth. Even if a particular essayist never watched movies or TV and ignored the Internet, the visual and verbal influences of these media on highbrow publications, among them *Harper's,* the *Atlantic,* the *New York Times,** and some academic journals, including the prestigious *PMLA,* are pervasive and inescapable. So there is more latitude, simply by means of the prevailing cultural climate, for writers who might have been more reticent in the far more discreet Victorian or Edwardian literary eras to present very human, intimate personae a century later.

---

*Indeed today's *Times* columnists not only write in a more personal manner, they encourage others to do so. For instance, in "Ants, Better With Dose of Humanity (and Humor)," James Gorman encourages scientists to present in their books and papers written for general readers personal "interludes and asides," little first-person "stories to go along with methods, discussion, and conclusions" that would release their writing from "the stranglehold of scientific jargon" and provide "a real glimpse of what science is and how it is done by human beings, rational and un-, grappling with technique, nature and the gathering of information" (sec. D, 3).

What, Me, a Human Being? Personal Academic Writing

By the 1980s, academic writers—at least, some with tenure who could afford the risk—began to come out as human beings, usually in less flamboyant ways than Wallace, but in style and orientation that seemed daring to scholars trained to consider the vertical pronoun taboo. Academics who write in a personal style understand very well that their human approach does not mean that academic essays are either simple-minded or innocent of theory, just that they are far more accessible than those written with large amounts of technical jargon, or in dense theoretical language and its accompanying unending syntax. Surprisingly a de facto coalition of feminist scholars, linguists, and neocons agree through pronouncement and performance that postmodern criticism, for instance, is both unintelligible and undemocratic, as Susan Peck MacDonald argues in "The Literary Argument and Its Discursive Conventions." MacDonald concludes, if "professional prose is so specialized that too small a circle of insiders can read it," if "novice professors and even seasoned professors" and students "have trouble gaining access because they find prestigious prose to be either unreadable or unwritable," "not because of the demands of the subject, but because it is professionally advantageous to appear 'difficult,' then we ought to stop awarding prestige to unreadable prose, and we ought to consider the social implications of reinforcing an elite caste system within our profession" (59).

The language itself of many contemporary academic essays is in fact returning to the clarity, simplicity, and honesty that George Orwell advocated in "Politics and the English Language," inveighing against "pretentious diction," jargon, other language designed to mask bias, sloppy thinking, bad ideas, and other forms of political manipulation. "The great enemy of clear language is insincerity," he said. "Political language . . . is designed to make lies sound truthful and murder respectable" (958–67). "What would Orwell say about X?" is a familiar, not-so-rhetorical question of commentators of all rhetorical and political persuasions. Thus in "So Help Me God," an analysis of fifty-four presidential inaugural addresses, Ted Widmer, National Security Council director of speechwriting during the Clinton administration, pronounces "Politics" "the greatest essay on speechwriting ever written." In support of this, he quotes the "lies sound truthful and murder respectable" (40–41) sentence.

From a post-postmodernist, neoconservative perspective, Stephen K. Roney, past president of the Editors' Association of Canada, uses Orwell's precepts, including the same "lies . . . murder" sentence, to undercut the stylistic propositions of postmodern critic Judith Butler, whom he is careful to identify at the outset has not only "been charged with bad writing, but has "won the annual 'Bad Writing Award' from the journal *Philosophy and*

Literature." In propositions adopted widely throughout the 1980s and '90s in the writings of academics whom MacDonald labels "vanguard" or elitist literary critics (such as Frederic Jameson and Gayatri Chakravorty Spivak, also winners of the "Bad Writing Award"), Butler claims that "clarity and simplicity are impossible if one is discussing a topic deeply." Difficult ideas "must necessarily be expressed in difficult language." Obscurity, rather than clarity, "is the proper medium to represent the obscure." It is "*necessary* to use bad style to be a good thinker" (all Roney's paraphrases, 13–20). Illustrating throughout this critique his understanding of Orwell's views that obfuscating language is a "rhetorical trick; a way for bad ideas to hide. . . . an obscure style is always a hindrance," Roney concludes that "Butler's challenge to Orwell cannot be justified on the grounds she has stated. Obscurity of style is still . . . and necessarily, a bad thing in itself. As for the true significance of the obscurity characteristic of postmodernism, I would only suggest that it is a symptom, not of a progressive or enlightened position, but of a vested interest seeking to secure its privilege" (21). That critics from potentially antagonistic ends of the critical spectrum, MacDonald as a liberal linguist, Roney writing in the journal of academic archconservatives, the National Association of Scholars, as well as Widmer in a centrist position, concur philosophically in their analyses may indeed signal, if not "the death of theory," then "the death of obscure academic discourse as we know it" and an indication that the academy is ripe for another kind of writing that is not only clear, but personal.

Recent academic essays seem smart in their intellectual range, depth of learning, and verbal wit rather than because of either obscure language or an abundance of citations, which diminish as essays grow more informal and authors trust their readers to get the point. Titles, too, become shorter. If the author relies on a few short, simple, perhaps witty or shocking words (read on!) to carry the freight, she is likely to skip the semicolon and its string of explanatory language. In "Me and My Shadow" (1987), Jane Tompkins initiated a vigorous defense of personal writing by lambasting the academic convention, "the public-private dichotomy, which is to say the public-private *hierarchy*" that had hitherto isolated her as a private person from her public writing: "I say the hell with it. The reason I feel embarrassed at my own attempts to speak personally in a professional context is that I have been conditioned [by men] to feel that way" (1104). Tompkins's prominence as a feminist critic assured notoriety to her other audacious confessions, among them that while meditating on the suicide of a young female colleague she was "thinking about going to the bathroom. But not going yet" (1107). This essay provoked a storm of controversy, neatly summed up by her champion, Nancy K. Miller, in "Getting Personal": "How can women get power from this

. . . self-indulgen[ce] . . . Is [her essay] about going to the bathroom? Or is it about critical authority? Or are they the same question?" (8). Miller also sagely observes, in a biographical aside that, though true, would have been taboo to New Critics and postmodernists alike: "One could argue that the [effect of the critic's authority] depends on the status of the writer. No one would care if Jane Doe went to the bathroom: it matters that Jane Tompkins is a known critical quantity, that (some) people will know that she is married" (27) to an even more prominent literary provocateur, the astute and flamboyant Stanley Fish. Defending such intimate personal commentary, Miller concludes that it "embodies a pact . . . binding writer to reader in the fabulation of self-truth, that what is at stake matters to others: somewhere in the self-fiction of the personal voice is a belief that the writing is worth the risk" (24). Carrying out the logical implications of her defense, Miller soon published "My Father's Penis" (1991), thereby exceeding Tompkins's daring in her very title.

As academic critics, women in the forefront, rushed to take up the challenge, a landmark essay in a personal style appeared in 1989, Susan J. Leonardi's "Recipes for Reading: Summer Pasta, Lobster à la Riseholme, and Key Lime Pie." Unusual for academic journals, "Recipes" is distinguished by its gracious persona, graceful style, traditionally feminine subject, unusual structure, total absence of footnotes, and paucity of sources—seven of the mere eleven "Works Cited" are primary texts. Leonardi's wit, too, is verging on mockery but not going there yet. Most important of all, however, "Recipes" is distinguished particularly by its locus of publication. That such a glamorous, groundbreaking work was published in *PMLA,* the most prestigious modern languages journal of its time in America, known for intellectual rigor and decades of male hegemony (including male editors), speaks volumes. How astonishing to find "Recipes," its intellectual daring, theory, and conceptual sophistication couched in thoroughly accessible language, dancing cheek to cheek with a clutch of *PMLA*'s customary, heavily theoretical articles, including " . . . the Self-Destruction of Modern Scientific Criticism," "Foucault's Oriental Subtext," and "Baudelaire's Theory of Practice."

"Recipes" begins with—*quelle surprise*—a recipe, for "summer pasta, lovely, sophisticated, delicious," adjectives that apply, as well, to the authorial persona. How odd—and how welcoming—to be invited to relax ("Let [the pasta] sit for a minute or two if you're not in a hurry, toss again, and serve") and to indulge one's own tastes ("You can leave anything out of this recipe except the pasta and the olive oil") as a way of making Leonardi's topic one's own: "the giving of a recipe" and its "interesting relationships to both reading and writing" (340). How startling for Leonardi's feminist literary analysis to begin with Irma Rombauer's use of rhetorical strategies in the canonical *Joy of Cooking*. But is a cookbook in the wrong (i.e., not literary) canon? After establishing a social community of women cooks and analyzing their behavior as readers and writers of recipes, Leonardi moves to similar considerations in E. F. Benson's *Mapp and Lucia* volumes and Nora Ephron's *Heartburn*. The author concludes by anticipating readers' potentially antagonistic questions: "What importance, after all, can recipes have to the reading, writing mind?" Echoing Tompkins, she asks, "Would the tensions that academic women face between the domestic and the professional make it more or less difficult for them to extend credibility toward a writer who begins with a recipe?" "Do I erode my credibility with male academics by this feminine interest in cooking, cookbooks, and recipes?" Leonaridi's final question, however, reiterates her initial invitation, "And, finally, will you try my summer pasta?" (347). Who could resist?

The generally enthusiastic response reinforced *PMLA*'s editorial decision to publish Leonardi's essay and gratified the author, who had taken the risk as an untenured assistant professor to submit to this "typically staid, dignified publication" a piece to which *PMLA*'s readers' initial reaction was "'the editors have gone mad'; 'this must be the April issue and it's an April Fools' Day joke'; 'they got mixed up and bound the wrong innards inside these sedate *PLMA* covers.'" However the correspondent, R. Baird Shuman, at the time a senior professor at the University of Illinois, Urbana, and respected critic, goes on: "I was absolutely dazzled by it. The piece is brilliant in every respect, combining valuable information on literacy embedding with feminist matters, with issues of kinship, with an analysis of symbolism" and much more. Shuman ends with congratulations to *PMLA* for being "willing to take a chance on a contribution as far out of the ordinary" as this (904). M. Thomas Inge, Blackwell Professor of the Humanities at Randolph-Macon College, reiterates, "The Editorial Board is to be congratulated for its breadth of vision in approving for publication Susan J. Leonardi's excellent essay. Seldom have methodology, form, style and content been so beautifully integrated in an article for *PMLA*, the first one I have wanted to read in ten years" (904).

If Leonardi could do it backwards and in high heels in *PMLA*, other academics, men as well as women, could publish personal-sounding essays. By the early 1990s, the floodgates were opening in literary criticism (though Leonardi's triumph did not signal a revolution in the usual *PMLA* article) as in numerous other academic fields: anthropology (Clifford Geertz, Ruth Behar), law (Patricia Williams), medicine (Atul Gawande, Oliver Sacks, Richard Selzer), linguistics (Deborah Tannen), computer science (Paul De Palma), information technology (Sven Birkerts), education (Shirley Brice Heath, Mike Rose, Howard Gardner), the sciences (Stephen Jay Gould, Isaac

Asimov); and the academy more generally as in such essay collections as Alan Shepard et al., *Coming to Class;* Deborah Holdstein and David Bleich, *Personal Effects: The Social Character of Scholarly Writing;* Joseph Trimmer, *Narration as Knowledge;* and Diane Freedman and Olivia Frey, *Autobiographical Writing across the Disciplines.* These writers and many more, trained in scholarly disciplines, have become accomplished at communicating ideas, however complex, by means of a human persona who writes without jargon.

A single example must serve as a synecdoche for this extensive body of contemporary work. In analyzing the impact of parenthood on his writing, Jeffrey Nesteruk's brief "Fatherhood, in Theory and Practice," published in the *Chronicle of Higher Education* in February 2005, makes explicit the ways many academic personal essayists conceive of style, rhetorical strategy, subject, and nature of their intended audience. Nesteruk, a professor of legal studies at Franklin and Marshall University, explains that before he became a father he used to develop "lofty thoughts" in his "intellectual sanctuary," his den, door closed, "deepening an intellectual insight, tracing a complex chain of logic, sifting carefully through conflicting bodies of evidence." His daughter's birth, three years earlier, opened that door as it humanized the author's style and altered his rhetorical strategy. Now, he says, "both my scholarship and writing have become more personal, more revealing. I tell stories along with arguing doctrine. . . . I also say things more provisionally. I let more of my uncertainties onto the page." Echoing Leonardi's invitation, he explains, "I'm less interested in winning an argument than in starting a conversation. . . . I want to give everyone, especially my critics, their due" (sec. B, 5; see also Olivia Frey).

The existential demands of parenthood have influenced Nesteruk's choice of subject as well. Reminded daily by his daughter of "how precious life is," he wants to concentrate on "enduring, basic questions" rather than "the latest academic trend or controversy." Thus he now composes essays "for larger academic audiences" and—because "having a child immerses you in a world of wider connections"—"the general public." In this more interconnected world, constraining "disciplinary boundaries . . . are slowly losing their sway." Fatherhood, like the "struggles of scholarship," first fragmented the author's world and "then put it back together in new ways," making him, like his young daughter, open to seeing and learning anew (sec. B, 5), exactly the way most creative writers function.

Invitation

You're invited to join us essayists on the porch, there's plenty of room. If it gets too crowded, we'll build a House of Essays; we'll use I-beams. Anyone (theorists included) willing to trade the language of dialogics, utterance, intertextuality, and the "anxiety of influence" for the friendly conversation of humankind, on any subject, is more than welcome. You'll need to be ready to present your specialist's knowledge with voice, panache, and a broad perspective, in language that doesn't grind gears on the uphill climb but sails up in overdrive. Feel free to bring your laptop, food, spouse, children, pets, the comforts of home and—dare I say?—traces of life's messiness and uncertainty that may even appear in your writing, as long as they suit your subject, in style and in substance. For, like Tompkins, Leonardi, and Nesteruk, in the vertical pronoun you'll be inviting readers into your own wondrous world, to engage in a hospitable, collaborative dialogue rather than competition to see who can score the most esoteric points. This writing will be very hard work; "we must labour to be beautiful," as Yeats reminds us in "Adam's Curse." But it will be the best fun you've ever had, I promise you. You'll get fan mail along with citations. Write—and see.

3

Teaching and Writing—
in the Margins, on the Edge

Teaching College English
as a Woman

Prologue

During my first year of doctoral work, I spent all my savings on a lifetime membership in National Council of Teacers of English. Already, in my first year as a TA, I knew I loved to teach. Nothing less than a lifetime commitment to the profession I was preparing to join could express that love.

It has taken thirty years to find the voice, the place in the profession, to tell the stories that follow. When the events occurred, I would never discuss them, silenced by guilt, shame, anger, and embarrassment. Like discussing childbirth (which for the same reasons I never did either until a recent reunion with college roommates), it would not have been ladylike. But at a summer conference in 1989, a one-hour session on "gender and teaching," attended by women and men alike, metamorphosed into two nights of telling life-saving stories. And so I tell you what it has been like to teach college English as a woman, to become a member of the profession I now and ever embrace anew. Call me Lynn.

My Job as Ventriloquist's Dummy

Once upon a time, as a newly minted Ph.D. with a newly minted baby, I got the best part-time job I've ever had, a half-time assistant professorship at a distinguished midwestern university. Unusual for the early 1960s, and unique to that institution, my job was created in response to the dean's estimate of an impending shortage of faculty. "It's going to be hell on wheels facultywise around here for the next five years," he said. So I was hired for exactly half of a full-time job: half the teaching load, half the advising and committee work, half the regular benefits. Our second child was born, conveniently, during my second summer vacation. Though not on a tenure track, I did have a parking space; it seemed a fair exchange. I taught freshman composition, of course, and sometimes sophomore lit surveys. I even taught in a room that overlooked the playground of our children's nursery school.

During the whole five years I taught there, I never expressed an original opinion about literature, either in class or out. In the course of my very fine education at one of our nation's very finest universities, taught entirely by men, except for women's phys ed where they allowed a woman to teach us how to develop graceful "posture, figure, and carriage," I learned, among other things, that only real professors had the right to say what they thought. Anyway in the 1950s there were no concepts, no language to say what I, as a nascent feminist critic, wanted to say. I tried, in a fifteen-page junior-year honors paper: "Milton's Eve did too have some redeeming virtues." The paper was returned, next day, in virgin condition, save a small mark in the margin on page two where the professor had apparently stopped reading, and a tiny scarlet C discreetly tattooed at the end. In shame and horror at getting less than my usual A, I went to see the professor. "Why did I get a C?" I was near tears. "Because," he said in measured tones, drawing on his pipe, "you simply can't say that." End of discussion. I did not sin again.

I had majored in English because I loved to read and to write, and I continued to love reading and writing all the way through graduate school. But somewhere along the line, perhaps through the examples of my professors, measured, judicious, self-controlled, I had come to believe that my job as a teacher was to present the material in a neutral manner, evenhandedly citing a range of Prominent Male Critics, and let the students make up their own minds. It would have been embarrassing, unprofessional, to express the passion I felt, so I taught every class in my ventriloquist's dummy voice. Indifferent student evaluations reflected the disengagement this approach provoked—"although she's a nice lady," some students added.

Editing textbooks didn't count. Only the other women who taught freshman composition part time took this work seriously. (Collectively we were known to the male full-time faculty as the "Heights Housewives," as we learned from the captions on the witchlike cartoons that would occasionally appear on the bulletin board in the English department office.) I had collaboratively edited a collection of critical essays on Faulkner's *The Bear* intended for freshman writing courses, signing the book contract in the hospital the day after the birth of my first child. I was working on two other collaborative texts. The English department invited my senior Faulkner collaborator, a gracious scholar of international renown, to come to campus to lecture on the subject of our book, but they did not invite me to either the lecture or the dinner for him. The university's public relations spokesman nevertheless called and asked if I'd be willing to give a cocktail party for him, at my expense. That may have been the only time I ever said "no" during the whole five years I taught there.

Freshman composition didn't count. I was so apprehensive about publishing original writing in my own name that when my husband, Martin, a social psychologist, and I collaborated on an article about a student's writing process, I insisted that we submit it in Martin's name only. Only real professors with full-time jobs could publish academic articles, and I knew I wasn't one. *College English* accepted it by return mail. "Now do you want your name on it?" Martin asked; "you should be first author." "Yes," I said, "Yes."

My work in nonfiction didn't count. I proudly told the department chair that I was beginning research on a biography of Dr. Benjamin Spock, soon to retire from his faculty position at the same university. I had access to all the primary sources I needed, including Spock himself. "Why don't you write a series of biographical articles on major literary figures?" asked our leader, whose customary advice to faculty requests for raises was "Diversify your portfolio." "Once you've established your reputation you can afford to throw it away by writing about a popular figure." I thanked him politely and continued my research, a logical extension of my dissertation study of biographical method. I could learn a lot about how people wrote biographies, I reasoned, if I wrote one myself. And because I couldn't say to the children, "Go away, don't bother me, I'm writing about Doctor Spock," I learned to write with them in the room.

Ultimately I didn't count either. A new department chairman arrived soon after I began the biography. His first official act, prior to making a concerted but unsuccessful effort to abolish freshman English, was to fire all the part-time faculty, everyone (except TAs) who taught the lowly subject. All women but one. He axed me privately, in person; a doctorate, after all, has some privileges, though my office mate learned of her status when the chairman showed a job candidate the office, announcing, "This will be vacant next year." He was kind enough to write me a letter of recommendation, a single sentence that said, "Mrs. Bloom would be a good teacher of freshman composition." I actually submitted that letter along with a job application. Once.

On the Floor with the Kitty Litter

After our move to Indiana, one of the textbooks so scorned during my first part-time job actually got me my first full-time job, two years later. The department had adopted it for the freshman honors course, and the chair had written an enthusiastic review. Then, dear reader, he hired me! This welcoming work enabled me to find my voice. After ten years of part-time teaching, as bland as vanilla pudding, I felt free to spice up the menu. Being a full-time faculty member gave me the freedom to express my opinions about what we read and wrote and to argue and joke with my students. My classes became noisy, personal, and fun. Two years later, I received tenure, promotion, and an award for good teaching. Then, after four years on the job, my husband was offered a professorship in St. Louis too good to turn down. I resigned to move.

My voice was reduced to a whisper. I could find no full-time job in St. Louis in that inhospitable year of 1974 when there were several hundred applicants for every job. In hopes of ingratiating myself with one or another of the local universities, I taught part time at three, marginal combinations of writing and women's studies. I taught early in the morning, in midafternoon, at night, coming and going under cover of lightness and darkness. It didn't matter, for no one except my students knew I was there anyway. Department chairmen wouldn't see me; with insulated indifference faculty, even some I'd known in graduate school, walked past my invisible self in the halls. For administrative convenience, I was paid once that semester, after Thanksgiving, $400. Fringe benefits, retirement, the possibility of raises or continuity of employment were nonexistent. At none of the three schools did I have any stationery, mailing privileges, secretarial help, telephone, or other amenities—not even an ID or a library card. I was treated as an illegal alien. Nowhere did I have an office, until I finally begged for one at the plushest school, frustrated and embarrassed at having to confer with my students in the halls on the run. After several weeks, the word trickled down that I could share space with a TA and, as it turned out, her cat, which she kept confined there. This office symbolized my status on all three jobs. It was in a building across campus from the English department, where no one could see us. It was under a stairwell, so we couldn't stand up. It had no windows, so we couldn't see out, but it did have a Satanic poster on the wall—shades of the underworld. The TA had the desk, so I got to sit on the floor next to the kitty litter. I stayed there, in the redolent dark, for a full thirty seconds.

Then my voice returned, inside my head this time. Its message was powerful and clear, "If I ever do this again, I deserve what I get." I did finish the semester. But I never went back to that office. And I never again took another job that supported such an exploitative system, even though that meant commuting two thousand miles a week to my next job, a real job, in New Mexico. "Go for it," Martin said and took care of the children while I was away.

Poison in the Public Ivy

Four years later, we moved again to eliminate my cross-country commute. Through research support, graduate teaching, directing a writing program, and supervising some sixty TAs and part-time faculty, my New Mexico job had given me a grown-up voice. I was beginning to talk to colleagues throughout the country, at meetings, through my own publications and those of my students, and I was looking forward to continuing the dialogue on the new job as associate professor and writing director at a southern, and therefore by definition gracious, public ivy.

As I entered the mellowed, red-brick building on the first day of class, a colleague blocked the door. "We expected to get a beginning assistant professor and wash *him* out after three years," he sneered. "Instead, we got *you*, and *you'll* probably get tenure." I took a deep breath and replied in a firm voice, "You bet."

"We" contains multitudes; one never knows at the outset how many. Although the delegated greeter never spoke to me again, it soon became clear that "we" meant a gang of four equal-opportunity harassers, all men, all tenured faculty of long standing, all eager to stifle my voice. Their voices, loud and long, dominated all department and committee meetings and, word had it, the weekly poker games where the decisions were really made. I could do no right. I was too nice to my students; everybody knows that undergraduates can't write. I was merely flattering the students by encouraging them to publish; that they did indeed publish showed they were pandering to the public. My writing project work with schoolteachers was—aha!—proof that I was more interested in teaching than in literary criticism; misplaced priorities. My own publications, ever increasing, were evidence of blatant careerism. I received a number of prestigious grants and fellowships; just a way to get out of teaching. The attendant newspaper publicity, though good for the school, reflected badly on my femininity.

Although I was heard in class and increasingly in the profession at large, I had no voice in the departmental power structure. The Gang of Four and, by extrapolation, the rest of the faculty, already knew everything they needed to know about teaching writing; they'd learned it long ago as TAs. Faculty development workshops were a waste of time. The college didn't need a writing director anyway; the students all wrote well, the faculty all taught well, and Southern Public Ivy had gotten along for two hundred years without a writing director. Why start now? As a way to forestall my imminent tenure review, this hospitable group initiated a review of the position of writing director. If they could demonstrate that there was no need for the job, despite the thousand students enrolled every semester in required freshman English, not to mention the upper-division writing courses, oversubscribed and with waiting lists, and the initiative in other departments for a writing-across-the-curriculum program, I would not have the opportunity to come up for tenure. Because the review was, of course, of the job and not of the person in it, I, of course, could not be consulted; that would compromise the impartiality of the process. Nor could I discuss the ongoing review with colleagues; ditto. Or the department chair; ditto. Or the dean; ditto, ditto.

The review began in September of my second year. Nobody identified its criteria; nobody told me what it covered; I could not ask. Occasionally a friendly colleague would sneak into my office during that very long fall semester and tell me that he was so anguished by the proceedings he wanted to resign from the review committee; *sotto voce* I urged him to stay on it. A borrowed voice was better than none. Rumor had it, I heard, that I was talking to a lawyer. How unprofessional. Oh was I? I whispered. The campus AAUP president heard about the review; write me a letter, he said, outlining what's going on, and I'll send it to the national office. So I did. And he did.

Then, on a clear, crisp evening in January, tenure became irrelevant. Our family dinner was interrupted by the phone call that every parent dreads. Come right away.

We saw the car first, on a curve in the highway near the high school, crushed into a concrete telephone pole. Next was the rescue squad ambulance, lights revolving red and white, halted amidst shattered glass. Then the figure on the stretcher, only a familiar chin emerging from the bandages that swathed the head. "He was thrown out of the back seat. The hatchback door smashed his face as if he'd been hit with an axe," said the medic. "I'm fine," said our son, and we responded with terror's invariable lie, "You're going to be all right."

After six hours of ambiguous X-rays, clear pictures finally emerged long after midnight, explaining why Laird's eyes were no longer parallel—one socket had simply been pulverized. The line of jagged-lightning stitches, sixty-four in all, that bolted across his face would be reopened the next day for reconstructive surgery. "Don't go out in a full moon," sick joked the doctor, howling like a banshee, "People will mistake you for a zombie."

Laird had to remain upright for a month so his head would drain, and our family spent every February evening on the couch in front of the woodstove, propping each other up. Every day the writing directorship review committee asked by memo for more information; every day I replied, automatically. I do not know, now, what they asked; I do not know, now, what I answered; or what I wrote on student papers; or what we ate, or read, or wrote checks for during that long month.

But I do know that in early March the AAUP's lawyer called me, and his message was simple: "A university has every right to eliminate a position, or a program, if there is no academic need, if there are no students in it, for example. But it cannot eliminate a position just to get rid of the person holding the job. If Southern Ivy does this, they'll be blacklisted." He repeated this to the department chair. When the department voted, in its new wisdom, in late April to table the review of the writing directorship until after I had been reviewed for tenure, a friend, safely tenured, whispered to me, "You just got tenure." The thick copies of the committee's review were never distributed; I was awarded tenure the next year—and left immediately to become department chair at an urban state university, tenured, promoted to professor, with authority to have an emphatic voice. The review was never reinstated, says a faculty friend still at Southern Ivy; for six years the writing directorship went unfilled.

Escaping the Rapist

Fortunately even as department chair I could continue to teach, and I often taught women writers. One day my class, not only writing-intensive but discussion-intensive, began arguing about Joyce Carol Oates's "Where Are You Going, Where Have You Been?" Some claimed that Arnold Friend, "thirty, maybe," who invades Connie's driveway in "an open jalopy, painted a bright gold," his eyes hidden behind mirrored, metallic sunglasses, is in love with the pubescent teenager about whom "everything has two sides to it, one for home and one for anywhere that was not home" (2278). Others asserted that from the moment they met, Arnold's "Gonna get you, baby" (2279) signaled the abduction with which the story concludes. Though he does not lay a finger on his victim, Friend does, they pointed out, threaten to burn down her house and kill her parents—scarcely acts of love. After screaming for help into a disconnected phone until she loses her breath, Connie has no more voice and walks sacrificially out into the sunlight and Friend's mockingly waiting arms: "What else is there for a girl like you but to be sweet and pretty and give in? . . . You don't want [your family] to get hurt. . . . You're better than them because not a one of them would have done this for you" (2290).

Such compelling evidence clinched the debate, and I decided to reaffirm the students' interpretation with a lifesaving story of my own. "A decade earlier," I began, taking a deep breath. I had never thought I would tell this story to my students. "My husband, adolescent sons, and I were camping in Scandinavia. But it was a dark and stormy night in Stockholm, so we decided to spend the night in a university dorm converted to a youth hostel for the summer. At 10 P.M, the boys tucked in, Martin and I headed for the showers down the hall. He dropped me off in front of the door decorated with a large, hand-lettered sign—*Damar. Women. Frauen. Dames.*—and went to the men's shower at the other end of the long corridor. As I groped for a light switch in the pitch-black room, it struck me as odd that the lights were off at night in a public building. The room was dead silent, not even a faucet

Lynn delivering the inaugural Board of Trustees Distinguished Professor address, University of Connecticut, 2001

dripping. I walked past a row of sinks to the curtained shower stall closest to the window, where I could leave my clothes and towel on the sill.

"As I turned, naked, to step into the shower, a man wearing a bright blue tracksuit and blue running shoes shoved aside the curtain of a shower stall across the aisle and headed toward me. I began to scream in impeccable English, 'Get out! You're in the women's shower.' He kept on coming. My voice had the wrong words, the wrong language. I screamed again, now into his face, looming over mine as he hit me on the mouth. I screamed again, 'Get out!' as he hit me on the cheek. My mouth was cut, I could taste the salty blood as he hit me again in the head. I began to lose my balance. 'If he knocks me down on the tile,' I thought, 'he'll kill me.' Then I thought, still screaming, 'I don't want my children to hear this.'

"Then time slowed down, inside my head, the way it does just before you think your car is going to crash when it goes into a skid, and the voices, all mine, took over. One voice could say nothing at all for terror. I had never been hit before in my life. How could I know what to do? The man in blue, silent, continued to pummel my head, his face suffused with hatred, his eyes vacant. Another voice reasoned, 'I need to get my clothes and get out.' 'But to get my clothes I'll have to go past him twice.' 'I should just get out.' Still I couldn't move, the whirling blue arms continued to pound me, I was off balance now and afraid of falling. Then the angry message came, etched in adrenaline, 'I didn't ask for this, I don't deserve it, and I'm not going to take it.' I ran naked into the corridor."

The bell rang. "You're right," I said. "Oates's story is about violence, not love." The students, whose effervescent conversation usually bubbled out into the corridor as they dispersed, filed out in silence.

That was on a Thursday. The following Tuesday, an hour before our next class meeting, a student, svelte and usually poised, came into my office, crying. "What's the matter?" I asked. "Saturday night," she said, "I was walking home alone—I live alone—and heard the phone ringing in my apartment. When I rushed in to answer it, I must have left the door open. Because after I'd hung up, when I went into the kitchen, a man stepped out from behind the curtain, grabbed me from behind, and shoved a gasoline-soaked rag over my face. As he began to wrestle with me, he ripped my shirt trying to throw me down. Suddenly I heard your voice in my head, repeating the words you'd said in class, 'I didn't ask for this, I don't deserve it, and I'm not going to take it.' I ran, screaming, into the street and flagged a passing policeman. You saved my life."

"No," I said, "you saved your own life."

Coda

The computerized NCTE membership card says that my lifetime membership expires in 1999. As the date draws closer, I write headquarters about this. Several times, and still no answer.

I will have to raise my voice. My commitment to teaching English is, after all, for life.

---- ❋ ----

Voices

Do I contradict myself?
Very well then I contradict myself,
(I am large, I contain multitudes.)

Walt Whitman, *Song of Myself*

The Authorial Dialogue: Talking to Myself

When I sit down to write, the voices arrive in my head, talking to me, with
me—for I have considerable say in this conversation—sometimes talking
with one another, occasionally interrupting the flow of conversation, rumi-
nation, meditation with arguments, shouts, shrieks, hoots of laughter, or of
derision. Lest this sound as if I belong in a madhouse (well, no more so than
any other creative writer), let me explain. The essay you're reading now will
identify and examine the voices that converse, chime in, chivvy—a colloquy,
sometimes cacophony of choristers that are present in my mind—with every
piece I write, sometimes in the foreground, at other times in the background.
They are never silent, as indeed a voice that I recognize as my own conversa-
tional voice reminds me in the course of writing this sentence. I consider the
dialogue that accompanies, that indeed drives my writing, as the writer's
composing community. Its constituent voices depend on the nature of the
work in progress, how far along it is, my mood, and a host of other factors,
calculated and less deliberate.

Even when I've finished the piece and am saying it aloud in my mind, listening for the sounds and the rhythm, the music as well as the words, this
conversation goes on beyond the ending. Did I get it right? Did I—as one editor's remark resonates—"stick to the point"? Does it sound better this way,
or that way . . . or some other way? (My eye doctor provides the calm voice-
over as he proffers lenses for sharpness of vision: "Does it look better this
way? Or that way?") Will readers understand what I've said? Will they follow
the intricacies of style as well as substance? Will they fathom the nuances?
(Another editor's observation invariably pops up: "If readers can find sex in

an ambiguity, they will.") Will they get the jokes? Although I'd like readers to love me, at least the Lynn they have come to know in the work, love is beside the point. More importantly, have I compelled their belief, their agreement? (Here Joan Didion chimes in with the observation that writers are always saying, "*Listen to me, see it my way, change your mind.*") Finally I have to turn off the conversation, let the piece go. I've done the best I could in the time allotted for the writing, the visions and revisions. But when I'm reading the page proofs, or even the published version, the voices start in again and point out countless changes I could have made had I world enough and time.

Do all writers have this running dialogue in their heads, I wonder? The most articulate composition studies commentator on voice is Peter Elbow, whose own writing reveals an articulate, engaging, inviting voice. This is an embodiment of the voice he encourages students, in such works as *Writing With Power,* to listen for and develop in their own writing, especially in chapters on "Writing and Voice" and "How to Get Power Through Voice." In "Three Mysteries at the Heart of Writing," Elbow defines the "virtues" of a "strong and lively voice in writing," which might be termed its *register:*

> (a) audible voice: writing that makes readers hear the intonation or
> that sounds lively and energetic, (b) dramatic voice: writing that gives
> readers a sense of a *person,* (c) distinctive or recognizable voice, and
> (d) voice with authority or courage to speak out, (26)

(elaborated on in his introduction to *Landmark Essays on Voice and Writing,* xi–xlvii). You will hear my own versions of these voices in the dialogues that follow.

Although other books of advice on how to write talk about finding one's voice as a writer, except for Elbow this is never very specific, and voice itself is seldom defined. Sometimes the advice books suggest that writers should hear the sounds of their own words—Elbow's advice focuses on this—but rarely do they indicate that others' voices should, or will, be intermingled. Now and again an essayist will create such conversation either by writing in a variety of diverse voices, or by creating characters who serve as mouthpieces for a phalanx of the author's alter egos. This Sam Pickering does with Slubey Garts, Proverbs Goforth, Baby Lane, Googoo Hooberry, Malachi Ramus, Loppie Groat, Turlow Gutheridge, and Josh, a surreal retinue who "wander in and out of his essays and from book to book" (Spinner, "Interview with Sam Pickering," 193).

I assume that all writers in fact converse with a multitude of voices in their heads as they write, but I don't know for sure. These days I am too shy to ask this question that I used to pursue intrepidly when I believed that writers could—and would—give precise anatomizations of their creative process.* Although the writers I know will talk at length about editors, readings, and royalty income (generally, its conspicuous absence), they usually don't talk about how they write. After eighteen years of writing creative nonfiction myself, I can understand why the extraordinarily articulate are not very communicative on this point: so much of what writers do is so intuitive—following trails of sound, sight, sense, silence—that it's impossible to analyze. James Thurber's self-portrait of the writer at work could limn us all: "I never quite know when I'm not writing. Sometimes my wife comes up to me at a party and says, 'Dammit, Thurber, stop writing.' She usually catches me in the middle of a paragraph. Or my daughter will look up from the dinner table and ask, 'Is he sick?' 'No,' my wife says, 'He's writing something'" (Plimpton and Steele, "James Thurber," 96). As Arthur Miller's Charley tells Willy Loman, in explaining why his son Bernard doesn't boast about trying a case before the Supreme Court, "He don't have to [talk about it]— he's gonna do it" (*Death of a Salesman,* act 2, line 95).

Allan Gurganus is one of the rare exceptions who both acknowledges and analyzes the multiple voices that participate in his creative process: "I believe in Whitman's vision that we're all composed of a thousand voices and that those of us who have chosen to use our imaginations on a daily basis instead of suppressing our imaginations, which is what the culture frequently demands, are very lucky because we are always in company. We are always surrounded by voices that are like and unlike our own and that are our own. And part of the joy of having written for twenty-odd years is that as I'm now sitting here, I seem to be alone but in fact I'm trailing about sixty people" (90). Although these voices belong to a universe of Gurganus's as-yet-unrealized characters, just waiting to be written about, rather than the clutch of editors, nags, and scolds that I'm discussing here, their collective presence occupies a comparable mental space.

To illustrate the many voices that constitute this authorial-editorial community of one that indeed contains multitudes, I will recreate the dialogue that went on in my head as I was writing "Teaching College English as a Woman."† This creative nonfiction essay tells four feminist stories—of

---

*When, in 1976, I interviewed Iceland's only Nobel Prize winner in literature, Halldor Laxness, and asked him, "How do you explain your creative process?" or variations, "How do you write?" every time he deflected the question: "Ninety-eight percent of the people in Iceland are literate." Thus rebuffed, I stopped asking.

†My thanks to Jesse Scaccia, graduate student in creative nonfiction at the University of Connecticut, spring 2003, for asking the right question—"What decisions do you make as you're writing?"—at the right time. I offer this as proof that I do listen to actual outside

discrimination, harassment, threats, and violence—shocking in their transgressive subject matter though sufficiently widespread for me to imagine from the outset that I was writing as Everywoman in Academia.‡

STAGE DIRECTION. I will indicate different speakers by different names, sometimes with descriptive labels as well. I had originally intended to further differentiate among speakers by representing each with a different typeface, but soon decided that readers would find this too gimmicky, too distracting, a privileging of style over substance. Furthermore they might be provoked into arguing with my choice of type—should the hostile reviewer be represented better by **Braggadocio** rather than by Century Gothic?—and be further diverted from the discussion at hand. Thus I have chosen, cribbed actually from a poet friend whose voice I admire, the gracious, capacious typeface, Palatino Linotype, instead of Times New Roman, my previous, somewhat stodgy, default typeface for my ordinary reflective voice. I am using this typeface for all the speakers below, even when it is nicer than they are. Although my own voice characteristically experiences some modulation, modification as any work in progress develops, I know from the outset that the voice I am attempting to represent here will be a voice as close to my natural speaking voice as possible. There will be no academic jargon (characteristic even in other pieces when I'm making very theoretical arguments for an academic audience), no convoluted sentences, no long words where short ones will do. If you don't hear Orwell's voice, speaking here straight from "Politics and the English Language," listen carefully. Better now? Can you detect a soupçon of Strunk and White? Although you may not hear the advice of my best professors in both grad and undergrad schools—Sheridan Baker, Austin Warren, Bob Super, and especially Eastman—these resound in my ears as well.

The Entire Essay: Call Me Everywoman

LYNN (as the essay begins to shimmer in the distance): The writing teachers at the workshop loved these lifesaving stories. In a practice run for what I would soon begin to write, I told them tales of subordination. "My Job as Ventriloquist's Dummy" distilled to the essence numerous instances where, as a part-time teacher and writer, I had no voice of my own, never articulating "an original opinion about literature, either in class or out." I spoke of

---

voices, as well as my own, in particular, early in the writing process—and again, very late when I ask selected friends and my husband to give the piece a tough, critical reading.

‡ Significantly this piece was governed from the start by the concept of voice; indeed one version was published as "Hearing Our Own Voices: Life-Saving Stories."

marginalization: the story that would become "On the Floor with the Kitty Litter" symbolized my lowly status as an adjunct, in the windowless office under a stairwell I was grudgingly allowed to share with a TA—and her cat. I told stories of confrontation and aggression that would take shape as "Poison in the Public Ivy" and "Escaping the Rapist." Singly and in combination these tales in and out of school illustrated what it meant, at least during the 1950s, '60s, '70s, and '80s, to teach college English as a woman. That these coalesced into an essay that continues to be reprinted, even included in anthologies for first-year writing students, implies that these stories are still, alas, alive and well in the academy of today, and that my voice does contain multitudes.

What follows is a compressed version of the dialogue in my head that took place over the months during the gestation and writing of "Teaching College English as a Woman." The title, incidentally, came last.

BEGINNING ASSISTANT PROFESSOR, female: Write these down. Publish them. We women need to hear about your experiences.

NEW WRITING DIRECTOR, male: Men do, too.

LYNN: But what right do I have to represent my situation as typical? Why should readers be expected to care about what happened to me?

AUTOBIOGRAPHY CRITIC, genre specialist: Oh, get real. Since your critical specialties are autobiography and personal essays, you already know the answer to these objections. A fundamental premise of autobiographical writing, as well as of much fiction, is that the author has enough in common with her readers so they can tap into relevant aspects of the human condition.

AUTOBIOGRAPHY CRITIC, feminist: Right! Remember Lejeune's concept of the "autobiographical pact," that the writer whose name is on the work is purporting to tell the truth about the character—herself—in the work, and readers expect a true representation. Your job here will be to tell the stories with no whining, no special pleading, no "O poor me."

LYNN: That part's easy. My knee-jerk reaction is to tell the truth and tell it straight, not slant à la Emily Dickinson. I can tell these stories now because I'm at the top of my game. I'm a tenured full professor, and unless I lose my mind or my head, my job is secure. I have an endowed chair in writing, one of the first in the country in the very field my string of antagonists (including the Gang of Four) dismissed as trivial, peripheral to "real" scholarship because writing required no brains, only grammar. The events I'm talking about in this essay are over—for me—and I have no personal stake in their outcome. In fact I couldn't write them down with the hope of publication until I could treat them dispassionately enough to be able to transform life into art. But comparable stories are still very much alive for innumerable other women.

MALE ADJUNCT: And some men, too.

SENIOR PROFESSOR, male: So you had some professional problems coming up through the ranks. So what? Everybody has to undergo hazing, rites of passage that show they're among the fittest and deserve to survive. No one is exempt from this; why should you expect your life to be any different? And why should we care about what happened to you?

LYNN: Because what happened to me happened to thousands, generations of women like me—adjuncts, women trying to accommodate feminist readings of works dominated and protected by male critics, women seeking tenure in undervalued and nontraditional fields, women being raped, literally and metaphorically.

MALE ADJUNCT: And some men, too; don't forget!

FEMINIST COLLEAGUE, black: Think of how long it took Harriet Jacobs's *Incidents in the Life of a Slave Girl,* tales of attempted rape and sexual harassment, to be authenticated and attributed to their rightful author, over 125 years. You go, girl!

LYNN: But where can I publish this, when all the journal editors are male? [Remember, I was working on this in 1990–91.] Academic writings in general avoid any suggestion that there's a real human being addressing the subject, sometimes even with (gasp!) passion. Nobody in English has ever written in such a personal voice about such personal issues. No journal has ever published such transgressive tales.

ASSISTANT PROFESSOR, female: But these are stories that have to be told.

LYNN: True. And they're the stories I most want to tell.

MARTIN: Then tell them. Go right to the top journal, *College English.*

LYNN: You're right. I have to send it there; the readers of *College English* are my friends, my colleagues, my primary audience. But the editor is not. The articles he's been publishing during the past five years are highly theoretical, full of jargon, devoid of humanizing examples. The authors in his universe tell no stories. No first person. Nevertheless I have to send it there; this is the one journal everyone reads. It's about time someone appeared as a living human being in the major journal.

MOM: Have you no sense of shame? No pride? How can you discuss [lowers her voice] rape?

LYNN: Well, Mom, it wasn't my fault. For a while I was embarrassed to acknowledge the attempted rapes—professional (by the Public Ivy Gang of Four) and physical (in the shower at the youth hostel). But I got over it. Except for the fact that in both instances I was a woman in the wrong place at the wrong time, I personally did not provoke these assaults. Any other woman who happened to be in those places, vulnerable and alone, could have been attacked just as I was.

*Lynn's mother, Mildred
Kisling Zimmerman, 1963*

MOM: You actually appear naked in that story.

LYNN: The readers can't see me. I offer no descriptions, no salacious language. I started to say, "If nakedness bothers them they should just turn off their imaginations," but I've changed my mind. Everyone in the profession needs to confront the issues raised here—in the open, unadorned. The nakedness of these issues, not of my body, should be profoundly disturbing.

MOM: Furthermore, you know our family never admits to having problems. Zimmermans are winners, not losers. We can only acknowledge successes, triumphs; never discouragements or defeats. If your boss or anyone else knows you're vulnerable, they'll pick on you. All they need to find is one flaw, and your reputation will be ruined.

LYNN: Well, Mom . . . I'll just have to take that risk.

MEMBER OF THE GANG OF FOUR: Be careful what you say. We might sue you!

LYNN: I'll take that risk, as well.

NCTE LEGAL COUNSEL: And NCTE won't protect you. No publisher would defend you against libel.

LYNN: Libel shouldn't be an issue. Every word I'm saying is true. I'm naming no names. My antagonists are so common they could be anywhere;[§] the reputations of the actual individuals aren't in danger.

FEMALE COLLEAGUE (mild-mannered) FROM PUBLIC IVY: We all know who they are. And we know that what you say is true. Still, publishing that article is a big risk.

LYNN: The stakes are worth the risk. Nothing will change for women if women don't stick up for themselves—and each other. So I'm sending the article to *College English*—and in so doing, I'm daring them to publish it.

The Single Sentence: "Call me Lynn."

Now that I've given you a sample of the dialogue running through my mind as I planned and wrote the piece, let's examine a characteristic conversation that occurred during the writing of a three-word sentence. I subject every word, every space, every punctuation mark, and every syntactic structure of everything I write for publication (including some e-mails) to the same kind of demanding dialogic scrutiny, a practice that I am convinced separates the professional writers from the amateurs. To those of us who do it, it seems as obvious and as natural as breathing. (Maybe that's why, like breathing and other natural processes, it receives so little discussion.) Students need to understand this essential concept as well, but it seems to have escaped all but two undergraduates I've taught in the past decade. Yet only through repeated modeling of this in writing classes—"Here's what I say on paper. Here's what was going through my mind"—am I able to persuade my undergraduate writing students that to exercise comparable rigor, the equivalent of subjecting every syllable of their writing to a hundred-pound bench press, holds the promise of a magnificent body of prose.

"Call me Lynn."

And so I tell you what it has been like to teach college English as a woman, to become a member of the profession I now and ever embrace anew. Call me Lynn.

LYNN: I'm trying to send a lot of signals with "Call me Lynn." Can I count on everyone to recognize the allusion to Melville's Ishmael?

MALE CRITIC: Yes, even people who haven't read *Moby-Dick* or can't remember it know that sentence. Just as Ishmael did, that invitation prepares readers to listen to the tales that follow.

§ The fact that various commentators on this essay have assumed the events took place in a number of different schools at different times attests to the ubiquity of the problems I address.

LYNN: But won't readers think it's the height of arrogance for me to imitate Melville, and his best-known line?

FEMALE CRITIC: They might, but so what? You want to convey the self-confidence that you're comfortable with the canonical authors. You can quote a major author without having to cite the source and figure your readers will pick up on the allusion. That's a witty way to let the cognoscenti know you're literate.

COMPOSITION STUDIES SCHOLAR: This is also a subtle way for a composition studies author to establish a bond between herself and literary scholars. And that's important!

LYNN: Well, it also signals that I'm friendly, open, nonauthoritarian—which the stories proceed to illustrate. In real life I would actually say "Call me Lynn" to people I'd just met—students, folks at conferences, research helpers, especially if we were going to continue talking.

FEMALE NEWCOMER TO THE PROFESSION: Do you really expect everyone to know who "Lynn" is? If that isn't arrogance, it's surely the height of self-confidence.

LYNN: The timid part of my mind wants to be self-effacing. That nagging voice says it's the height of hubris to call attention to yourself. But the stories I'm telling in "Teaching College English as a Woman" deal with various ways in which women have been silenced in professional situations. As a student in the 1950s, not being allowed by male professors—that's all there were in my Big Ten alma mater—to present feminist interpretations of literature. As a part-time faculty member, being fearful of expressing any independent opinions in class about the literature I was teaching. As a teacher, having my published pedagogy denigrated as "merely textbooks." As a scholar, going underground with my research on *Doctor Spock,* because the male establishment saw it as a women's subject, too accessible and too popular. As a candidate for tenure at Public Ivy in the 1980s, being obliged to remain totally silent while factions of men debated for and against the writing directorship I held. When I finally did raise my voice, it was a terrified scream as I was being pummeled by a rapist—but no one else was in that empty, echoing room to hear me.

So the assertive side of my mind tells me to talk. Indeed, how could I not speak up, when the whole thrust of my essay is that it's time for women to find their voices and become publicly articulate on their own behalf, and on behalf of other women? Who will do it if we don't? The time has come to attach our names to our actions—so yes, call me Lynn, and listen up.

FEMALE COMPOSITION STUDIES COLLEAGUE: You shouldn't be too modest; people *do* know who "Lynn" is, and it's you. Your professional reputation is out there. Even if readers don't know your other work—which, admit it, has been published widely—they'll be reading "Teaching College English as a Woman." People will want to hear these stories. And from then on they'll call you, as they know you, "Lynn."

INCOMING FEMALE COLLEGE ENGLISH EDITOR [who accepted "Teaching College English as a Woman" without revision, after the outgoing male editor handed it off to her with two conflicting external reviews—"Powerful personal testimony, compelling and timely. Publish immediately!" versus "So she made unwise decisions. Who cares? Reject!"]: Mention of your name in the text will also send readers to the brief bio at the bottom of the first page of the article. Those forty words identify your Establishment credentials. Readers will quickly learn that you are a full professor and endowed chair at a class 1A research university (OK, so it's not an ivy!), the University of Connecticut, which established one of the first writing chairs in the country. They already know that an endowed chair is a rare academic job with perks, privileges, and high status. They'll also learn other high-status, high-stakes information: that you've been president of a national professional organization, the Council of Writing Program Administrators; and that you've chaired a division in the major establishment organization, the MLA. These affiliations show that you can cut it in both composition studies and literature, that people respect and trust and like you enough to elect you to speak on their behalf. Most particularly, they show that you've come out from under the stairwell and the kitty litter. You're an insider, now, not an outsider.

LYNN: You mean, they'll recognize that I've overcome the difficulties and succeeded in the academy on the academy's (read: men's) own terms.

COLLEGE ENGLISH EDITOR: Yes.

LYNN: And finally found a voice. Yet to ask readers to "call me Lynn" is also to admit that I'm vulnerable. I can come out as a human being—from behind the titles, the rank, the professional offices. How liberating! And how unconventional in academic writing at the beginning of the '90s.

CRITIC OF STYLE: And how unconventional to put so much weight on such a short sentence so early in the piece, and in such a pivotal position.

LYNN: Well, I like it. "Call me Lynn." Those three short, one-syllable words sound good. Like a number of other succinct phrases—"I love you"; "I came, I saw, I conquered"—they mean a lot more than they say. Such high compression with explosive impact; it doesn't get any better than this!

ANONYMOUS [and therefore genderless?] MANUSCRIPT REVIEWER: Now that it's been accepted, what do you think will happen when it's published?

LYNN: I think it will make a huge impact. I'm not saying this from vanity, or from the naive writer's belief that everything she says will change the world. Twenty years ago I expected my biography of *Doctor Spock,* my first major book, to do that, yet despite favorable reviews and being selected for distribution by Book-of-the-Month Club, it barely repaid the expenses I incurred in writing it. Even with that harsh dose of reality as a warning, I know this is a breakthrough piece in composition studies—in its storytelling mode, in the stories it tells, in its feminist stance and firm voice against the oppression of women in academia.

DIFFERENT ANONYMOUS [and therefore genderless?] MANUSCRIPT REVIEWER: As I said in my review, this is a totally original work. *College English* has never published anything like this.

LYNN: I'm banking on the compelling power of the stories, on the honesty of the voice to expect that it will make my reputation as an essayist, a teller of true stories. Of course, I could be wrong and thus ignored, or worse, derided, my veracity called into question. I might even be sued—at least that's what NCTE feared when they arranged for libel insurance before they published the piece, for the first time in their eighty-year history. I'm willing to take these chances in my writing; they seem almost trivial in relation to the high stakes and vulnerabilities these stories reveal.

The Last Word(s)

Well, here I am, still talking to myself in order to talk to my readers with clarity, authority, power, and elegance. It should be apparent from the illustrations in this essay that the author, nominally a community of one, is actually a buzzing beehive of communication. The particular voices that resonate in my head may not be those that anyone else hears (do you know my eye doctor in Manchester, Connecticut?), but their roles are comparable in this colloquy. Although I am listing them in their order of frequency, sometimes those with but a single remark ("Stick to the point") exercise an influence far greater than their verbiage. The voices that constitute this author's community include:

MY OWN AUTHORIAL VOICE, in whatever tone and range I will be employing in the work at hand.

VOICES I EXPECT, of those I've "talked to" in preparing to write the piece—scholars, critics I've read, colleagues, or others I know personally. Antagonists, too and always. I can "hear" their voices in the appropriate accents.

VOICES THAT SURPRISE ME—often those of other writers, favorites I hope to echo or imitate; sometimes authors, or their characters, or their stylistic traits that arrive from inner—and outer—space.

VOICES OF PEOPLE I LOVE—family, friends, people I admire; alive or not, they are never dead.

AN EDITOR'S VOICE, usually mine, in the voice I use with my writing students. This editor never sleeps. Although the tone is kindly (why should I scare myself?), the attitude is unsparing, with "so what?" and "prove it" as the unremitting questions. In the final edit, "How does this sound?" comes to the fore, and then I read the part in question out loud or in my mind to make sure that the sound suits both the sense and the sensibility.

Thus I have an entire community in my head as I'm writing, all imagined, all under my control, but yet citizens of the "real world" as well. With every piece I write, I expect to engage in a dialogue, an interrogation, that I can tune in and out as the work proceeds. Only as I reach this, the very end of the piece, do I realize that one salient group often considered in scholarly commentaries about writer-reader relations is missing here—the generic intended audience. Although some or all of the voices I do examine may represent specific people whom I want or expect to read the work, I am not writing to satisfy a poll or to feed the perceived tastes of large groups. I'm writing from passion, and love, and delight with the discovery, the subject, the expression, the innovative ways I expect to present the material. I am, as Gertrude Stein says, writing "for myself and strangers." If I'm happy with the result, I expect that my readers—at least a significant portion of those strangers I want to make friends of—will be drawn in, engaged, impelled to read all the way to the end. In my voice, they will find voices of their own.

Six Degrees of Separation, Six Degrees of Disclosure

In most books the I, or first person, is omitted; in this it will be retained. . . . We commonly do not remember that it is, after all, always the first person that is speaking. I should not talk so much about myself if there were anybody else whom I knew as well.

Henry David Thoreau, *Walden*

The essayist . . . selects his garb from an unusually extensive wardrobe: he can pull on any sort of shirt, be any sort of person, according to his mood or his subject matter—philosopher, scold, jester, raconteur, confidant, pundit, devil's advocate, enthusiast.

E. B. White, *Essays*

Prologue: The Art of the Art

Whether we write in the humanizing first person, or in a human voice, or about our very lives, the self in the text is always a constructed, created self. Professional writers create this self both automatically and deliberately, as E. B. White says, pulling on the shirt that suits the subject, the mood, and the mode of their writing. Indeed in much professional writing, one could find an infinite recess of constructed selves; what appears to be progressively more intimate is nevertheless carefully controlled. This is the expected, professional norm, as it is with any other public, professional performance. If there is a vulnerable self, admitted and acknowledged in the writing, this too is a construct analogous to Judy Garland's ability to cry on cue every time she sang "Somewhere over the Rainbow."

Readers, like students or clients in a variety of fields, want and expect such control. It would be an affront to expose the unwary to the terrors, traumas, or temptations occurring in the writer's private life unless they were germane to the subject at hand. And it would be very unprofessional. We like our professionals to appear, well, professional, yet humanly so. From newscasters to teachers to our "personal" physicians, we want them to be gracious, concerned, caring, engaging, but we really don't want to know about the beating, if not bleeding, hearts behind their cheerful visages. It would be unfair for professionals to impose their personal problems on the members of their audience, each of whom has problems of his or her own.

Nevertheless the life that is being scripted for us, not necessarily the one we write about, is running forward, whether steadily, or in a repetitive loop, or out of control. Although our writing may provide the voice-over, with sufficient volume to override the undertones, there is no pause button in the flow of time, in the stream of events and phenomena to which we have no choice but to respond. That is the human condition. And although the persona in the text is not equivalent to the person behind the text, that person "bleeds" through as a pentimento image, the original version seeping into the painting superimposed on it. This process of transforming life into art, of coming out as a human being as we come into the text with care and calculation, does not make writers any less human. But it does give priority to the work of art and to the artistic control—and the writer's common sense —that mitigates against the kind of rampant, unguarded confession and narcissism that some critics wrongly attribute to personal writing (see Gass, "The Art of Self"; Patai).

Six Degrees of Separation, Six Degrees of Disclosure

I am using the concept of "six degrees of separation" to designate the degree to which the writer's actual self, whatever that is determined to be, emerges in and through the work. The research of Stanley Milgram in the 1960s (see Milstein), reiterated in the conceit of John Guare's play *Six Degrees of Separation* (1990), posits that everyone in the United States is connected by six or fewer stages of circumstance or acquaintance. Through an interlocking chain, the most intimate connections provide ultimate access to the most remote, often unlikely people. In part, I am using this concept as an index of how close the writer's self-presentation is to the unguarded, "inner" self; in part, as an indication of how close the writer is to the intended audience.*

---

*My theory of the way to conceive of an audience in relation to the presentation and development of the author's persona differs in orientation from the concepts of audience presented by Ong, Park, Ede and Lunsford (1984) , and Elbow ("Closing"), to identify only some of the best-known discussions of the subject.

From left to right rear: O. T. and Mildred Zimmerman (Lynn's parents), Marie and O. A. Zimmerman (Lynn's paternal grandparents); left to right front: Burke Zimmerman (Lynn's brother, age two) and Lynn (age four), Detroit, Michigan, 1938

On this scale the sixth degree of separation, the most remote end of the social continuum, reflects the fact that there are many people—either individuals or members of groups—whose existence we know of in this world but with whom we have no contact, either through ignorance, deliberate exclusion, mutual indifference, or geographical remoteness. These people are not part of the target audience of our writing. If they do encounter it, they will probably need to know a great deal about the cultural, political, historical, and other relevant contexts not only of the author's particular life, but of the entire culture and society in which that author lives. Yet they may not care at all about any of this; such a distant audience does not concern us here.

At the other end of the continuum, on a scale of zero to six, zero means that the writer is talking primarily to him or herself; anything an external reader encounters in zero degrees of separation is the equivalent of reading the writer's mind. One degree of separation includes the writer's most intimate relationships—perhaps only the spouse, best friend, or most significant other. Two degrees, intimates still—selected family members, friends, or colleagues with whom one has fairly continual contact and who share knowledge of each others' major life events and a significant segment of common culture. Axiomatically, the greater the degree of separation the audience is from the writer, the more information they need about the writer's life, personality, habitual way of looking at the world, for the writer to seem real. For intimate audiences, less is more; minimal cues are sufficient to trigger responses in one's readers, based less on what the writer actually says than on what it evokes.

Family Jokes: Zero, One, Two Degrees of Separation

Here, for example, is a collection of favorite family punch lines, any one of which sends me, my husband, or our sons into uproarious laughter: "It's a piston engine" (spoken in a fake Cambridgeshire accent); "Why doesn't he ride his bicycle?"; "No, it's only an ordinary *brown* whale"; "He's running around like a chicken with its legs cut off"; "Nonny-nonny noo"; "Ah'm tard, awful tard." Our daughters-in-law, though admirable in all other respects, don't always get these jokes; when they do, they don't always appreciate them. They were not present at the creation, nor have they experienced the aging of this wit, like fine wine, over the years. Our grandchildren, however, are beginning to accept some of these as their birthright, along with others of their own contribution: "It's doing the backstroke"; "A bowing groy"; "a'a" (but not pahoe'hoe); "Just use the quasenbö pan"; "Suave [pronounced "swayve"] dog." There is no point in trying to explain these jokes to you here; I could recite the words, but the music would be off-key.

The Writer's Presence in the Middle Distance

The third, fourth, and fifth degrees of separation are equivalent to the distancing that occurs in the most common of our social conversations. To "Hi, how are you?" there is only one acceptable answer, "Fine." If one were to answer truthfully, as I might have done at any time during the last three weeks, "Well, my mother just died. And I'm facing shoulder surgery," this would have nonplussed the casual greeter, to whom "Hi, how are you?" really means "I see you and I acknowledge that you and I are, if not friends, at least colleagues, casual acquaintances—people who meet and greet in public places." Or "Hello, Professor. It is I, your student, passing by."

To give a truthful answer might provoke clichés on the part of one or both of us: "Oh! I'm so sorry to hear it." Or, like the family jokes, a truthful answer would require a great deal more explanation than I would want to give or the greeter would want to hear. My mother was ninety-four and in a precipitous decline after ninety-three years of robust health. The truth would provide the necessity of more intimacy or even empathy than we might want or have time for, given the many unresolved issues that festered during her lifetime. Because this doesn't fit listeners' conventional expectations, it is hard to explain, especially with the conciseness a casual conversation requires. A truthful elaboration would indicate an equality of status and friendship and a reciprocity of intimacy with the hearer, when in fact we are merely passing one another in the corridors of life. If I'd added another true fact, "A pre-op EKG for the torn rotator cuff disclosed that I've had a heart attack sometime in the last two years," that would have freaked both of us out.

We are not throwing a pity party here, and so I say, "Fine, just fine." But that answer, though appropriate for a casual conversation—even though I am aware that it is a lie every time I utter it, and as an honest person this bothers me—will not suffice in creative nonfiction or other personal-sounding writing intended for this same audience. Although writers and teachers of academic articles adhere to the deceptive conventions that the author (even if evacuated from the text) is a "finished" character, a public persona speaking with certainty, confidence, and a sense of resolution or completeness (Gass, "Emerson"; Olivia Frey), personal essayists employ other conventions.

Personal essayists present the author as a character in the "author saturated text" as a private person, speaking from a stance of uncertainty and vulnerability in a world where matters are incomplete and unresolved (see Ruth Behar, "Dare We Say I?"; Peter Elbow, "Reflections"; Nancy K. Miller, *Getting Personal;* and Scott Russell Sanders, "The Singular First Person"). Thus it's much easier to explore troublesome relationships, such as my lifelong struggle with my mother, in personal essays, a capacious, elastic genre that does not require closure, rather than in casual, social conversation that mandates superficiality. I have done so in many of the chapters in this book. So too, like talking to fellow passengers on airplanes, I can tell members of an audience I don't know personally about the heart attack message (scare? diagnosis?)—it's still in flux, and I don't know what label to settle on—that I will not discuss with colleagues and students, who are nearer if not closer. At school I am taking care that this aspect of the pentimento image does not bleed through.

I used to believe that readers were not seeking the author either in or behind the text, that they mostly wanted to hear a compelling story. But personal experience belies this; while academic articles provoke citations, letters to the editor, even whole articles or books of rebuttal, personal essays are likely to engender all of the above, as well as mail written to the author constructed within the text, and sent to the author behind it.[†] Best of all, they

---

† This outpouring of fellow feeling is not confined to human beings; witness the outpouring of love for the iconic racehorse Barbaro, an athlete dying young whose noble image (not, of course, a self-construct) captured the public's passion after he broke a leg in the Preakness, two weeks after winning the Kentucky Derby in 2006. As Joe Drape reports:

The gates of the hospital here have been adorned with signs proclaiming love for Barbaro and beseeching him to heal—"Grow Hoof Grow"—since his arrival. The fruit baskets filled with green apples and carrots, elaborate flower arrangements and get-well

engender more stories; readers of others' true stories find in them an invitation to tell their own right back. Although I tell some of these stories to my students in autobiography and creative nonfiction classes to model the personal essays I'm asking them to write, I will not tell them about the current, pending medical issues.

I had intended to use "Stress Test," which follows, as an example of private, zero-degree-of-separation writing, just for myself. But I couldn't do it, for reasons that I'll soon explain.

Stress Test

"Will you need a wheelchair?" asked the nurse who was calling to schedule the echocardiogram and stress test at the hospital. Six weeks earlier, our family—my husband, Laird and Sara, and Beth and Paul—had spent four days hiking on and around Mt. Rainier at eleven thousand feet. After a day on the trail, we'd hit the lodge pool for an hour, followed by immersion in the hot tub. Yes, I'd been winded on some of the steeper trails; one photo shows all of us looking bushed. But in another, the one I can see out of the corner of my eye just to the right of the computer screen on my desk, taken ten minutes later, we're alert, smiling, and ready for more. There is no wheelchair in this picture. And there were no symptoms of a heart attack between the baseline EKG two years ago and the EKG I'd just had in preparation for the shoulder surgery that showed a level spot on the third lead readout—indicating damage to the heart muscle—where there had been a gentle spike two years before. No symptoms at all, no pain, no indigestion, nothing. "No, I won't," I said.

"It's a long walk from the parking lot to the cardiac unit. Are you sure you can make it?" Her voice had the kindly solicitude, slightly condescending, that I myself often use when talking to—gasp—little old ladies. I wanted

---

cards arrived by the truckload. Since early June, a Barbaro Fund has attracted more than $1.2 million in donations for the hospital, which is part of the New Bolton Center at the University of Pennsylvania.

Online message boards were swamped with Barbaro news and for months became a virtual waiting room. On Monday, one of them . . . had its daily traffic nearly double to 15,000 visitors in a single hour. . . . "I love you Barbaro," read one message . . . "Everyone in my family is praying for you & lighting candles. Stay strong & don't give up! XXOO."

Barbaro was eulogized as well as euthanized by his doctor, grieving veterinarian Dean Richardson, who said, "People love greatness. . . . People love the story of his bravery" (Joe Drape, "After 8 Months Filled by Hope, Setback Ends Barbaro's Battle," 17).

to tell her, "Furthermore, my total blood pressure is usually around 120/70. My cholesterol is 186 (desirable is under 200); *my triglyceride level is 70* (again, desirable is below 200); *my HDL—the "good" cholesterol—is 68* (under 130 is desirable); *my LDL is 104.1* (low risk). *At 5'3" and 115 pounds, my body mass index is 20.36* (overweight starts at 26, obesity begins at 30). *I've never smoked, and I don't eat junk food, and I exercise every single day of the year."* I wanted her to know that I am, really, a healthy person, and I wanted her to reply, "Well, then, that EKG must have been a fluke." But all I said was, "Yes, I can." Was this what it meant to be a "heart patient?" I scarcely knew how to behave; I hadn't even had the tests, and already I was swearing never to fit the stereotypes.

It is clear that I am not writing this exclusively either to or for myself. I know what our family did on our summer vacation. I am well aware that my medical profile exudes good health; I already know all of the data I'm presenting here. I don't need to write any of this down. Although before I wrote this I hadn't articulated my intention never to succumb to the stereotype of an invalid, it is certainly apparent to all who know me that I am as unlikely to accept that stereotype, or any other, with docility. But readers of this essay, whoever you are, don't know me or any of this inside information, so I have to tell you something to enable you to know me from the inside out and thus to be as surprised by the "heart attack" diagnosis as I, my family, and my doctor are. Moreover I also realize, although I personally love these stellar test results, to announce them to external readers would be regarded as boastful and therefore offensive, were it not for the mitigating effects of the possible heart attack. With its potentially devastating consequences in the balance, I receive the sympathy vote. I can get away with a lot as an essayist, taking risks with its form, characterizations, tone, for readers are a great deal more forgiving of the vulnerable writer than of the securely smug. However I neither ask for nor expect pity as a "heart attack victim"; no "poor me," no "why me?" The irony of fate, life's joke on life for the preventively oriented, is that the joke will be on us, and it will not be funny. However I refuse to succumb to, as *New Yorker* critic Arlene Croce calls it, "victim art" (55).

I don't think I personally could ever attain "zero degrees of separation"— an intimate heart-to-heart with only myself—even if I were keeping a private diary. In fact Sara asked me during our recent vacation, "Why don't you keep a journal?" since both of our grandchildren have been trained in school to do so, and they keep them voluntarily on trips. I replied that as a professional writer I eschew the elliptical. I always have in mind an audience who doesn't know me, and whenever I start to jot down the bare bones (which in this case would have been simply the dialogue with the nurse), I begin to tell the story, fill in the details, play with possibilities, even to revise the text as

I'm in the process of writing it. So I might as well just go straight to the essay itself, even though I realize that such prolific writers as Charles Dickens, Mark Twain, Henry James, and Virginia Woolf kept detailed notebooks that they later drew on for fiction and nonfiction alike. That many of the entries can be understood by readers remote from these writings in time and context attest to their high amount of significant detail.

Of course I have constructed a self in the "Stress Test" episode; I tried to pick out only details that were unique to myself. Thus I intentionally omitted thoughts that I figured were so common everyone had them and would recognize them in the undercurrent of what I did say. Here's what I left out, in the order the questions arrived as my doctor, Rick, called with the news of the aberrant EKG. "Sit down," he said in a kind voice, "take a deep breath. Take two." He paused a beat. "The readout looks as if there's been some muscle damage to your heart." "Does that mean I've had a heart attack?" I jumped the gun. As he asked whether I'd had any symptomatic pain or indigestion during the past two years since my previous, normal-looking EKG. "Surely," I thought, "there's been some mistake. Could the lab have sent him someone else's EKG?" Then, "Am I going to die? How soon?" Then, "I'm not ready to die yet—I need more time in this life." But all I said to the doctor was, "How could I have had a heart attack and not know it?" "That happens sometimes," he said. "But you're so healthy I wouldn't have expected it to happen to you."

By this time Martin was on the phone as well, in time to hear the doctor say, "I've told the orthopedist to cancel your shoulder surgery until we figure out what's going on with your heart." "Can I continue my daily swim?" "No, and no fast walking, either. Just ordinary walking." "Am I going to be a permanent invalid?" I was thinking, "I don't want to learn how to live like that." Then Martin asked, "What about sex?" "Only with one person at a time," replied Rick, and I said, "Be still, my beating heart." We hung up, laughing. Martin came in and put his arms around me as I sat there in shock, too stunned to cry. When I finally relaxed enough to be able to cry, I willed myself not to; it would only give me a bad headache, and I had a manuscript to finish and papers to grade. I would have to hold onto hope, and keep the sick jokes coming. When I arose to walk across the room, I wondered whether my steps would be shaky as a result of this dubious new knowledge, but my stride was firm and brisk. The same as before.

If what I have said here does not surprise you, then in "Stress Test" I got it right, and the self behind the text is congruent with, if not a twin of, the self within that text. If I got either version wrong, then I will have to back off until I have sufficient distance to see clearly what to revise.

Teaching Self-Constructions and Genre

What I have told you of these most intimate matters and the genre in which they are expressed, my audience of professional peers with four (if you know me or my work) or five degrees (if you don't but are reading this essay) of separation, I also tell my students (three degrees of separation) in a more general way, and with different examples. I am currently teaching a graduate seminar in autobiography; my students have read "Living to Tell the Tale," and that's the only autobiography they'll get from me all semester. This is not a course in Lynn Z. Bloom, though I am intentionally modeling, in a somewhat personal style, collaborative teaching and learning during every class meeting. I want my students to love the subject as I do, to see its power and glory and excitement, and so I wear my heart, but not my medical chart, on my sleeve. I want my students in their own work to experience the inseparable interconnections among humanity, artistry, and intelligence. My understanding of the issues as a teacher is profoundly influenced by my practice as a writer. "Although the essay as a genre gives the impression of being tentative, casual, laid back, searching," I tell them, "it is nevertheless written by a person in charge, though one who admits she doesn't have all the answers." Here are some of the suggestions I offer to enable students to create that character, the central consciousness of a compelling tale.

Authorial persona:
Issues of self-construction, self-transformation, self-disclosure

How do I want my readers to see me? In what role(s), relationship(s)?

Do I want them to like me? If yes, it cannot be for sentimental reasons or on account of special pleading. If I don't want the readers' affection, why not?

What conspicuous values, beliefs, actions will demonstrate my character and personality in this story?

Why am I (as a character) not perfect? In what areas am I vulnerable that matter in this story?

What behavior, scenes, details can I incorporate to illustrate the character I'm presenting?

What seemingly insignificant details, idiosyncrasies, habits can reveal larger truths about this character?

In what language will I talk? And the others in my writing? (Try reading the dialogue aloud, and the rest of the narrative, to see if it sounds realistic; change it if it doesn't, but eliminate the repetition and the clichés unless you're striving for a comic parody of people who talk that way. Of course contractions are all right, and slang, even profanity if that's the way you talk.)

What do I need to leave out, even if it's true, to keep the focus where I want it?

Finally, is there any significant disparity between my private and public self? Am I really the same person as the one I write about? Should I be? Does it matter?

Genre: What are the conventions of the kind of essay I'm writing, the story I'm telling?

Before we get to the questions student writers can ask themselves, I have my students unpack the implications of the dead-on definition of "true story" Tim O'Brien offers in "How to Tell a True War Story." This applies to all sorts of creative nonfiction and personal essays, as well as to the fiction in which it appears.

"True war stories do not generalize. They do not indulge in abstraction or analysis."

"Often in a true war story there is not even a point, or else that point doesn't hit you until twenty years later, in your sleep. . . . "

"You can tell a true war story by the questions you ask. Somebody tells a story, let's say, and afterward you ask, 'Is it true?' and if the answer matters, you've got your answer."

"In the end, of course, a true war story is never about war. It's about sunlight. . . . It's about love and memory. It's about sorrow. It's about sisters who never write back and people who never listen." (*The Things They Carried*, 84–91)

After we've derived from O'Brien some operative parameters of this open-ended genre, I remind them that "true stories" can have exactly the same characteristics as fiction: a central character (see above) and subordinate characters, a theme, a plot, setting(s), action, dialogue. The main difference is, as Philippe Lejeune contends in "The Autobiographical Pact," the author's claim that what (s)he writes is true, and the reader's expectation that this is so: "When we recognize the person who claims authorship of the narrative as the protagonist or central figure in the narrative—that is, when we believe them to be the same person—we read the text written by the author to whom it refers as reflexive or autobiographical" (Smith and Watson, 8).

From these considerations derive questions student writers can use to guide their construction of the genre:

What's my narrative about? Can I focus on a single topic?
How overt or indirect do I want this to be?

133

Should my narrative follow the conventions of any particular type of autobiographical story? (The following are the most common in student writing, among many possibilities—all elaborated on in Smith and Watson's *Reading Autobiography,* appendix A, "Fifty-two Genres of Life Narrative," 185–207.)

> *bildungsroman*—initiation, coming-of-age, sense of emerging identity
> *discovery or learning* (something or about oneself; how to accomplish or overcome something); a literacy or education narrative
> *watershed, turning point* (when life was one way before something occurred, another way—usually fairly dramatic—afterward)
> *adventure, travel, narrative of exotic escape*
> *witness or eyewitness*
> *apologia*—a justification of one's own deeds, beliefs, and way of life (Smith and Watson, 184–85)
> *family memoir,* focusing on the author's relation to one or more members of the immediate family; if this involves first- and second-generation immigrants, then this may become an ethnic narrative, as well, that negotiates boundaries, identities, hybrid, or conflicting cultures (see Smith and Watson, 104)

What tone best suits my subject? Straightforward and serious? Humorous? Ironic?

Conclusion: Laying Our Lives on the Line

Two issues of the writer's self-confidence intersect with the writer's self-consciousness. Although these usually bedevil students more than professional writers, the issues are the same when one undertakes the deliberate construction, presentation of a self in the text. Writers have an immense personal stake in their personal writing, and in that character who lives in and through their work. "Love me, love my story"—or the reverse, "Love my story, love me." But for the readers, love is not the issue; engagement is, and whether or not the tale is compellingly told. Students have to be reminded that the grades are awarded not on the merits of the character presented (who may be annoying, boorish, despicable . . .) or the life depicted (whether saccharine, sensational, sordid . . .), but on the quality of the writing, with no special pleading from the author beyond the text. Additionally students, like all writers, have to be encouraged to trust themselves to get it right, to tell the essence of the true story in an economical way but to set it up in such a way that the readers can fill in the blanks, flesh out the tale for themselves. I tell my students to go heavy on the nouns and verbs and core dialogue, light on the adjectives, adverbs, and descriptive passages. Then I tell them to read their work aloud to each other, and if it passes that muster, to someone four or five degrees of separation from them. If it compels those readers' attention, belief in the author's point of view, and engagement with the central character, then the author has successfully come out, as both a writer and a human being in—and behind—the text.

Oh, one other thing. It has not escaped my notice that you might be sufficiently interested in the life of the writer of this essay beyond its textual parameters to want to know the results of my heart examinations—the echocardiogram, the stress test, the hundreds of gamma camera photographs of my radioactively injected heart after exercise and at rest. I should tell you the score, but at this writing I don't know what it is. I, who love ambiguity in literature, have little tolerance for lack of clarity in real life. Although I have told you punch lines without the jokes, I do not want to tantalize you with the story of life's big joke on my life and then pull the punch. If this were fiction, I could invent alternative endings. What would you like—happy? sad? melodramatic? sweet and touching? stiff upper lip? I could write it to order. But this is a true story, and truly I don't know what to say. Pending the results, I take brisk walks, hang out with family and friends, end the evenings with a single glass of cabernet. As usual. And every day I sit at the computer and write my heart out.

Subverting the Academic Masterplot

Teachers' Tales—the Masterplots

Teachers' tales out of school, the stories we love to hear, seem to have two basic masterplots, both with happy endings. Plot One shows the teacher-as-practitioner playing the role of what Stephen North calls "television doctor." In this "miracle-cure scenario" (46), the teacher is confronted with a new, or chronic, problem that defies solution. This mystery malady infects the entire class or individual students, who for unfathomable reasons can't master the requisite skills or learn the lessons du jour. The tortured teacher, who has previously leapt all problems with a single bound, is stymied. She paces and ponders, buttonholing colleagues with the Problem That Will Not Die.

Picture, for example, Mina Shaughnessy "sitting alone in the worn urban classroom" where her "severely underprepared" freshmen have "just written their first essays." In astonishment and despair, the Master Teacher ponders their "stunningly unskilled" writing. However, unable even to "define the task" or "sort out the difficulties," she can "only sit there, reading and re-reading the alien papers, wondering what had gone wrong and trying to understand what [she] at this eleventh hour of [her] students' academic lives could do about it" (*Errors and Expectations*, vii).

The universe is out of step until the teacher, through accident or intention, stumbles on a solution, trying first one, then another remedy until fortune favors the prepared mind and—voilà! The miracle cure is at hand. *Errors and Expectations* metamorphoses into *Great Expectations;* Shaughnessy now has "no difficulty assessing the work to be done nor believing that it *can* be done" (vii). The students' problems are solved; "'Oh, Dr. [Shaughnessy], this is so much better! How can I ever thank you'" (North, 46). Other teachers are inspired; Shaughnessy's ragtime band marches on in triumph.

Although Plot Two might be considered a variation of Plot One, for it too ultimately has a miracle cure, this version is inspired by the Book of Job instead of the Book of Mina. In this story, for whatever reasons, the class begins to deteriorate; students and teacher are either marching to different drummers, or else not marching at all. Unless a dramatic change happens in a hurry—prompted by the teacher's agonizing reappraisal, the students' spontaneous turnaround, or some form of deus ex machina—the class is doomed to entropic disaster. The teacher, formerly arrogant in her confidence that she can work miracles, has been thoroughly humbled by forces greater than she. The dark night of the soul infects students and teacher alike; Dostoyevsky reigns in a Kafkaesque universe.

But wait! The dramatic change does in fact happen, and redemption, resurrection, are at hand. Teacher and students have learned An Important Lesson together and, sadder but much, much wiser, have achieved Victory Against Great Odds. Praise the Lord; the beat goes on. I myself have structured "Finding a Family, Finding a Voice" according to this plot, which tells how my course in teaching composition for new TAs had become an unstructured, off-balance response to a crisis (no textbooks, students who themselves were not teaching). In this weekly guerilla theater, by sharing my own risk-taking writing in progress (a very personal, very exploratory version of "Why I Write"), I and the students "effected a paradigm shift. Within two months' time," I wrote, "my class had changed from students in the process of learning about teaching in order to teach writing, to students in the process of becoming writers in order to teach writing" ("Finding a Family," 22).

We live by these masterplots; they exalt every valley and make the rough places plain. These are the success stories that, in one form or another, teachers love to hear, and live to tell. But the story I am finally able to disclose to you here, nearly two decades after the dismal events, fits neither of these ultimately exhilarating plots. It is the story of the worst course I have ever taught, the worst teaching I have ever done, the most students who didn't stay the course—and right they were. Since even the greatest of teachers must have dwelt in Disaster City on occasion, I assume that such stories are legion, buried in the secret files of our minds. Like accounts of illegal abortions, these seldom attain the public status of lore or legend—and when they do, they happen to someone else.

Well this one happened to me, with my unwitting, indeed eager, complicity. It is, at best, a cautionary tale of some of the bad things that can go wrong when a course and a teacher and a class and a curriculum inadvertently conspire to subvert the academic rhythm of a semester, flexible and forgiving, by trying to cram what should have occurred over fifteen weeks into a five-day summer session. When I began to write this, I continued to attribute all the difficulties to the course's truncated time frame. But no longer. As I wrote and rewrote, I came to understand that yes, the compressed format provided insurmountable constraints, but these were exacerbated by my own ignorance. I was a stranger in strange lands, in a university new to me, in an unfamiliar school (of education) with its own (and to this English professor) strange culture, trying to introduce new doctoral students to a new discipline that neither they nor I could have mastered in a week's time, that included concepts I didn't understand very well (statistics) or knew nothing about (ethnography—O fatal concept). The redemption from this disaster lies in the warning I offer here.

Academic Rhythm

I live by the generous rhythm of the academic year. Martin and I, already wedded to the semester system, were married during the shimmering legato of a summer vacation between master's and doctoral study. Our children were born during summer vacations. We've always moved, for new academic jobs, during summer vacations. Indeed vacations, particularly summer's three capacious months and the punctuation of Christmas break, which always proceeds presto, no matter how many calendar days are actually allocated, serve a myriad of academic purposes. For vacations make possible the time out of time—an increasingly rare luxury in today's downsized, outsourced, overstressed, workaday world—that provides the steady heartbeat for the entire academic year; the opportunity to read, write, do research, reinvent old courses, and create new ones; the time to travel.

Summer school courses disrupt two sets of natural academic rhythms, the summer's stately pace and the semester's measured tempo. Attempts to adapt the semester's customary pace to summer school's double, or triple, time may work in courses that consist primarily of reading as the way of learning—students can read more, or read faster. Or they can read less. Or teachers can expect less, although I am in Shaughnessy's camp and teach with great expectations in all seasons. Indeed I've found that the summer school mode most conducive to student learning without compromise on my part is the intensive workshop format, such as that used in the numerous sites of the National Writing Project, and in the Martha's Vineyard Summer Workshops. The long days, happy nights where students can get to know and work (and yes, play) with one another, the built-in two- to three-day breaks (good for library or field work and major writing), are supplemented by an extra month after the course ends so the students can complete an extensive term project. This schedule gives the students, mostly full-time teachers themselves, ample time to read widely, to reflect, to engage in various modes of research, to write, and to revise—maybe even more than an ordinary semester would allow.

Perhaps it was three satisfying summers of teaching in a National Writing Project five-week intensive workshop format that led me to accept an invitation from Prestige U to teach a summer school course, "Research 1, Introduction to Research Methods." Those summers of team teaching with an education school colleague and a veteran high school English curriculum supervisor, as well as the Writing Project participants, smart and energetic, led me to believe I understood, even shared, the schoolteachers' view of the composition studies universe.

"You can use whatever time frame you want," offered the dean's henchperson, "three times a week for the entire summer, every day for six or eight weeks, half days for two weeks, or," when I still did not answer, "full days plus some evenings for a week." Even the anemic salary, scrunched into a single week, appeared robust. So I leapt like a trout at the one-week format, the one most congruent with our family's summer plans. That this format proved totally uncongenial to every principle of teaching and learning that works well in a semester format should have been no surprise to me or to the sponsoring institution, for that matter, especially in the bailiwick—devoted to the study of education—where I was to teach.

A similar, so I believed, course had been the capstone of my own formal doctoral study, required of all students not the moment they entered the program but after they'd passed the doctoral prelims. Its virtue lay in the enforced opportunity to write one's dissertation prospectus, and to rewrite it dramatically, under supervision, every week for fifteen weeks until we got it right. As a consequence of innumerable visions and revisions, the project, always intellectually interesting, became manageable, elegant, and refined—and of course refined and adapted again many times during the actual research. "No problem to condense that course," I thought, for at the time I had never met a course I couldn't teach, "as long as I can plan it thoroughly in advance." A meticulous syllabus would see me through.

Alien Nation

I had come, fresh from the country, to the holy city of Byzantium on a blazing July Sunday afternoon loaded, I thought, for bear. I had already sent ahead a syllabus, detailed hour-by-hour, and a stack of journal articles to be xeroxed as the required reading. My underventilated undergraduate dorm room, windows sealed shut, accessible only by elevator and a fistful of keys, was home away from home. It reeked of eau de Big Mac and throbbed around the clock with heavy metal pulsations. When I finally fell asleep, these even penetrated the anxiety dream that reliably precedes each semester. This one differed from the usual in which I'd forgotten my books, or syllabus, or critical article of clothing—only to discover its absence when I faced the students and opened my book bag—or took off my coat. In this one, however, the dean called me the night before class was to start to say that he'd changed my assignment. Instead of teaching composition, I was to teach calculus. "But I don't know anything about teaching calculus," I responded. "You can *read,* can't you?" he thundered. "Just pick up the book and go to class and read faster than the students."

On Monday morning, I arrived a half hour early at the frigid seminar room in which the class was to meet from 8 A.M. to 5 P.M. for the next five days, to find several students there already. Greying and grave, they eyed my cotton shift and sandals with calculated impassivity. I began to shiver, but here, too, the windows were sealed shut.

The early arrivals' not-so-casual conversation made their agenda very clear. "Our own schools have recently let out. We're glad to be here for only a week; it won't interrupt the rest of the summer very much," said a woman in a twin sweater set and pearls. "With Prestige's evening and summer courses, we can teach full time and still work on our degrees. And of course we expect As," spoken with a smile. "We're entitled to As," quickly added another, whose navy suit and pumps signaled a person accustomed to being in charge—whether of a classroom, a department, or an entire school didn't matter. "Admission to the doctoral program automatically guarantees this." There was no smile. What did an A here mean? I wondered. Were As in fact a doctoral entitlement? Well they'd have to do the work, and then we'd see.

By 8 A.M. the room, designed for twenty, was crowded with double that number around the seminar table, an astonishing enrollment even for a required course. "Let's get acquainted," I chirped. "You don't know me"— how could they when I had no reputation at that school as a teacher, nor anywhere as a researcher in the field of education. "You can call me Lynn, and I'd like to call you by your first names."

"Here we call our professors by their titles, and they call us by ours," shot a slender, bearded young man in jeans. His glittering eye fixed on mine. "You *are Doctor,* aren't you?" Ordinarily I'd have joked, "Not a *real* doctor." That morning I simply said, "Yes. A Ph.D."

"My name is *Mister Barber, ABD,* and I want to know why you don't have an Ed.D. This is a school of education, and an Ed.D. is our normative degree."

"What's the difference?"

"*You* should know."

Even though he shouldn't have asked, he was right. I should have known that as the creation of an English department, my understanding of the meaning of research was very different from that of the education school faculty and students. Research in English, at least in the research institution from which I had come, was theoretical rather than applied; text-oriented, not classroom-based; qualitative rather than quantitative; analytic rather than descriptive. When I'd taught a comparable course to English grad students, we always skipped the math to cut to the humanities chase—theory; philosophy; rhetorical analysis; case studies replete with character, plot, and resolution. I recognized that *College Composition and Communication* and *Research in the Teaching of English* of the time revealed very different research paradigms, but since I'd never had a doctoral student in education before, I'd never had to figure out why.

As I distributed xerox after xerox, other questions began. Most of the students, I had been told before I came, were newly admitted to the doctoral program. All that I knew about Prestige's expectations of the course came from the catalog description. I told them, "Research 1 will be, as the catalog explains, your introduction to the specialized professional literature and to the methodology of composition studies research. Because the scope of this course, like many that focus on the state-of-the-art in any field, exceeds that of the existing textbooks, I—and you—will have to do a lot of talking to integrate the journal articles I've brought. Stories about our teaching experiences can make important connections."

I ventured a smile at the noncommittal faces. "As you can see by the syllabus"—I felt as if I were droning on, even though the class had been in session less than five minutes, "we'll be spending half-day segments on overviews of some of the major methodologies of composition studies research, as represented by well-known, well-regarded studies in the field. We'll look at methods ranging from teacher lore and teacher-as-researcher to case histories; to clinical research emphasizing small- and large-group studies, short- and long-term; to assessment of reading and writing. Because the field, new as it is, is changing so fast, these methods are exemplified primarily in the journal articles I'm giving you."

This scheme anticipated a combination of the topic areas and procedures of North's *Making of Knowledge in Composition* and Edward White's *Teaching and Assessing Writing*. Indeed, had both these books been available at the time—along with Lauer and Asher's *Composition Research: Empirical Designs*, Tate's bibliographic overview in *The Writing Teacher's Sourcebook*, and alternative paradigms to North, such as Kirsch and Sullivan's *Methods and Methodology in Composition Research*, Gere's *Into the Field*, Farris and Anson's *Under Construction*, and Ede's *Braddock Essays 1975–1998*—the course, even in a one-week format, might have been manageable.

It occurred to me as I was talking that I should have asked a Prestige faculty member what the course usually covered. Now, even if the map I had prepared was inadequate to navigate this unknown territory, it was already too late to change. So I soldiered on. "As you can see from the syllabus, this course, short though it is, will culminate in a term project that requires you to conceptualize and design a research project. With luck, it will prove to be a model for your dissertation research."

The class erupted with questions. "How much time do we have after this week is up to turn in our papers?" "Would three months be enough—by mid-October?" I replied. "I'd like to allow some turnaround time so I can comment on a preliminary draft." "Our annual bonuses depend on the grades being turned in before Labor Day"; what I saw by then would be all I'd get. "How long do the papers have to be?" My usual answer, "Write until you've said what you have to say and then stop," would hardly suffice. "How many outside sources do we have to use?" How could I answer that when I didn't know what they were writing on? "Where can we find them?" "What are the summer library hours? Is it open on Sundays?" I didn't even know where the library was. "What else will our grades be based on?" Attendance and class participation seemed too juvenile for this obviously mature group. There would be no time for them to prepare reading-response notebooks or literature reviews during the week we were meeting, and it would be hard, in these days B.C.E. (Before Computer E-mail), to collect and respond to such work once we left campus. "I'll . . . I'll have to let you know."

During these preliminaries, I became aware of considerable rolling of the eyes among Mr. Barber and two other blue-jeaned peers. And then it hit me. What was an ABD doing in this course for new doctoral students? I could have asked, but the answer, any answer, would only create complications. We were going to stick to the syllabus, by God, so that I, at least, could stay afloat for the week.

And so we did, at least on Day One. Contrary to my preferred format of interactive class discussion interspersed with small breakout groups focusing on particular issues, I did most of the talking—all morning about writing process research, all afternoon about issues of language teaching and linguistic research. The strict constructionists, ardent champions of current traditional grammar, listened with distant politeness to my explanations of other systems of grammar—structural, transformational, formal, and informal. Then they asked, "But how can the pupils do sentence combining properly if they don't label the parts of speech?" "Why should we bother with deep structure when the students already have trouble diagramming the surface structure?"

"You'll be better able to answer those questions tomorrow morning," I said, wondering if my own sentences were still coherent after eight hours of practically nonstop speech. I continued, "After you've read the Chomsky material from *Syntatic Structurer* tonight."

The class jerked to attention. "What reading tonight?" asked Mrs. Sanders, a woman whose take-charge manner pegged her as a principal.

"What's on the syllabus, of course."

"Doctor Bloom," she enunciated with precision, "You need to understand that most of us have a long drive to get here in the morning, and we'll be going home in the rush hour. We have other responsibilities once we're there. There's no way we can read a dozen articles a night, let alone absorb them. Especially," she said, "when we already have a backlog of today's articles that no one could read in advance."

She added, "Just tell us the two most important ones, and we can at least skim those."

"Every single reading is important," I replied. "Every single reading deals with a different aspect of the field, and every single hour of the day's lectures is predicated on your knowledge of the readings. Except," I paused, trying to calm down, "Wednesday afternoon, when another lecturer will run all of us through the boot-camp basics of statistics"—concepts I barely remembered from the single undergraduate course I'd taken fifteen years earlier: ANOVA, beta weights, chi-squares, Likert scales, multiple correlation, one- and two-tailed statistical tests, threats to internal validity, and Type 1 and Type 2 errors. "You won't need to be able to do the actual math at this stage," I offered, "but knowing the terminology will help you read the research articles." Which they weren't about to do.

"Well," I finally said, as the silence continued, "if you have to choose, start with Elliott Mishler's 'Meaning In Context: Is There Any Other Kind?' It's just come out, and it will help to make sense of everything else you read. And the xeroxed section of Emig's *The Composing Process of Twelfth Graders.* We'll be discussing narrative research methods in the afternoon."

"Such as . . . ," asked Mr. Barber.

"Oh, teacher stories focusing on practical wisdom and teacher-as-researcher, some interviews, and case histories, mostly."

"Anything else?" he persisted, his gaze unflinching.

What was he driving at? "We'll take it up tomorrow." The students talked among themselves, but not to me, and surged into the steaming summer sunset.

The Cooked and the Raw

The next morning, I began with "What are good research questions?" in hopes of warming up the room, which was even colder than the preceding day. "How do we know they're good?" "How could a question be translated into a workable research design—say, for your term papers?" "Excuse me," offered a middle-aged woman who had taken notes nonstop on Monday. "My name is Mrs. Miller. This is my first doctoral course. You just gave us the syllabus yesterday, and we haven't had a chance to read much." She looked embarrassed. "I'm sorry, but I can't answer your question responsibly until I've done more reading and thinking. At the moment, I haven't a clue about what would be a good question to ask, or a bad one. Until now I'd never thought about research designs, ever. How can I invent one out of thin air?"

"You're right," I began, ignoring the groans of Mr. Barber and his two pals. "It's not possible for someone new to research, no matter how experienced you are as a teacher or writer"—I smiled and she smiled back—"to understand at the outset the research issues and models that you're here to learn about. This five-day seminar will just scratch the surface."

As I spoke, the import of these words began to sink in. How, indeed, in this brief span of time could the students even learn enough terminology, let alone the research literature in their chosen area, whatever that was to be, well enough to join in the ongoing dialogue in the academic parlor, as Kenneth Burke envisioned? Even when they did find a research focus, they'd need to let the ideas marinate long enough to make them their own. Would it be possible to devise a workable research design at this stage of their graduate study? Any design would predictably require a number of revisions, and consultations in connection with each one. Even with express mail, this would be a stretch to accomplish at long distance. But the entire course was built around this task.

"I'll try to confer individually with everyone this week, and we can at least map the terrain." Where would the extra twenty-five hours come from in the next three days to make good on this desperate promise?

"Well, I know what I'm going to do," announced a pretty peroxide blonde. "In my experience, rule-oriented grammar drill is the best way to teach students to write well. My students always ace the SATs, and their newspaper—I'm the adviser—has won state awards three years in a row." Her crimson smile was triumphant. "In fact," she asserted, "drilling the rules is the *only* good way to ensure that students will write properly. My term paper will prove I'm right. That paper will be the basis of the thesis that my dissertation research will prove." Several of her peers nodded in approval. "What a wonderful subject," said one, ignoring my surprised silence.

I couldn't imagine that Prestige would let its students investigate an issue that even at the time had been thoroughly discredited. However there were already so many things I hadn't anticipated at Prestige that I asked, "So what else do you think would be good term paper topics?"

"What about an ethnographic study?" interposed Mr. Barber.

My hesitation did not escape his notice. What was "ethnography?" I was as startled to hear this unfamiliar term as I had been when someone complimented me at a professional meeting for having done "a pioneering study in protocol analysis," a method so unusual at the time that it had no label. Mr. Barber had me exactly where he wanted—up against the wall. With no context, I hadn't a clue. I took a deep breath and said, "What's ethnography?"

"You don't know what ethnography is? Well, let me tell you. We've"—he gestured toward his two companions—"just finished a research course in ethnographic methodology with Shirley Brice Heath." Her early innovations and methodological sophistication had yet to appear in *Ways With Words,* the transformative work that would make ethnographic research as standard a tool in schools of education as it was in anthropology; it would later win her a MacArthur "genius" award. "We can't do our doctoral research with her, because she's moving to Stanford. But we signed up for this course to lay out the groundwork for our dissertations. If we get the methodology worked out this summer, we can do our classroom fieldwork in the fall. But you," his face reddened with anger, "you don't even know what ethnography is. I didn't pay eight hundred fifty dollars in tuition for this course to listen to low-level grammar projects. I know how to do statistics. And I can't stand your silly stories." Telling stories was for me even then as natural as telling the truth.

"Why don't you drop the course?" I could hardly get the words out.

"I've tried. There's some rule that the registrar won't waive."

"I'm sure if you hold your ground you'll get a refund." Mr. ABD Barber and his two colleagues quickly stuffed the day's xeroxes into their book bags and marched out. "If anyone else wishes to leave, please go now." My words reverberated in the frozen air.

No one moved, but I knew that from then on the course was irredeemable. I would never be able to regain the authority that for Mr. Barber and associates I had never held in the first place. I would like to be able to say that with the malcontents' departure the course immediately shifted into the overdrive I work for in all my classes—high energy, low friction, full speed ahead.

But when I try to recollect the particulars of the rest of that very long week, it is as if I had been anesthetized. Through memory's translucent scrim, the course topics, the visiting statistician, the students pass in slow motion, with the sound turned off. I am giving lectures no one can hear, holding soundless conferences with every student before class, during lunch, late in the afternoon, throughout each exhausting evening. But this class has shattered into discrete fragments at the utterance of "ethnography," and its members float off into space, some beyond reach, the rest to alternative universes, from which they send me term papers better than they should be. The best is on teaching writing by teaching grammar.

4

The Arts of Living

Writing and Cooking,
Cooking and Writing

And a Recipe for the Best Blueberry Pie

Writing and cooking are two of the things I like to do best. Indeed they're a lot alike—a messy mix of knowledge and improvisation, experience and innovation, and continual revision with a lot going on in between the lines. For years I've toyed with writing a cookbook. But although I'm willing to revise my writing indefinitely until I get it right, I'm not willing to revise my cooking the way that Rose Levy Beranbaum did when she wrote *The Cake Bible*. She baked draft after draft of yellow cake, the subject of her master's thesis, until it floated out of the oven, light as a whisper, flirting alternately with sweet and with tart. Fifteen versions in two weeks, or so I imagine.

That's about right for revising a manuscript, but what would my husband and I do with a cake a day? We had enough trouble getting rid of the Friendship Bread, a millstone in doughy disguise. I've never learned to make bread as Martin does that so well I don't need to learn. Today he's making sourdough baguettes with sun-dried tomatoes from our own garden. A dozen years ago, returning from the Sierra Nevadas, where I had gone to edit the wartime diary of Margaret Sams, I had carried back to Virginia her gift of a sourdough start, a bubbly descendant of pioneer stock Margaret's great-grandmother had transported to Sacramento in a covered wagon 140 years earlier. Mine made the return journey by jet, its adolescent vigor threatening to break the mason jar in transit. A neighbor once gave us, in desperation, we later realized, a starter for Friendship Bread (aka Hermann Bread, aka Amish Bread), a sweet, yeasty concoction calculated to create enemies, because it doubled daily in bulk and had to be fobbed off on still other neighbors. They grew as quickly sick of it as we did until we hustled it off to the compost heap, where for weeks we'd catch glimpses of it creeping, amoeba-like, from beneath rotting cabbage leaves.

Lynn's paternal grandmother, Marie Kadow Zimmerman, on her ninetieth birthday in 1969, with great-grandchildren Laird (age five) and Bard (age seven)

But I digress. This is much easier to do when I'm cooking than when I'm writing, unless I'm writing about cooking, which is a continual digression, for every recipe is full of stories. Although writing, like cooking, demands an audience for the finished product, the dialogue in my head when I write— with other writers, readers, myself—is spoken aloud when I cook. If no one's in the kitchen with me, I'm on the phone, a cordless model in perpetual danger of dropping into the dish du jour while I talk to students, family, friends, editors, and colleagues. The night before last, for instance, I peeled ten cups of Ida Red seconds for a pie while helping a grad student, herself a pie baker, explore a dissertation prospectus on working-class autobiographies. During the next conversation of substance, I'll peel and sauté the onions for the onion soup I've been contemplating making for several wintry weeks. In fact, writing this sentence has impelled me to call the butcher to make sure he has beef bones in stock. He does, but how many pounds? A frantic flipping through Julia Child yields only vague clues, but there, on page forty of *The New All Purpose Joy of Cooking*, lies the answer, "5 pounds." I'd guessed 6, and I can relax. I'm planning to make the salad for our impending dinner party during a long-distance call to my mother. "What are you cooking this week?" she invariably asks, anticipating the obbligato of chopping and dishwashing.

But the cooking is more fun when the kitchen is full of those very people who make the phone calls, as it has been since the day my German grandmother wrapped me twice round with an apron and I climbed up on a chair to pinch fanciful shapes from leftover strips of pie dough stretched on the floury, red vinyl counter. I learned to cook by watching my grandmother and my mother and through considerable experimentation, as well as from a stew of cookbooks. My recollection is that Mom did all the fun parts while assigning me to peel the potatoes and scrub the carrots, but since I have always loved to cook, there must have been pleasure beyond root vegetables. I learned to write by total immersion in a broth of books and a lot of practice and false starts and careful attention to the sounds as well as to the sense. So I absorbed Dr. Seuss, my earliest favorite author, followed soon by Louisa May Alcott, and later by Dr. Spock. If to write was to join the conversation of mankind, to cook as an adolescent was to join the conversation of womankind, expanded in adult life to a colloquy with the world. Scraps of that communion over the years remain in the exchange of recipes, and the resulting recipe file, a history of friendships over time and distance.

As I write this, I flip through my bulging recipe file, crammed with recipes like rings on a redwood. The scent of chocolate wafts up from clippings and cards written in diverse hands. A card with a patina of tomato-y fingerprints is labeled Lentil Soup from Fifi, a neighbor in Indianapolis thirty-five years ago. This succulent concoction includes lots of carrots, dried mushrooms, "a slug of red wine," and seasoning with basil and vinegar instead of salt, in deference to Jim, her husband's, high blood pressure. It remains the gold standard of lentil soup and memento of a golden friendship, imbued with the absent presence of Jim, who has since died. Indeed this recipe file contains a moveable feast, my lifelong dialogue with fellow cooks, a history of friendships. The card for Kleff's Kale is suspiciously clean. Could wariness of that aggressive leaf have kept us from recreating this standout from the marathon Middle Eastern cooking sessions in our Williamsburg kitchen? With Ramsey Kleff, Martin's social research colleague, as impresario, we always made so much food we had to call up extra guests on the spot to share the overrun. I learned the labels—dolma, baba ghanoush, kibbeh, tabouli—long after the orderly chaos in our kitchen had subsided. But when Martin and I visited Ramsey's mother in Haifa, we came to understand essence and substance alike, for she stuffed us with food and tales of compassion, Christian and Jewish, Arab and Israeli, and blessed us with two baskets of savory leftovers for the road.

On a besplotched index card is Jerry's Salad Dressing, vinegar and oil with two surprise ingredients, onion juice and Worcestershire sauce. Along with Chicken-Sparerib Adobo, this is a lagniappe from my research in 1965 in

151

Cleveland, where I began to edit Natalie Crouter's *Forbidden Diary,* a record of her family's imprisonment in a Japanese camp in the Philippines in World War II. Natalie herself could scarcely boil an egg, even when her life really did depend on it; Jerry, her husband, did the cooking in prison camp and invented these recipes that survived two world wars. When the prisoners were weak from hunger, they would "spend hours talking of food," feeding their imaginations with prewar repasts, "gingerbread with whipped cream or hard sauce, apple sauce, whole wheat bread with gobs of butter—endless lines of dishes parade in our talks," Natalie wrote, "each talker going the other one better. Clara copies British cookbook recipes all day and reads them out to us" (November 4, 1944). My own children didn't dare complain about the food at home, for they knew I'd retaliate with paragraphs from the Crouters' starvation diet at the end of the war, two handsful of dirty, moldy rice garnered bit by bit from "cracks in the storeroom floor" (November 12, 1944). Writing long accounts of camp life daily in her clandestine diary, an activity punishable by death had the diary been discovered, was for Natalie as life sustaining as eating. "This diary," she wrote after eight months' incarceration, "is a safety valve! It is a rock through the window!" (October 5, 1942).

As I write this, I am interrupted by a phone call from Waldo, Martin's colleague. "What can we bring for dinner?" "Dessert," I say without hesitation, hoping secretly for a rhubarb pie from the fruit of their garden. Even if it's technically a vegetable, rhubarb works like a fruit. Turning again to the recipe file, I encounter Polly's Microwave Risotto with Asparagus. She'll be at dinner next week, too. She's an economist and collector of antique children's books, and I am as grateful to her for giving me a book-sale find of Julia Child's *Mastering the Art of French Cooking,* first edition, as I am for her lucid explanation of the euro. I don't know how she found such a pristine volume. In my kitchen, good cookbooks get so sticky and spotted from service on the front lines that I don't dare borrow library copies. The cookbooks likely to turn up at library sales run to specialized exotica, *The Whole Anchovy Cookbook;* outmoded tastes, *The Joys of Jell-O;* or astounding concoctions of *Radio Recipes,* heavy on oversalted combinations of canned mushroom soup, ketchup, fake bacon bits, and crushed potato chips. Good cookbooks, tattered and grubby from honorable use, stay home where they belong.

How happy I have been to have a second chance for rapprochement with Julia. When I was writing *Doctor Spock: Biography of a Conservative Radical,* my futile hope to end the Vietnam War, I gave Fifi my copy of Julia Child; (Julia salts with discretion.) This was the very bonus I'd joined Book-of-the-Month Club to get, along with the *Compact Edition of the Oxford English Dictionary* in two hefty volumes. So absorbed was I, however, with my preschool children and my writing ("Move over, Ben," Martin would say night after night as we climbed into bed, when I was writing Spock's biography) that I could scarcely even read Julia's long, detailed recipes straight through. Everything I tried was a failure, for she demanded a concentration and devotion to nuance at a time when I needed to get to the point in a hurry. So I relied at the time on two svelte paperbacks, Peg Bracken's *I Hate to Cook Book* and Marion Burros's *Elegant but Easy*. With the children grown, I am happy to return to the kitchen with Julia, even though Boeuf à la Bourguignon takes two fat pages to one skinny column of Beef Stew with Wine in *The Joy of Cooking*. I usually make this toothsome dish two days in advance of the day my grad students come to dinner, a recompense for reading their term papers aloud, and reheat it in the oven so the succulence will permeate the house when they arrive. I want their reading to be imbued with the subtle essence of the climactic dinner party scene in Virginia Woolf's *To the Lighthouse,* Mrs. Ramsay's gift to the guests and family she loves and whom, with her own death imminent, whe will never see again.

What recipe did Mrs. Ramsay give her cook to use, I wonder. Probably none at all. For the language of food is not the language of recipes but the language of cooks, communicated as surely and eloquently through their creations as the most sophisticated discourse emerging through scholarly articles. Neither my grandmother, who went through eighth grade, nor my college-educated mother relied much on cookbooks. The only cookbook in my mother's house to this day is a 1944 *Woman's Home Companion Cookbook,* its daunting advice (such as to cook spinach, brussels sprouts, and cauliflower a full forty-five minutes) ignored. That their breads were light, their piecrusts flaky, their pot roasts tender, and their chicken soups full-bodied with falling-off-the-bone chicken chunks and golden homemade noodles attests to the wisdom of long years of practice—and Mom's desire to beat her mother-in-law at her own game. They never wrote down recipes, never tried to transform an art into a science, in tacit acknowledgment of the fact that most good cooks regard recipes the way good writers regard dictionaries, as sources of inspiration—when they use them at all—with license to improvise.

Although grammar books would be a closer analogy to cookbooks than dictionaries are, such comparison would be not only infelicitous but inaccurate. I don't know any real writer who reads grammar books or even uses them for reference, though I've met a couple who have written them. In a moment of weakness, over a very elaborate, very costly lunch in Manhattan, I once agreed to write a very large handbook of grammar and mechanics for a very large publisher. It was to include all the rules college freshpersons would ever need to know, and many they would not. Over dessert, Chocolate Damnation, a seductive blend of chocolate and raspberry I recall to this day,

I agreed to write a workbook, and over espresso I said sure, I'd do a teacher's manual as well. Today, with further infusions of butter and sugar, I'd have agreed to prepare a CD and a Web site as well. Once I was safe at home, however, and on leaner cuisine, I found many other projects to write on the new computer that came with the contract. Journal articles, book reviews, conference papers, forays into autobiography, even another whole book, *Fact and Artifact: Writing Nonfiction.*

While my professional vita grew fat, the folder labeled "Handbook," never more than a generic name, remained thin. Every time I thought about all those rules, I found compelling reasons to go into the kitchen and reaffirm my burgeoning relationship with Elizabeth David. Her cookbooks, embodiments of summer, *A Book of Mediterranean Food, French Country Cooking,* and *Summer Cooking,* were an emblematic choice, for her impressionistic recipes call for a backbone of experience, a deft hand, and a willingness to take risks, to experiment and invent. Lemon Chicken, for instance, begins, "Poach a chicken with turnips, carrots, onions and a large piece of lemon peel," clearly an invitation to improvise. As I read it, a chicken of any size will do. One can omit the turnips or substitute parsnips, expand or contract the ratio of onions to carrots in the poaching stock, use more (or less) wine, white or red, tarragon and parsley instead of watercress, and on and on. Just the way real writers do it. A little of this, a little of that, add and subtract and move things around until the result is elegant simplicity—or abundance if that's what you're after. Exactly the advice I'd given in *Fact and Artifact.* Just as Huck Finn couldn't pray a lie, I couldn't in honesty write a handbook of rules. I canceled the contract, the only time I've ever done such a thing, and returned the advance. They let me keep the computer, but it was already obsolete. Then I celebrated by making David's Cold Chicken Véronique, which begins with her characteristically casual enticement: "Divide a carefully boiled chicken into several large pieces." What, I wonder, does it mean to boil a chicken "carefully," or recklessly, for that matter?

My grandmother was not a reckless cook, but she was a generous one. When I was growing up in New Hampshire, heavy wicker hampers would arrive from Grandma in Detroit right after Thanksgiving, redolent of cinnamon, ginger, and anise. Pfeffernüsse, springerle, lebkuchen, gingerbread, mandelplaettchen, and Christmas stars with red and green sugar marked the delicious days of Advent. Their essence is so powerful in memory that I have had to get up from the computer—right in midsentence—not only to tend the beef stock that has to simmer for three more hours before it will be ready to make onion soup, but to eat a leftover Christmas cookie, a snowman made of two stacked, nut-studded balls rolled in powdered sugar. (I eat when I write, but I scarcely even taste anything when I cook, for the process provides its own nourishment.) Yet no recipes corroborate this legacy or Grandma's other specialties—Dutch Apple Pie, and Sauer Klops, ground meatballs in a sour cream sauce with whole allspice. Or is it Klups? I have never seen the name written down, and indeed had to look up the German cookie spellings in a cookbook rather than a dictionary. Writing about this abundance is the best way I know to preserve it, whether I get the spelling right or not.

Our immediate family dotes on recipes even as we recognize that much of their meaning, as with any other writing, lies in between the lines. We knew Sara was destined to marry Laird when we saw the pictures from her first Christmas visit to our house in rural Connecticut. Martin, Sara, and I are bending over pots on the stove, heads atilt at the same angle, spoons astir in each right hand, a cheerful chorus of cooks. They commemorated their marriage by making a three-tiered wedding cake from *The Cake Bible,* chocolate cake with chocolate frosting, raspberry ganache, and fresh raspberries. The next Christmas, we began what has become a family tradition, extended to Bard and Vicki when they married six years later, the annual purchase of a cookbook that we can all share. Because each household already had copies of *The Joy of Cooking,* 1975 edition; Jane Brody's *Good Food Book;* Marcella Hazan's *Classic Italian Cooking;* and Claudia Roden's *Book of Middle Eastern Food,* each with a distinctive literary flavor that complements the food, we began with the Silver Palate's *New Basics Cookbook. The Joy of Cooking,* 1997 edition, is too indispensable to share; we've given copies to each other. Bard and Vicki keep Madhur Jaffrey's *A Taste of India,* Bard having been influenced at a critical age by a month's apprenticeship to our houseguest from Bombay, Grace Chellam, truly a mistress of spices, and of amazing free-form aromatic cookery. Bard and Vicki are also custodians of the parent *Moosewood Cookbook* and its offspring, and *The Thousand Recipe Chinese Cookbook,* a fat book with a thin one—a dozen basics—inside yearning to escape. Laird and Sara have the *Bon Appétit* subscription, whose relevant issues promise sustenance, both literary and culinary, during family vacations. We trade back and forth Judith Olney's *The Joy of Chocolate* and Maida Heatter's *Book of Great Chocolate Desserts,* inspired by Laird and Sara's annual gift of homemade chocolate truffles, in which their children, Beth and Paul, now have a hand. Indeed in our annual orgy of Christmas baking, it was Paul, then five, who assembled and rechristened the Snowman cookies—aka Mexican Wedding cookies, aka Pastelitos de Boda, aka Pecan Butter Balls, only we like walnuts better. But none of us can cope with Marcel Desaulniers' opulent compendium of lavish desserts from our favorite restaurant in Williamsburg, Virginia. Death by Chocolate, Tuxedo Truffle Torte, Pillars of Chocolate with Cocoa Thunderheads all seem to require costly ounces of Valrhona chocolate (Sam's Club, our chocolatier, purveys ten-pound bags of Guittard bittersweet chips at $15.95) and four days' preparation time. The pages of this gift from Maureen, a Williamsburg friend and fellow cook during ten years of collaborative monthly dinners, got stuck together during a dishwater spill, and we have been too intimidated by the contents to pry them open.

Vicki, a food scientist, has provided enlightened redemption from the only formal cooking lessons I've ever taken, obligatory domestic science in eighth grade. There we were taught to prepare bland, colorless, mushy foods that have never since blighted my kitchen—custard, tapioca, tomato aspic, oatmeal, cream of wheat, and omelets that everybody burned. Mrs. Wilcox, who also taught grammar, another complexity of rules that we had to follow to the letter, regardless of the literary flavor, imposed comparable rules on our cooking classes. We had to make sure the kitchen was spotless before we began. What a waste, since we were only going to mess it up. We had to suit up, in calico aprons and despicable hairnets. We had to arrange all the utensils and ingredients in the order we expected to use them, and turn the oven on to preheat, even if what we were baking wouldn't be ready for an hour. When we finally got to muffins, the only redeemable recipe in our repertoire, we had to sift the flour three times before measuring, and once again after adding the salt and baking soda. Teaspoons, tablespoons, cupfuls had to be level or the results would be doomed to disaster.

When I began my first full-time teaching job, I hired a volunteer from among my freshman English students as cook's helper. It would make literary sense to say that I taught Susan how to cook every Friday afternoon for four years until she graduated, but in truth she was a home ec major, and we taught each other how to cook. I don't remember the exact recipes, except for Fifi's Lentil Soup and Linda Kraus's Brisket—they probably weren't very exact—but we laughed a lot and spilled a lot and often had to adapt what was simmering on the stove to compensate for crucial ingredients omitted because, as Mrs. Wilcox would have chided, we were talking too much instead of concentrating on what we were doing. One year Susan gave us a yogurt maker for Christmas, but Martin and I soon backslid into our warm-oven method. When Susan and her husband came to dinner years later, I served the brisket—a flat-cut beef slathered with chopped onion and garlic, baked for four hours, then covered with a mixture of chili sauce (one eight- or twelve-ounce bottle), Worcestershire sauce (two tablespoons), and dark brown sugar (a half cup) and studded with whole cloves and baked another hour with parboiled potatoes and carrots. "Whoever finds a clove will have good luck," I would tell Bard and Laird, who understands why now that he lures Paul and Beth to the dinner table with the same enticement. A recent e-mail correspondence tells me that Susan's daughter Laura, now a college sophomore, an English major and aspiring professor, will be joining our household for a summer internship and a taste of what it's like to prepare a book manuscript for publication. I will be surprised if our collaboration doesn't spill over into the kitchen.

Vicki explains the chemistry that underlies the recipes, reinforcing the intuitive wisdom of my ancestral cooks: why jelly jells better when you add pectin; why water ruins melting chocolate; why a food processor turns potatoes into a glutinous blob instead of mashing them. In *Cookwise: The Hows and Whys of Successful Cooking,* a fortieth wedding anniversary gift from Vicki and Bard, Shirley Corriher, research biochemist-turned-cook, clarifies further cooking conundrums. None of us, however, knows the verb for what happens when the yogurt is done. We make four big tumblers every week. In the interests of economy and elegance, I have deleted extraneous ingredients, such as condensed milk and softened gelatin, from the recipes others have given me. Although I work from memory, in the recipe I give people I always say, "Blend together five cups of nonfat milk powder, three and a half cups warm water, and two tablespoons live yogurt start, fill the glasses, and keep in a warm water bath at a constant 110 degrees, the temperature of a gas-oven pilot light, until the mixture *yogs.*" *Yogues* might be a better spelling, although my computer spell-check resents both versions. Even Claudia Roden, who recommends wrapping the bowl in an "old shawl" and letting the mixture sit overnight, circumnavigates the verb with "thick like a creamy custard."

Slow Cooking

It has taken me four days, much faster than my usual writing pace, to write this essay. But then I actually began this piece a decade ago and revised it four times in the following year. While this has been simmering for nine years, out of sight and conscious mind, I have concentrated on researching and writing other scholarly articles and books and creative nonfiction. Yet all the while I've been writing, I have also been cooking, a practice continued during the writing of this piece. I've interrupted this text to stir the soup bones and vegetables browning in the oven, then gone back to the computer, transferred the soup mixture to the stove top and added liquid, returned to write more, and finally strained the cooled beef stock at midnight before going to bed. *The Joy of Cooking* promised that the congealed fat would form an airtight seal that would preserve the stock. I checked this morning, and so it had. I could postpone slicing and slowly browning the onions for the soup until I'd finished this writing.

Because of its long simmer, I thought that "Writing and Cooking" would be a piece of cake to finish. But as I tried to knead it into shape, I realized that during the intervening years, without even looking at the earlier version,

I had cannibalized it for parts of other essays. So I started again from scratch. I am a better writer of personal essays now than I was nine years ago, less fearful of spilling the beans, more willing to improvise with a pinch of this, a soupçon of that, confident (originally I said "condiment," a Freudian typo) that what begins as potluck will, with proper seasoning, provide a feast for the eye and nourishment for the mind. (I am tempted to leave every one of these food metaphors in this paragraph just to see whether I can get away with them. The presence of this parenthetical remark signals that, by Julia, I could.)

I always try out my academic writing on readers before I send it off to editors. Martin and a colleague or two can be trusted to give tough critiques, smart and thorough. After the editors and reviewers have weighed in and the work is published, I usually receive congratulatory e-mail messages from a few friends, and gradually the citations of my work appear in others' publications, missiles launched in the wars of the words. Such is the way of the academic world. My creative nonfiction, however, stories embedded in stories like raisins in scones, is intended for a much wider audience—anyone who likes stories. And who doesn't? Accordingly I've given earlier drafts of "Writing and Cooking" to friends and colleagues, cooks and non-cooks alike. Everyone likes to eat, and I have yet to find someone who doesn't like to read about food. I asked them the same questions I always do: "Is this clear?" "Do I need to add anything? Omit anything?" "Have I avoided sentimentality?" But what I really want to know is, "Do you love this piece? Did you savor it? Would you come back for a second helping?"

What I don't dare ask for is, fortunately, what I get. Whereas the reader response to my academic writing, even the hot topics, is invariably cool—intellectual if not disengaged—the reaction to my personal essays sizzles. Writing about food whets the readers' appetites. They reminisce about good cooks in their own families. They revisit the menus of family gatherings. They correct the seasonings. They try out the recipes embedded in the text. I had a long conversation with Lori, who had copied the yogurt recipe, on why you only use two tablespoons of yogurt start. (Any unpasteurized yogurt will provide one, but I gave her some of mine.) More than two tablespoons crowds the growth of the culture, the mixture won't *yog* properly, the result is too runny. "My yogurt came out very firm, and shrank to half its original volume. Why did it do that?" I don't know. "Can I add fruit or flavoring to the mixture as it yogs?" I don't know that either; for thirty years I've only made additions after the yogurt was done. "Vicki will have the answers," I say. "Let's send her an e-mail." Or readers counter my favorite recipes with recipes of their own. Jenny's Mint Chocolate Chip Cookies calls for, and I've never seen this anywhere before either, a quarter cup of dried mint—"if

Cooks at work: Lynn, Bard, and Rhys in the Blooms' kitchen, Christmas 2006

grown in your own garden, all the better." Those who know this piece is coming in the mail salivate in expectation.

Whether I am a better cook now than I was nine years ago is incidental, as long as my family and guests are satisfied. I was going to add, "after all, my life doesn't depend on it." But writing this essay has made me realize that in many ways my life, and the lives of those I love, does depend on the cooking, even more than the eating. The morning after Thanksgiving we were at Laird and Sara's in Boston amidst a houseful of other relatives, including a dozen children under ten. Beth, then two, got up at six, and I got up with her to keep her from waking everyone else. After an hour's reading, we grew tired of *Double Trouble in Walla Walla*—a wild and wonderful book whose rhyming principle is signaled in the title; *Cloudy with a Chance of Meatballs*—food rains from the sky and nearly swamps the village's satiated inhabitants; and *June 29, 1999*—a small book about giant vegetables. "Let's make something good for breakfast," I said, "scones." "What are scones?" she asked. "Flattish biscuits with raisins in them." Beth pulled a chair up to the kitchen counter, I wrapped an apron twice around her, propped open *The Joy of Cooking* to Classic Currant Scones, and measured the flour and sugar while she stirred. Then she dropped in the butter, a tablespoon at a time, while I stirred, and then the raisins. I beat in the egg-and-milk mixture, and together, my hand on hers, we began to pat out the dough. "Take your hand off, Grandma Lynn! I can do it myself!" she ordered. "Gently," I said, "don't pound it flat!" and showed her how to fit the cookie-cutter shapes—stars small, medium, and large—efficiently onto the doughy rectangle. After the stars got boring, we switched to pigs and Scottie dogs, and by the time Beth was sprinkling the tops with cinnamon and sugar, the rest of the family was filtering into the kitchen ready to snatch the scones from the oven before they'd even cooled. "Let's do it again," said Beth the next day. She beamed when we gave her nested real measuring cups for Christmas, with matching measuring spoons for Paul.

During our most recent visit to Boston, Paul, age five, presented us with a large, flat, cardboard box, carefully wrapped in paper of his own design, with P-A-U-L crayoned over it in his favorite color, green. "You can't unwrap it until you get home," he said, "but your clue"—he has discovered mystery stories—"is sticking out the top." An eight-ounce raspberry yogurt cup, filled with the wad of black Polartec that transformed it to a flowerpot, sprouted a large, red carnation. "A flower," he assured us, "*not* an umbrella." When we tore off the paper, what to our wondering eyes should appear but a miniature garden: a green felt rectangle expanded by a sheet of paper colored green, with bright felt vegetables taped to the surface, carrots, tomatoes, cucumbers, eggplant, green beans, pumpkins. No kale. "Exactly what we grow in our garden," Paul said when we phoned to thank him, "and exactly what we cook." We did not discuss the two untethered genuine theater tickets resting atop two of the pumpkins. "Admit one," says each. We have given the garden pride of place on the pass-through counter between the kitchen stove and the center hall; anyone who enters the house will spot it on the instant. With this Eden in view and tickets to get us in, I finish making the onion soup.

The Best Blueberry Pie

Serves 6–8
Preparation time (exclusive of crust): 10 minutes actual cooking time, plus 2 hours for cooling cooked berry mixture.

To eat this pie is like eating fresh berries, only better. Use the largest, plumpest berries to fill the pie shell.

4½ cups fresh blueberries
1 9-inch pie shell, baked and cooled
¼ cup water
¾ cup sugar
2 tsp. salt

2 tbsp. cornstarch
1 tbsp. butter
1 tbsp. Grand Marnier or Cointreau
¼ cup fresh raspberries (optional)

1) Spread 2½ cups fresh blueberries in cooled pie shell.

2) Cook water, sugar, and salt over medium heat until sugar is dissolved.

3) Mix cornstarch and 2 tablespoons cold water into a paste; to this paste add 3 tablespoons dissolved sugar mixture (boiling hot), stirring until blended; then whisk into rest of sugar mixture and cook over low heat, stirring with wire whisk until the mixture thickens slightly.

4) Add remaining blueberries, and stir over low heat until the mixture has thickened. Some of the berries should burst during this process, turning the mixture beautifully blue, but they should not have cooked enough to become mushy and shapeless.

5) Remove from heat. Add butter and Grand Marnier. Cool and chill.

6) When cool but not congealed, pour sauce over berries in the shell. Chill until ready to serve. Before serving, decorate with fresh raspberries, if desired.

Fresh strawberries, peaches, or nectarines may be used instead of blueberries. With these fruits, spread cooled crust with 2 tablespoons softened cream cheese—this keeps the liquid (it's runnier than the blueberry version) from soaking into the crust. Or, omit the cream cheese, and fill the pie shell just before serving. Use fresh blueberries for garnish.

Or: Fill shell with fresh strawberries, peaches or nectarines and top with blueberry sauce made by above recipe.

Bon appétit!

The Dinner Hours

We live our lives, do whatever we do, and then we sleep—it's as simple and ordinary as that. . . . There's just this for consolation: an hour here or there when our lives seem, against all odds and expectations, to burst open and give us everything we've ever imagined, though everyone but children (and perhaps even they) knows these hours will inevitably be followed by others, far darker and more difficult. Still . . . we hope, more than anything, for more.

Michael Cunningham, *The Hours*

Potluck

It's four above zero when we arrive home in a rush from Costa Rican rain forests the night before classes start. In addition to hordes of howler monkeys, we have seen 151 species of birds in twelve days, among them the brown booby and the resplendent quetzal, but only birders will want more details, which our level of avian voyeurism—"Oh, look at that pretty green bird with the long tail!"—cannot supply.

We will, however, tantalize the appetites of our friends and family with the unpredictable foods we've discovered on our trip that we no longer want to do without. This time it's bottles of Salsa Lizano; bags of *café* from Boquete, Panamá, where we toured a mountainside organic coffee farm; and aromatic packages of coffee beans covered in chocolate. I have in mind a Costa Rican feast for the next overnight visit from our family, which everyone but three-month-old Rhys can be counted on to help cook. At the moment, hospitality will have to wait. But not for long, for I have volunteered to host a potluck in six days for twenty-five—our creative writing faculty, student prizewinners, and the evening's speaker, essayist Anne Fadiman, her visit booked a year in advance, whose essays I have admired in the *American Scholar* under her editorship. But first it's necessary to slog through the morass of mail, read two dissertations, advise some graduating seniors, finish

an article with an imminent deadline, write a conference paper, weather per-
mitting (I have not yet heard the long-term forecast) take the car to the auto
emissions inspection, and while I'm at it, buy groceries. Welcome home!

Whether we are expecting company or not, on the seventh day of any
given week, I don't rest, I cook. Why make only single recipes when it's efficient to double them? Then we need company to eat up the excess. Thus
through impulse or by design, we have dinner guests once or twice a month,
not counting the casual drop-ins. I love to plan dinner parties as much as I
love to plan classes. The platonic possibilities—ideal combinations of guests,
menus, occasions—stretch before me like an ironed tablecloth, waiting to
be laden with good food. The delight is in the invention, in the search for
recipes, not fancy, but sources of inspiration and free-ranging modifications.
It's fun, too, to select heritage vegetables from the farmer's market, and to
pick the fruits from the nearby farm itself, but for local bounty we should be
having this party in August or in Costa Rica rather than in January in Connecticut.

My favorite moment, if all goes as planned, occurs about a half hour
before the guests are due to arrive, when calmness suddenly supplants the
cacophony of chopping, beating, grating, grinding, and diverse clattering
from the *baterie de cuisine*—now washed and put away. The house is in order,
the table set, Martin's bread is baked, the menu du jour is either on ice or
wafting welcome from the oven, except what we will prepare (say, pasta or
risotto or stir-fry or a simple salad) with the guests on the scene. Even if the
preparation has taken much longer than anticipated, as it always does, it now
seems worth the effort. I wish, fleetingly, that this rare serenity would remain
in stasis, that—like Keats's lovers on the Grecian urn—consummation of the
anticipated delight would be frozen in time, the meal ever awaiting guests
who have yet to come. This is the time just before the anticipated hour when
our lives might, as Michael Cunningham conceives, against all odds and
expectations, burst open and give us everything we've ever imagined.

This is what I am hoping will occur in the potluck planned for Anne
Fadiman's visit—the singular, perfect, dinner hour, which is actually about
all we'll have together before we have to rush off to campus for her reading.
Writers all, real-world lives fragmented and frayed, woven together in authorial camaraderie, welcome warmth on an arctic night. Though snow is forecast, even if Fadiman can't get here, we can nevertheless celebrate good
writing with Ken's gorgeous guacamole, Jenny and Peter's potato pancakes
with goat cheese, and Suzanne's "Fabulous Chocolate Cake." What a wonderful way to segue back into the workaday world, mixed maybe with a culinary
memento from our Costa Rican travels. I've already promised beverages
and Martin's baguettes. But, afraid we'll run out of food (does that ever really

happen in a potluck?), I decide to volunteer a backup pasta dish, just in case, that will have to be made just before people arrive, to keep it hot.

The night before the guests are due, we clean the house, move the chairs into companionable groups, arrange the tableware, cups, and glasses, and go to sleep with the ominous knowledge that the Carolinas are iced in and D.C. is being battered by heavy snow. The storm is no longer a question of *if*, but *when*, as morning opens to a sinister grey horizon. Because Fadiman's transportation requires a drive of two hours to Northampton and two back, the decision (not mine) to proceed or abort must be made by 1 P.M. After a morning of meetings and a swim at school, I return to a flurry of e-mail and phone messages—what to do?—and finally the verdict arrives, "Cancel," though not a flake has fallen. I could be pleased; I have a lot of work to do, as usual. But I am not. I am teaching "Coming of Age in American Autobiography" this semester, which begins with Benjamin Franklin's *Autobiography* and Frederick Douglass's *Narrative*, and as I reread these works, I am convinced that these founding forebears would not have allowed themselves to be deterred by the wildest of weathers, let alone weather reports. I continue to read, but by 5:15, under sullen but still snowless skies, I can't stand the foodless frustration anymore and head for the kitchen, compelled to cook, company or no.

I've discovered "Midnight Pasta with Tuna, Pancetta, and Spinach" in *Food & Wine*, a magazine we've been receiving lately because of frequent flyer miles, use them or lose them. Earlier *F&W* dishes, "Spinach and Cheese Grits Frittatas" (November 2003) and "Garlicky Cherry Tomato and Bread Gratin" (January 2004) have prompted requests for second helpings, even when the Yankees found out they were actually eating grits, and for copies of the recipes. Tonight's experiment is essentially linguini tossed with garlic, canned tuna (supplemented with a can of crabmeat), a little hot red pepper (omitted), and frozen chopped spinach (I incorporated the whole ten-ounce package, triple the designated quantity, and added two big handfuls of plum tomato wedges), sautéed in thinly sliced pancetta or bacon (I used bacon), and kept moist with a mixture of dry white wine, olive oil, and some of the cooking liquid from the pasta.

After dark, Martin drives in from a long day of classes in Hartford, still no snow, expecting a dark, chilly, chaotic kitchen full of potluck remnants and dinner debris, since there would have been no time to clean up before a hasty departure for campus. Surprised by the light streaming from the windows—we have no curtains in this house too far from neighbors to need them—he walks in the split second that I am dishing up the pasta, a side dish of fresh asparagus, and the promise of a glass of wine at bedtime. If we drink it now, we'll both fall asleep at the dinner table, so pristine tonight that dining in seems like dining out. Points of flickering candlelight illuminate our own multiple, moving images refracted in the panes of the dining room's large bay window that insulates us from the starless night beyond; we become guests at our own party. Warmed by the food, we share as we have done for forty-five years, tonight newly savored. "Good enough for company," the pasta wins our four-star rating; we will serve it at a party next week. We postpone dessert until bedtime, to accompany the wine.

Simmering beneath the Surface: The Analysis

I originally intended to write this paper as a critical analysis, beginning with commentary on the magnificent cuisine (read: splendid symbolism) of dinner parties in *The Awakening, To the Lighthouse,* and *Larry's Party,* suitable critical fare. But I wanted my readers to come alive as intimates, inside the writing rather than outside it. So I decided to invite you to dinner, enacting the meaning of "The Dinner Hours," rather than analyzing it. With "Potluck" on the front burner, I served forth the savory truth—that writing about food engages the mind, the heart, the senses, and sensibility of writers and readers alike. Even people on diets that require abstemiousness and calculation can indulge themselves at the literary dining table, where no one counts calories. For to write about food is to write about life itself. If "Potluck" has provided an aperitif, so much the better.

M. F. K. Fisher articulated the human essence of these moments, these hours. She introduces *The Gastronomical Me* with "it seems to me that our three basic needs, for food and security and love, are so mixed and mingled and entwined that we cannot straightly think of one without the others. So it happens that when I write of hunger I am really writing about love and the hunger for it, and warmth and the love of it and the hunger for it . . . and then the warmth and richness and fine reality of hunger satisfied . . . And it is all one" (353; ellipses Fisher's). I had not explained to myself this understanding of what I knew in my heart, and my gut, when I wrote "Potluck." I encountered Fisher's keen analysis later and realized that she understands what all good hosts, and food writers, know intuitively, including Kate Chopin, Virginia Woolf, and Carol Shields, creators of the memorable dinner party scenes in *The Awakening, To the Lighthouse,* and *Larry's Party,* that we'll visit soon.

As I wrote "Potluck," I wanted to convey the experience of this intermingling of life's essential needs—food, security, and love—amidst its concomitant uncertainties. I wanted readers, whom I regard as an intimate, friendly audience, however large or dispersed in actuality, to savor the fact that such parties, even potlucks, are not casual events; they require planning, organization, and yes, housecleaning. Most of all, they require the sense of hospitality that makes all this work worthwhile. Kathleen Norris, in *Amazing Grace*, quoting St. Benedict, "A monastery is never without guests," observes that "only people who are basically at home, and at home in themselves, can offer hospitality" (263, 267), a phenomenon that with its intimate intertwining of guest and host represents the essence of communion. I wanted readers, invited guests to the feast, to want that potluck to take place. I wanted your investment, even in advance of the party, to be as great as mine, even though you had been spared the housework. I wanted your disappointment when the party was cancelled to be as palpable as mine. So I had to offer you some food, as consolation for both of us.

Creative nonfiction not only helps us to understand the unfathomable, but to gain literary command over events otherwise beyond our control. I couldn't change the weather, threatening and problematic. But because food writing is, or should be, I believe, full of hope and promise, an essentially positive genre, I could invite you—even people whom, as a writer, I don't know—in from the cold, offer you good food, and the recipe, and warm friendship. You all could be guests at our table for two. To suit my taste, the offering had to be simple, straightforward, no strings; if it turned out right, I'd expect you to dig in, with relish. Yet if I were a rotten cook, if the pasta had emerged gummy from the pot, the sauce bland, the asparagus mushy, you'd never need to know as long as the writing sounded succulent and redeemed the forgone party. I like to think that good writing and good cooking are reciprocals. In truth they are not. For readers the quality of the writing is more important than the quality of the food. James Joyce won his four Michelin stars not for preparing colcannon and fried kidneys, but for immortalizing, among other subjects, the warm hospitality and feasting in "The Dead," "the fat brown goose . . . at one end of the table and at the other end . . . a great ham, stripped of its outer skin and peppered over with crust crumbs, a neat paper frill round its shin" (*Dubliners*, 252), a stay against life's encroaching bitter chill.

To observe that food writing often focuses on small details, seemingly trivial minutiae, the material aspects of domesticity—often but not necessarily bourgeois—is to note a conspicuous similarity between a great deal of creative nonfiction and fiction writing, whether minority or mainstream. From a variety of orientations that have engrossed theorists and scholars of anthropology, medicine, history, sociology, cultural studies of all sorts, multiethnic literary studies, and a greater academic focus on children and families, the stuff of life has today become infused with a high-profile legitimacy in academia, from freshman composition, to autobiography and advanced composition, to analytic dissertation research. (See, for instance, works by

Avakian, Haber, Inness, McFeely, Marranca, Montanari, Theophano, and Tisdale.) We are what we write what we eat.

Whatever the cuisine or raw ingredients, ranging from the wholesome to the sinfully indulgent, whether treated literally or metaphorically, writing about food is usually engrossing (if not always pleasurable) to read—even when the diet is problematic, representing the malnutrition of poverty, famine, or war. Because cooking and eating are social acts, evocative of a host of familial and communal relationships and cultural practices, writing about food—in the language and stance of cooks and eaters rather than that of critics—becomes inclusive rather than exclusive, welcoming rather than distancing, collegial rather than authoritarian. This writing, like the activities it represents, holds forth the Platonic ideal of perfection, the possibility of the perfect hour epitomizing the best of human relationships, whether through everyday cooking, international potlucks, courtship dinners *à deux*, holiday feasts, or the Eucharist.

The Literary Feast

Through hospitality, knowledge of the medium, foresight, and whatever control is possible in the fluid stream of time, both hosts and writers seek to create these hours, and to capture them. In *To the Lighthouse*, Virginia Woolf depicts in two striking sentences this evanescent perfection in the most luminous moment of Mrs. Ramsay's dinner party. Here this "astonishingly beautiful" (182) domestic muse and goddess, mother of eight, brings together the individualistic and quirky Ramsay clan and kindred guests. Among them are Mr. Ramsay, the paterfamilias scholar "scowling and frowning," and his acolyte, "miserable specimen" Charles Tansley (15); Rose and Roger gazing at their father; William Bankes, the self-styled "old fogey" whom Mrs. Ramsay is trying to marry off to "skimpy" Lily Briscoe, an aspiring artist with "Chinese eyes"; "monumental" poet Augustus Carmichael, devoted to abetting youthful Andrew Ramsay's discoveries; and Paul Rayley, "a nice young man with a profile like a gem's," and his new fiancée, Minta Doyle, in a "golden haze" (139–55). This party is the last public act readers see before we learn of Mrs. Ramsay's premature death:

> Now all the candles were lit up, and the faces on both sides of the table
> were brought nearer by the candle light, and composed, as they had not
> been in the twilight, into a party round a table, for the night was now
> shut off by panes of glass, which, far from giving any accurate view of
> the outside world, rippled it so strangely that here, inside the room,
> seemed to be order and dry land; there, outside, a reflection in which
> things wavered and vanished, waterily.

Some change at once went through them all, as if this had really happened, and they were all conscious of making a party together in a hollow, on an island; had their common cause against that fluidity out there. (146–47)

That such stasis is temporary, that unanimity among diners of diverse ages, interests, stages of life as those at Mrs. Ramsay's party, is so rare as to be remarkable, is an aspect of life as well known to planners of dinner parties as it is to writers. Even as she helps the guests to the succulence of the *boeuf en daube*—"'There is plenty for everybody'"—feeling "a coherence in things, a stability" when "everything seemed possible. Everything seemed right"—Mrs. Ramsay is aware that "this cannot last." Her thought, echoed by "somebody's" (it could have been anyone else at the table) "'Ah, but how long do you think it'll last?'" is affirmed through subtle, kaleidoscopic changes among the diners themselves, aware of the omnipresent passing of time. As the dinner hour ends, Mrs. Ramsay views the "scene which was vanishing even as she looked," and by the time she has left the room, it is "already the past." Hosts and hostesses, like writers about dinner parties, are aware of their attempts to create the utopian moment, time out of time, which becomes precious both in the experiencing and in the recollecting, made even more precious, for we know it is rare and cannot last. Indeed, as soon as Mrs. Ramsay "went a sort of disintegration set in"; the diners "wavered about, went different ways" (157–68). Thus guests depart for their ordinary lives, postparty depression or not. Though the aura of intimate goodwill may linger on, we who are without Mrs. Ramsay's Swiss maid and Mildred in the kitchen know that the dirty dishes invariably await.

In food writing that conveys the essence of such fleeting moments, the ambience of these dinner hours is comic, in the cosmic Aristotelean sense, as long as there is food in sufficiency or abundance. In *Larry's Party*, Larry, as host in the climactic scene, proffers carrot soup, garlicky roast lamb, and a "gorgeous" chocolate cake to eight guests, including his two lovely ex-wives, Dorrie (from Winnipeg) and Beth (from England), who by coincidence are in Toronto at the same time. Larry is a nervous host—and why not? He has grown up "ignorant of the shaping impulse that blows a party into being." His wives have always taken care of taking care—"Nothing had been expected of him," and this is "his first and only party." Moreover each guest has arrived with an agenda, from his cohost, Charlotte, who not so subtly wants to marry him; to Beth, who elected to divorce Larry three years ago, is now seven months pregnant by artificial insemination, and hunting for a job—and more—in Larry's vicinity; and Dorrie, who inquires crisply, "Yes . . . tell us what it's like being a man these days" (316).

As they devour the food with delight, Shields replays their dinner-table conversation, evocative of the indiscreet charm of the bourgeoisie. A characteristic exchange moves so rapidly it scarcely allows Larry, increasingly apprehensive, to get a word in edgewise:

> "My therapist believes that most cancers are caused by anger, by not recognizing and embracing your anger. He says I'm a case in point . . ."
>
> "Do you have a family back in Spain, Samuel?"
>
> "My brothers, my sister—"
>
> "But are you married?"
>
> "She has been dead one year. My wife. It was a depression. She took some sleeping pills."
>
> "My therapist says—"
>
> "That's one reason I accepted to take this project in Canada. To make some air between my sorrow and myself."
>
> "To put some distance."
>
> "Yes, precisely! To put some distance."
>
> "Who was it who said 'only disconnect?'"
>
> "Forster, wasn't it? But I think he actually said—"
>
> "If no one would like another helping of the soup—" (314–16)

We have ourselves participated in enough of these fragmented dinner conversations—note how many sentences are interrupted or never end—to understand why Larry believes that the party is in "ruins." "If this party were a play the curtain would come down," thinks Larry, "Right this minute" (327), when it becomes apparent to Beth—and all the others—that he doesn't want her to move to Toronto and resume their relationship.

Nevertheless the same party unites, in "the dinner hour," Larry and Dorrie, "partners in a long marriage, survivors of old quarrels long since mended. The journey they appear to have taken separately," during the fourteen years since their divorce, "has really been made together." Dorrie and Larry "have brought this evening into being, and here . . . are their friends and family, warmly invited, encouraged to talk, comforted with food and wine, adored, embraced," just as they will embrace each other and remarriage when "the hour is winding down. Soon the old friends will be gone. Soon they will have only each other," as long as they both shall live, when they can say with profundity in private what might sound merely saccharine in public, "'I love you. I've always loved you.' 'I love you too. I've been waiting'" (327–28; 336). That neither speaker can be identified doesn't matter; they speak as one.

Martin and I can wish the newly-reunited the transcendent happiness of the long married that is epitomized in *To the Lighthouse* by the quiet scene of Mr. and Mrs. Ramsay, sitting together reading and knitting after the guests are gone and the children are tucked in:

> Knowing that he was watching her, instead of saying anything she turned . . . and looked at him. And as she looked at him she began to smile, for though she had not said a word, he knew, of course he knew, that she loved him. . . . And smiling she looked out of the window . . . (thinking to herself, Nothing on earth can equal this happiness)— (185–86)

Thus, replete with these postparty images, we head for the kitchen, smiling, for the cleanup.

Yet as Michael Cunningham observes, these precious, perfect hours in life during which we experience perfect communion are rare indeed; desire exceeds fulfillment far more often in life, as it does in literature. Cunningham's Clarissa, a contemporary fulfillment of Woolf's Mrs. Dalloway, has planned a cocktail party to honor her dear friend Richard, recipient of a major literary award. He does not want to attend either the party or the award ceremony; he is dying of AIDS and wants to be alone. To hasten the inevitable, Richard jumps from his apartment window to his death. His last words are to Clarissa, who is trying to dissuade him: "'I don't think two people could have been happier than we've been'" (200). And so the elegant food for fifty, "spirals of grilled chicken breast . . . miniature onion tarts . . . steamed shrimp . . . dark triangles of grilled eggplant . . . the crab casserole," Richard's favorite, that "Clarissa made herself," becomes the funeral baked meats for but three survivors, Clarissa, Sally (her partner of eighteen years), and Richard's mother. Clarissa realizes that "it's time for the day to be over. We throw our parties. . . . We live our lives, do whatever we do," hoping for that unsurpassable hour of utopian fulfillment, hoping "for more" (223–25).

In Kate Chopin's *The Awakening*, Edna Pontellier stages an elegant dinner party for ten, on her twenty-ninth birthday, eager too for the hour that, as Cunningham says, "against all odds and expectations [will] burst open and give us everything we've ever imagined" (225). She even thinks of it as "the 'coup d'état.'. . . [It] will be very fine; all my best of everything—crystal, silver and gold." How can she miss? Edna's soiree is intended as a farewell to her opulent life as Léonce's pampered spouse, though he is away, allegedly on business, and her paramour, Alcée Arobin, serves as host. On the verge of moving out of her husband's elegant house to the "little house around the block," Edna treats her guests to an "extremely gorgeous" table covered with "pale yellow satin under strips of lace-work . . . wax candles in massive brass candelabra. . . . full, fragrant roses, yellow and red. . . . silver and gold and crystal." So enchanting is "this effect of splendor" that readers scarcely realize that

Chopin proffers no food at all, only a cocktail emitting "marvelous . . . garnet lights," accompanied by offstage mandolin music, a splashing fountain, and "the heavy odor of jessamine that came through the open windows." Although the guests experience "a feeling of good fellowship pass[ing] around the circle like a mystic cord, holding and binding [them] together with jest and laughter," they are unaware that the "regal" Edna herself, never a nurturer, is emotionally absent from her own party as she is throughout much of her life, overpowered by "the old ennui overtaking her; the hopelessness which so often assailed her" (965–72). The disjunction between host and guests in *The Awakening* far exceeds that of Mrs. Ramsay, Larry, and Clarissa, who despite moments of annoyance and distraction, proffer the gift of food, delicious, appealing, to those they cherish.

Whereas works about disaster, divorce, death may elicit critical indulgence because of their difficult and depressing subject matter, critics cut serious comedy no slack. They have in the past considered food writing—when they've noticed it at all—as lightweight and relegated it to the scullery rather than to the literary canon. Thus to be treated with respect as well as relish, food writing has to be very tough-minded, though encased in an accessible vocabulary and a style good enough for readers to devour, to savor; to convey a relaxed ambience with tight literary control. As with any artistic performance, good writing, like good cooking, must appear effortless irrespective of the work required to attain it. This is evidenced both in the works of the great food writers—A. J. Liebling, M. F. K. Fisher, much of Calvin Trillin—and in great food scenes from novels across cultures and generations, from seduction in *Tom Jones* to hunger in *Oliver Twist* to contentment and curiosity as Leopold Bloom, who "ate with relish the inner organs of beasts and fowls. . . thick giblet soups, nutty gizzards, a stuffed roast heart," grills his favorite, the breakfast kidneys in *Ulysses*, "which gave to his palate a fine tang of faintly scented urine" (55).

Space constraints allow only one more example, that of a most delicious scene in M. F. K. Fisher's garden of earthly delights. Although her own life was compounded of joy, disappointment, early sorrow, and later pleasures, it is these precious hours so poignantly illustrated by Michael Cunningham that prevail in Fisher's writing. For Fisher, one paradigmatic moment involves peas. In *With Bold Knife and Fork* (1968), more recipe-oriented than many of her writings, of "PEAS" she says simply: "The best way to eat fresh ones is to be alive on the right day, with the men picking and the women shelling, and everybody capering in the sweet early summer weather, and the big pot of water boiling, and the table set with little cool roasted chickens and pitchers of white wine. So," she asks, how often does this ideal moment—the sweet summer "day with stars on it" (for the "first mess of peas")—happen, a

Left to right rear: Sara, Lynn, and Laird; left to right front: Beth and Paul, on vacation in Switzerland, 1999

day indeed for "capering" (189), rather than the stately minuet of the formal dinner party? In fact, Fisher has unpacked this perfect picnic time twice before, in *The Gastronomical Me* and in *An Alphabet for Gourmets* (1949), where we learn that with her on their small farm in Vevey, Switzerland, in June of 1938 are her parents, several friends, and Dillwyn Parrish, whom she would marry in 1940: "There sat most of the people in the world I loved, in a thin light that was pink with Alpen glow, blue with a veil of pine smoke from the hearth. . . . [A] cow . . . moved her head among the meadow flowers and shook her bell in a slow, melodious rhythm, a kind of hymn. My father lifted up his face at the sound and, his fists all stained with green-pea juice, said passionately, 'God, but I feel good!' I felt near to tears" (*An Alphabet for Gourmets*, 666).

Fisher's writing, elegant and eloquently understated, like that of Woolf, Shields, Chopin, and Cunningham, too, captures the essence of a lifetime, a universe of the rare, best hours of life, bursting like meteors to illuminate the rest of the cosmos, difficult, dark, and deep. That is the essence of good food writing, of potluck, of life itself.

After the Party

On this second coldest night of the year in Connecticut (in Costa Rica, we missed the first one), dessert seems more a necessity than an indulgence, a sweet salve to our frustrated hospitality. We would ordinarily choose chocolate, anything chocolate, but because we were expecting others to bring that succulent substance, Martin has prepared a backup dessert, an apple cake that will keep. He used the recipe surfacing from "the small mountain of apple cake recipes" that survived the ruthless rigor of the *Cook's Illustrated* team. As with many recipes, this Apple Cake offers the hopeful promise that it will be easy, quick. But like everything else in this life, it wasn't that simple; to get the cake, well, as right as anything ever gets in our household, has taken time, patience, perseverance, and a reliable oven. The generous cake ("serves 10 to 12") that emerged from the Bundt pan fulfilled the *Cook's Illustrated* description: it "practically glowed with a haloed ring of lovely, flaxen gold apples." This apple cake "was the one—tall, bountiful, and with great apple flavor" (334). We light the candles, turn out the lights, raise our glasses, and become, again, our own dinner party. We go to bed early to hold in the heat.

The Two-Thousand-Mile Commute

"I hate to wash floors," I announced. "If you love me," said my fiancé du jour, "you'll wash the floors after we're married." "I might do it," I said, "but I'll always hate it"—grounds sufficient in what they implied to break off our engagement. Martin responded to this litmus test, "I'm stronger than you are. Either I'll wash the floors or we'll get someone else to do it, but you'll never have to wash a floor." Thus when Martin and I married in 1958, just before we began doctoral work at the University of Michigan, we adopted a single principle to govern our lives together: We would do whatever we could to enhance each others' personal and professional lives. From that, all else has followed, for the next forty-eight years and counting . . .

This principle, our version of the Golden Rule, made de facto feminists of us both, before the term was common. It meant, at the outset, that we would both work on our doctorates full time, that we would share the responsibilities for earning money and running the household (the proportions of each have varied over the years, with each of us assuming responsibility for what we could do—or liked to do—best), and that if one or the other of us needed extra help to accomplish something important, they'd get it. It also meant that when some male students in my doctoral program would say to me, "I'm glad *my* wife isn't in graduate school," I could cheerfully reply, "I'm glad I'm not *your* wife."

We moved to Cleveland from Ann Arbor when Bard was ten days old, and nine months later I finished my dissertation. I wrote the last hundred pages with a squirming baby on my lap by day and rewrote them again at night and on weekends when Martin was home to handle Bard's round-the-clock energy. Laird was born two years and one textbook later. Although I was teaching part time, by design I was away from the children no more than eighteen hours a week until the boys were in school full time, because

Martin and I felt very strongly that if we wanted our children to grow up the way we thought they should, we'd better spend lots of time with them. As a social psychologist, Martin could earn a great deal more money than I could in English, so we agreed that I'd postpone full-time teaching until the boys were in school. Thus during our sons' preschool years, I was never away from them overnight, with the exception of a single week's research trip to Boston and a few one-night research trips during the five years I spent writing the biography of Benjamin Spock, M.D. Little did I know that six years later I'd be commuting a thousand miles each way to work every week.

Martin's research job kept him out of the house, alas, during most of the children's waking hours, except on weekends, when the Three Musketeers hit the trail and I hit the electric typewriter full speed ahead. But on weekdays I could hardly expect Bard and Laird to leave my child-centered study, where they were playing as I wrote. So I learned to work in short batches of time, and late at night. By the time *Doctor Spock: Biography of a Conservative Radical* was published, we had moved to Indianapolis for Martin's first academic job and its more accommodating schedule.

In—and Out of—a Real Job

A year after our move to Indianapolis, our children started school and I got my first real job, at thirty-six, a tenure-track assistant professorship at Butler University, a convenient five minutes from home, teaching four different courses every semester. Martin saw the boys off to school so I could teach in the mornings and be home by the time they arrived for lunch (no school lunches at this '70s neighborhood school), and he did bedtime duty on the nights I taught. I loved the job—my colleagues, the students, and the variety of courses, and I received early tenure and promotion.

After five happy years in Indianapolis, Martin was offered his dream job at Washington University in St. Louis. I cheerfully resigned from Butler for the move. Our overarching operative principle was intact, and I was confident—with the arrogance of a Michigan Ph.D. who came of age during a seller's market coupled with the ease of finding the job at Butler—that I could again get a good job in the best place in town.

Wrong! In 1974's dismal job market, I could find no job except part-time work as an adjunct at three universities, where I came and went, invisible, under cover of lightness and darkness, as I have explained in "Teaching College English as a Woman." As a consequence, I made two resolutions: never again to take another job that supported such an exploitative system and, when and if I ever got another tenure-track job, to do what I could to help to change that very system. (The latter is another story.)

Martin, Laird (age seven), Bard (age nine), and Lynn Bloom at home in Indianapolis, Indiana, 1971. Photograph by Bob Stalcup, Butler University

The Critical Job Search

That year of miserable marginality impelled me to look in desperation for a full-time, tenure-track job. I would soon be forty-one and feared my career would end before it had scarcely begun. While our sons, now in junior high, were doing their homework, Martin and I took long evening walks around the neighborhood, exercising our eager border collie and entertaining options. Should I stay home and write full time? I enjoyed that; I was publishing apace; and I'd gotten two new book contracts during our first four months in St. Louis. I could be home when the boys came home from school, which I insisted on, and cook ad lib. Nevertheless I hadn't spent all that time earning a Ph.D. not to use it and to get paid appropriately. But the real reason was that I loved to teach; real students in actual classrooms were adrenaline to my teacher's blood. As a faculty child myself, I loved the rationale and rhythm of the academic life, even committee meetings. I loved being identified as a college professor, as much as I loved being identified, in other contexts, as Martin's wife, or Bard's and Laird's mother. With that identity gone, too soon, too soon, I felt bereft, in anticipatory mourning for an unlived life.

For a while it was hard for Martin to understand the intensity of this desire, especially given the appeal, though not the financial assurance, of a writer's career. I really wanted both; actually, I wanted it all, however immodest those aspirations might have been. "I'm your best friend," he said, and I hurt his feelings when I told, as usual, the truth: "Yes, but you can't be my *only* friend." As we renegotiated our Golden Rule, it became clear that "to enhance each others' personal and professional lives" meant arranging our family life so we could each have equivalent careers. Since we had comparable academic training and I had been off the career track when our children were little, I needed to scramble to get back on the train. I thought I would have to settle for a local—although the options in St. Louis ranged from dim to nil, if my experiences as an adjunct were prognostic. But what I really wanted was a fast express.

In his new understanding, Martin encouraged me to apply for jobs the length and breadth of the MLA *Job List*. With no institutional affiliation to provide an entrée, I was surprised to receive invitations for a dozen interviews at the MLA meeting from schools around the country. Two I remember very well, even three decades later: the worst, where the yawns of the three interviewers eager to escape to the convention bar reaffirmed the in-house favorite daughter's hammerlock on the job. And I remember the best, because it was so much fun, with the University of New Mexico. Fourteen faculty crowded the department chair's small hotel room, sitting on the bed, the floor, or standing; as candidate, I got one of the two chairs. Although the job had been advertised as Renaissance lit, which I had taught at Butler, the interviewers had picked up on my work in biography and autobiography and composition, all my favorite subjects, and geared the interview to these. The discussion was verbal volleyball, with myself the only player on one side of the net. Someone would lob a title over the net, and I'd hit it back; I'd read every book and article they mentioned, and more. We talked about big ideas and invented whole programs in that interview, which, though scheduled for forty-five minutes, lasted two hours. These people could be friends, I thought, and I could hardly wait to meet the students—a mixture of Hispanic, Native American, and Anglos, from an exotic culture far beyond the Mississippi.

As the results of the interviews came in, with invitations to visit campuses far beyond driving distance, the reality of what I might be getting into began to dawn. To accept a tenure-track job with all its attendant rights, responsibilities, and privileges, I would have to commute overnight or longer. Could I really do this? To even contemplate a long-distance commute violated my whole understanding of what marriage and motherhood meant. Despite the fact that Martin and I considered ourselves feminists, given our operative principle that translated into a marriage much more collaborative than many we knew of at the time,* I believed that a mother who loved her family and wanted them to thrive was always available to her husband and children.

A call from New Mexico in February wonderfully focused our minds. "Come for an interview," invited the cordial chairman, Joseph Zavadil—to whom I dedicate this chapter—himself the father of seven. "I must tell you," he said, "that state law says that if we pay your expenses for an interview, you have to be willing to take the job if we offer it to you." "I'll call you back," I said. This was the perfect job, a chance to teach autobiography, women's lit, and graduate courses in composition research—three new fields that were just beginning, in the flagship school of the most exotic stateside location I could imagine, with research support and the chance to direct the writing program. "What if they offer me the job?" I wailed to Martin. "I can't take it. Albuquerque is a thousand miles away; I'd have to be there three or four nights a week. I can't be away from home so long." "Oh yes, you can," he said, without hesitation. "I'll come," I told the chair.

---

*To celebrate finishing *Doctor Spock,* Martin and I took the boys camping throughout Europe for a summer, renting out our house in Indianapolis to an older law student and his family whom we had never met. The wife met us at the airport on our return, with a defiant welcome: "I've seen how you live, I know there's a different way to do it than the one I have, and I'm divorcing my husband." And so she did.

I loved New Mexico but was convinced I'd blown the interview. My interview talk was on point of view in Gertrude Stein's autobiographies. In my innocent heterosexism, I didn't realize that to talk about Stein was to signal UNM's large lesbian community that I was ready to join them. So from all venues of the campus they arrived for the lecture, their blue jeans and cowboy boots a frontier contrast to the sedate suits I was used to in the effete East. Although the English faculty seemed happy with my interpretation, the lesbian contingent was growing restless; their unending questions pushed for a lesbian reading, and I resisted—gently, at first, as I tried to escape a confrontation. "How can you *not* read Stein as a work of lesbianism?" someone asserted, and I got mad. (A decade later, I'd have agreed. One learns.) Into my mind came my favorite scene from *Huck Finn,* when Huck refuses to turn Jim in to the slave hunters, in defiance of the law and the locals. "You can't pray a lie," I thought. "OK, I'll go to hell, and lose this job"—which by then I desperately wanted—"but I have to say what I think." So I took a deep breath, clung to the podium, and said, "Any set of readings that allows only a single -ism, whether it's Freudianism, Marxism, feminism"—I paused—"or lesbianism, is too narrow." Whereupon the hecklers rose and strode out as a white-maned English professor shouted, "Gertrude Stein was a beautiful woman." I returned home, convinced that the beautiful job had fled the room along with my antagonists.

Even if I were to get an out-of-town job (others were emerging; I had even had one interview in an airport phone booth as I left for New Mexico), we never entertained the option of moving the children, then in seventh and eighth grades. We had a big old house in St. Louis in a superb school system. The boys were well ensconced in school. Martin's office was two blocks away from their school and four blocks from our house, so he could easily bike home to be there when they got home from school. Besides, he said, on any new job I'd need to concentrate on learning all of the complicated things I'd need to know to do the work well; I shouldn't be bothering about housework or child care. "But what if something goes wrong at home while I'm away?" "I'll handle it," he said. My protests were getting weaker. Then Dr. Zavadil called to offer me the job. "We were impressed with the way you stood up to the hecklers. We didn't care what you said, just the fact that you didn't back down under all that pressure was important. Come ahead." Then he offered me an associate professorship at double my previous salary and a teaching schedule tailored to my commuter flights. Yet I hesitated. "My commuting expenses will cost half my salary," I said to Martin. "Yes," he replied; there went the raise. "Go for it." And so I did.

The Exhilaration of the Long-Distance Commuter

Every couple invents their own marriage and has to reinvent it as life circumstances change: geographic and career moves; the arrival and departure of children, aging parents, and other relatives; the waxing and waning of income, health, and affairs of the world. For many of these changes we have models. We can talk the situation over with those who have preceded us, we can read up on it, and nowadays we check it out on the Web. But in the mid-1970s, if there were precedents, especially for the wife and mother as the commuter, we didn't know about them. Marital lore says that extreme commuting works if the couple has a very strong marriage, which can literally "go the distance," or a very weak one, which benefits from separation, but that uncertain marriages can't take the instability and are likely to dissolve. With no model for long-distance commuting—we came from traditional families and lived in a neighborhood where the mothers who worked were within easy reach of home—we had to invent and reinvent new and capacious dimensions. We didn't ask our sons' opinion, but they seemed unfazed by the prospect of my absence. I was afraid my neighbors would shun me, but they seemed as intrigued as I by the prospect of my new job and said they wished they'd had comparable opportunities. The women's writing group I'd been leading decided to adapt their meeting times to my commuting schedule.

We soon settled on the model that worked well during my three-year affiliation with UNM. Three weeks out of four I flew from St. Louis to Albuquerque—a straight route, no change of planes—on a Monday or Tuesday morning and returned home on Thursday night. The fourth weekend, I stayed in Albuquerque to cut down on costs, catch up on work, cook meals to freeze and thaw during my shorter stays, and explore the state. I worked hard, in my office with a balcony and huge windows facing the ever-changing Sandia mountains; fourteen-hour days and evenings meant I could get most of the class preparation and administrative work done in situ. I was so busy I scarcely had time to get lonesome except during the occasional solitary dinner and at bedtime. I graded papers on the plane; the two-plus-hour flight was just long enough to finish a set. That left the three-day weekends in St. Louis free to write—a great deal, as it turned out; to spend lots of time with my family; and to cook meals for them to eat during my absence, thus assuaging my initial guilt at leaving the children during the week. Martin's and my Friday trips to the grocery store had the frisson of a honeymoon. The boys, busy with school and after-school activities, accepted my departures and arrivals with aplomb. After all, they could count on their dad to be home when they were, and—especially after he had switched from full-time research to a professorial job—Martin had always given them a lot of attention, even for a time becoming Cub Scout den mother (the Scouts had no alternative language at the time for den fathers).

Indeed when I asked Bard and Laird as I began this essay how they had felt about my commuting, each shrugged. "No big deal. That was just what you did." "We were busy all the time you were away." "We expected it, just as we expected a scramble of housecleaning on Thursday nights before we went to pick you up at the airport." This experience also set a pattern that our sons' wives have benefitted from, as they freely travel on business while their husbands tend the household. So I soon got over the guilt, though I kept on cooking and acting as communication central, in charge of scheduling everyone's appointments and serving as a concierge for the family's social life and recreation. By this time, however, Martin was baking bread regularly, which he does to this day; as his culinary repertoire expanded, the boys too were developing a lifelong love of cooking. When we were interviewed about our "alternative lifestyle," Martin and I always maintained that it wasn't alternative, it just occurred in two different places.

Not only was the New Mexico job the right job, it came at the right time in my life, and that of our family. I wanted to get in on the ground floor of research in the areas I was hired to work in; as it has turned out, all three—autobiography, women writers, and composition studies—have moved since then from far left field to the mainstream. I wanted to direct a big undergraduate writing program, do research on it, and help train TAs how to teach it. UNM not only provided research funding, but a crack typist; a program secretary, herself a fine creative writer; and an administrative assistant who handled with aplomb all queries, including the usual grammar mavens and threats of lawsuits over grades. She also took me to the airport, a fast mile from campus. I learned a lot about multiculturalism in this state where Anglos were in a minority; I taught a much wider range of students in income and age, as well as ethnicity, than I'd ever taught before. I learned about high- and low-stakes testing of writing; I learned, often the hard way, about academic politics, for good and for ill. Thanks to the mentorship of many, particularly my last and best landlady, retired political science professor Dorothy Cline (to whom this essay is also dedicated), who had been the first woman commissioner of Bernalillo County and knew everyone in the state, I learned from the inside what it was like to live in the still fairly wild West, with mountains and canyons and mesas and Indian reservations that our family explored during spring breaks. What I learned would have been utterly impossible had I never left home and settled for the alternative—part-time adjunct jobs in St. Louis.

I learned, too, that it was possible to take huge risks, with my family and my career, because the foundation was in place. All the things that might have derailed either the commuting, our marriage, or our children didn't happen. Although I was three weeks late to school at the outset of the job because of recuperation from unexpected gallbladder surgery, all of us stayed healthy, and happy. Martin and I had neither the time nor the inclination to develop dangerous liaisons. Our sons' grades remained stellar, their behavior (to our knowledge) wholesome, as might be expected of the children of nerds. The airline crews never struck, the flights were never cancelled or rerouted, and in those innocent times I could rush from class through the Albuquerque airport's adobe corridors and onto the plane in ten minutes flat. By chance, trouble struck only when we were together. Our dog was mangled to death by a mastiff; Laird broke a tooth in a sports accident; on a camping trip in Sweden, I was attacked by a rapist on drugs within two hundred feet of my sleeping children.

On the Road Again

The attempted rape, coupled with the unavailability of jobs for Martin in Albuquerque, for UNM had no social work school, made us decide after three years that it was time to stop commuting. Because English positions were still scarce, we agreed that I would find the job first. Fortunately the range of my new experiences, particularly as writing director, provided a plethora of possibilities in cities and towns where Martin could also find work. For this move, the boys had a vote; Williamsburg, Virginia, beat San Diego four to nothing. As an enticement for Martin to stay at Washington University, his social work dean offered me the best part-time job I'd ever encountered: to teach a course in social science writing and edit a social work journal the school published. If that had been an option four years earlier, I'd have accepted it; no question. "I'll take it if you want me to," I told Martin, for his job was both agreeable and prestigious. "Nope," he said cheerfully, "you deserve the best job you can get in your field, not mine. Here, you'd be just as isolated professionally as you were when we first came." And so we moved, where I encountered nonstop professional harassment, beginning the day I arrived; Laird was nearly killed in a car crash; and Martin was diagnosed with a brain tumor. We all survived.

Except for the traumas just identified, this story sounds too good to be true. To ensure reader sympathy, I or my family should have experienced a major crisis, trauma, breakdown, or horrendous problem that we overcame only after great storm and stress. Preferably more than one, to make the narrative of the two-thousand-mile commute compelling. But those bad things didn't happen as the consequences of commuting; they are not inevitable. The many morals of this story of personal and professional risk taking are evident. Like many other adventures in life, the big risks that could have culminated in catastrophe had even greater potential for change, growth, and a great deal of fun, not only for myself but for our entire family. We chose the long, adventuresome open road over a dead-end street. That two-thousand-mile journey, back and forth, back and forth, a dozen times a semester, led not only to the Land of Enchantment, but to the wide world of the possible, from that day to this.

(Im)Patient

Patient at Work, 1

I am writing this on the computer, with my right arm in a sling, resting on a pillow on my lap. This is the forty-first day after the first of two rotator cuff surgeries on my right shoulder. As I begin to write, "This is the first post-op day that I can move my fingers in reasonable comfort for any length of time in order to press the keys," my right hand is seized by a cramp that shoots bright steel rods of pain from my fingertips to my shoulder socket. I stop. Should I take an Aleve, the only painkiller I can tolerate? I haven't had one for ten hours, which I took at 4 A.M. to still the throbbing pain that woke me up. No, I'll wait and see if the pain gets worse. It subsides, and I start again.

Today is also the first day since the surgery that my mind can focus coherently on telling a story, figuring out what it means, writing it down, getting the words and the rhythm right. I need to write this particular story at this time, to write through the pain (though I do not intend to say much about the pain itself—who needs more of that?) while I am experiencing it, to provide both the necessary understanding and the necessary edge to what I write. A psychotherapist friend tells me that healthy people can't make themselves hurt by thinking about pain. It doesn't hurt, he says, to recall labor pains months or years beyond childbirth; after the pain has subsided, women can remember having been in pain, but they can't recreate it. So I must write about this experience while it's hot.

I also need to write this to see whether I am able, once again, to do what I most love to do—to write, which has been the lifeblood of my professional commitment over the years. Has this ability been dissipated entirely in the mist of anesthesia and its aftermath, or only temporarily subdued? During the past six weeks, as the usual invitations to present papers at professional meetings, contribute chapters to others' books, come up with research and book proposals of my own, have flowed in at their usual pace, I have let them float right on past, vaporized in my mental fog. Try me again in another six weeks, I've said to the more tantalizing requests. While floundering for a month to proofread page proofs for a 627-page book that would have ordi-narily taken five days, max, I have been wondering whether my mind will ever again be agile enough, imaginative enough to write with originality and insight, about anything at all. I have to find out. So when I see the call for papers on "Disability and/in Prose," I think, "Aha! The right subject at the right time." Even if I fail in the attempt, the subject is so common, though never commonplace to those undergoing it, that it's worth the effort—the risk of the undertaking, and the pain of the execution—to explore it.

I have written these last five sentences with my left hand, to give my right hand a rest. Even with the aid of a gyroscopic mouse, which I have learned to manipulate, clumsily, solely with my left hand, I make many typing errors, erase, and write again. It has taken two hours and forty-five minutes—which just morphed into three hours, no, make that three hours and fifteen, nope, three and twenty-five minutes—to write these four paragraphs, double my usual time. I am exhilarated, and exhausted. My arm pulses pain. I will resort to that Aleve, followed by the respite of a little nap. (Actually, I don't take the Aleve, and the nap lasts an hour.)

How fortunate I am that my profession, as a college English professor and a writer, affords the luxury of slow healing—including an accommodat-ing schedule that has enabled me to miss only one class, once, during this time, though much of the convalescence has taken place during Christmas break. And how lucky I am that Martin, on the same academic schedule, is cheerfully willing to serve as a good right arm—in virtually all the tasks of daily living that I can't manage with my awkward left hand alone—from cooking, driving, and housecleaning to tying my shoes and flossing my teeth. Although I quickly learn to dress, shower, and eat left-handed, there are many other things it's not worth the struggle to learn for the nine or ten weeks that my arm will be restricted in a sling. Newly dependent, I hate to ask for all the help I suddenly need, but Martin anticipates nearly everything.

Betrayed from Within

I never expected to be sidelined with a jock injury, because, daily exercise notwithstanding, I am not a jock. I've never been on a winning sports team, ever, from elementary school to the present, not even in our family soccer games—the Percales versus the Flannels, team assignment determined by sheet preference. There I get to play goalie, a post where I can do and receive little harm.

Throughout elementary school, I was invariably picked last for the team sport du jour—softball, tag football, volleyball, basketball. As team captains called out names of the chosen, my face burned with anxiety and shame at my inability to pitch, bat, throw, pass, shoot a ball—or for that matter, run or swim, with any accuracy, speed, or distance. Year after year, I never got any better. In high school, I wised up and wimped out by scheduling orchestra practice and student newspaper editorial meetings during gym times. In college, "lifetime sports" finally came to the rescue: noncompetitive tennis, golf, swimming, and figure skating—which I loved despite my lack of grace and the toll it took in wickedly skinned knees and gouges up and down my shinbones from repeated falls. The incredible lightness of being I enjoyed then persists to this day, in fast walking around campus or doing errands, moderately paced hiking on family vacations (last summer, six of us, including grandchildren ages eight and eleven, spent two weeks hiking in the Canadian Rockies, six-eight-ten hours a day), and the slow but steady lap swimming I've engaged in nearly every day for the past thirty years.

I enjoy the activities themselves, and the conviction that they're helping to ensure good health. Indeed I believe my body owes me reciprocity. If I treat it right, my body should enable me to perform the full range of activities involved in an active personal and professional life. Given appropriate rest, nutrition, and exercise, I expect my body to function without fail, seven days a week, 365 days a year.

So nine months ago, when the pain in my right shoulder persisted, I picked up the pace of my swimming, firm in my belief that an invigorating swim cures just about everything. The pain just got worse, even after I modified my overarm stroke, and when it began to keep me awake at night, I reluctantly consulted my trusted primary care physician, Rick, who treats his patients as happy collaborators in the maintenance of good health. After—in succession—rest, a cortisone shot, and physical therapy made no significant difference, an MRI revealed a torn rotator cuff, caused by a bone spur in my shoulder that created a "medium tear" (as opposed to "small" or "large") in the muscles. This is, as I have learned from all the jock jokes tossed my way by the cognoscenti, an injury common among baseball pitchers. I have been betrayed from within, perhaps by the very exercise I have counted on to keep me healthy, and though I would not have forgone a single lap of the swimming, there is no way I could have prevented the injury. There is no choice but to have the bone spur filed down and the tear sewed up, under ordinary circumstances an hour-long arthroscopic surgery. The orthopedic surgeon, Dr. Jay (not his real name)—keen, cheerful, and gung ho—who repairs the knees, elbows, and shoulders of my university's varsity athletes and is known for successfully redoing other surgeons' botched work, performs the initial operation. But because the stitches and the screw inserted into the bone to hold them tear out as a consequence of aggressive post-op physical therapy, which I have followed to the letter (and thus been labeled "noncompliant" by both therapist and doctor), he performs a second operation three weeks after the first to repair the repairs—another hour under general anesthesia.

Ambulatory Surgery

"Ambulatory surgery" strikes me as an oxymoron. Are patients—as an impatient person I think of us as victims, scarcely patient at all—expected to walk around while the doctor operates on the run? The term conjures up a Monty Pythonesque hospital scene of a clutch of the halt and the maimed, bandaged from head to foot, being lashed into a quick march on crutches through the exhortations of a gaggle of manic doctors and nurses. "Faster, faster," they cry, as the patients struggle to keep up. This worst nightmare serves as a metaphor for my attitude about the impending surgery, and I suspect I am not alone.

Nor am I alone in the hospital wing where the outpatient surgery (another oxymoron) is performed. The curtained-off section for each patient is barely wide enough for a hospital bed and the small chair crunched beside it, an uncomfortable space for my husband or the attending nurse. No verbal privacy is possible within this sheeted tent, whose impermanence confirms the fact that I'll be out of there soon. Perhaps "ambulatory surgery," like dry cleaning, means in by ten, out by two, although I don't know whether all patients are supposed to be able to walk into the hospital and, four hours later, rise up from the operating table and walk away from the scene of bloodletting. I know that's what I expect. Can so transient an operation be a very big deal?

In the old pre-HMO days, when patients stayed a week or two in the hospital after surgery, we knew we were there to heal, and we expected to spend another month recovering at home. The process, like that of an ocean liner on a stately trans-Atlantic crossing, was clear, its schedule certain, its comforts as gracious as bouillon at eleven and lap robes at the ready for naps on the deck chairs. Today we "ambulatory outpatients" are traveling coach on low-budget airlines, carrying our own luggage so we can be up and out and back to work in record time. True, the much less invasive techniques of contemporary microsurgery make operations far easier to recover from than they used to be. But what's a realistic timetable for recovery from any specific surgery, and how are patients to know and deal appropriately with this?

The amount of time the actual postoperative healing process will take seems to be a lot clearer to medical personnel than to patients. A friend's situation is typical. Shortly before my own initial operation, I encountered him walking across campus, pale and doubled over on a surprisingly hot October afternoon. "What's the matter?" I asked. "I had my appendix out four days ago, an emergency, and today I needed to get back to the lab." "But," I was trying to be tactful, "you seem to be having trouble walking." "Well," he smiled wanly, "I did stay home for three days. But it's so boring to spend all that time in bed."

By sending us home once our eyes begin to focus and we can maneuver in a straight line, doctors reinforce this macho behavior. I know the surgeon has said it will take several weeks for the muscle repair to heal up, a process extended by the second operation. I understand that physical therapy might proceed for another six months, even longer, until I can do everything with ease again. Nevertheless once I leave the hospital, about an hour after emerging from the recovery room, in my mind I am already on the mend. In fact before the second operation (which I optimistically expect to take ten minutes, Dr. Jay's minimum estimate, instead of the hour, his outer limit, that it actually requires), I have accepted an invitation to a party set for six hours after the surgery. How invasive can a ten-minute operation be, I speculate beforehand, and never recalibrate my thinking to the hour-long reality, which should have registered, but doesn't. Only when I am overcome by nausea and head-to-toe itching that invades every bodily orifice, reactions to the prescribed painkiller, Tylox this time, am I forced to acknowledge that we're not going anywhere that night. Samuel Johnson's assertion that a second marriage is a triumph of hope over experience reverberates in my foggy mind. I call the hostess and croak a cancellation; after each operation my voice—surprise!—disappears for two days.

Academics ("like yourself" is the unspoken qualifier), Dr. Jay observes during a follow-up visit, are used to attaining high levels of success, often competitively—through rational means, an insider's knowledge of the profession, and force of will. "But no matter how hard you try, you can't speed up the body's natural healing process." I could use a bumper sticker to reinforce this reminder: "You are mortal. Live with it."

Patient at Work, 2

It is three weeks after the second surgery, and I have resumed physical therapy, this time on campus, very close to my office. Because I have changed locations, I have to fill out all the admissions paperwork again, and one form has me stumped. The Pain Scale: "How severe is your pain (on a scale of zero [no pain] to ten [worst pain imaginable]) at its worst? When lying on the involved side? Reaching for something on a high shelf?" And the Disability Scale: "How much difficulty do you have Washing your hair? Washing your back? Putting on . . . a pullover sweater? Putting on a shirt that buttons down the front? Putting on your pants? Placing an object on a high shelf? Removing something from your back pocket?" (J. W. Williams, "Measuring Shoulder Function"). I haven't done any of these things—at all—with my afflicted arm since the operation; wearing the sling continuously except for bathing, dressing, and physical therapy is designed to inhibit all the motions these taken-for-granted activities entail. But these routine tasks must be done, and although my left arm lacks dexterity, I must use it exclusively to tug, push, and pull whatever is necessary to do the job—taking twice the time with more than double the effort.

Paul, the therapist (he's conducting his dissertation research on tears in rotator cuffs and knees as a result of athletic injuries) solves the problem of how to answer by drawing a slash through the whole list. He puts me through a routine of exercises—some familiar, several new—and I am astonished to be able, with trembling effort, to raise my right arm over my head. Paul does an excellent job of explaining the physiology and mechanics of each exercise, which embeds the rationale for doing it. But when it's time to practice at home, one of the reasons why I have always been such an inept athlete becomes very clear. I find it very hard to understand or remember the specifics of how to perform a particular motion, any motion except those, I remember, that relate to cooking—currently off-limits. I lack what Howard Gardner, in his concept of "multiple intelligences" has called *bodily-kinesthetic* intelligence. So when I look at the instruction sheet and see—under "Lying on back with cane" (any sturdy rod will do)—"Bilateral shoulder flexion, elbows straight," I don't know what it means. Has Paul, who knows I'm an English professor, used those very words when he showed me what to do? "Bilateral shoulder abduction with elbows bent" connotes, to me, a villain skulking off, elbows crooked, having tucked a cowering maiden under his cloak, surely not an aspect of physical therapy as we know it. Pictures would have helped, but in their absence I call Paul for clarification. With the memory of last month's ripped-out stitches still fresh, I'd rather ask than to risk a third surgery.

Information supplied, directions at hand, I work my way with all deliberate caution through the exercises: "pendulum," "sawing modified," "table slides" straight forward and at an angle, the aforementioned shoulder flexions and abductions, ending with "internal and external rotation"—the latter done lying on my back, elbow on a pillow, forearm up, rotating my hand back and forth. Or should it go around and around? As I'm writing this, I begin to wonder, have I remembered correctly? I'll have to call again in the morning. The familiar exercises now seem easy, comfortable, but I cannot relax, because I know what's ahead. Each new exercise is uncomfortable at first, verging on painful, though I try to stop just short of pain; it requires careful thought, deliberate motion—and more patience than I thought I had. The exercises also require counting—numbers of repetitions, amount of time to hold a particular position. That I lose count helps to explain why I'm a bad knitter and an impossible bridge player. I've never been able to concentrate on numbers, even single digits, narration is my preferred mode. It's a relief to reach the final instruction, "ice—20 minutes," and to sneak in a nap or some reading for pleasure while the ice bag rests on my shoulder. Can learning to write be this hard, even painful, for my undergraduates? This much work? And this slow? It's useful to be reminded from time to time what it's like to be a novice learner rather than an expert, slaloming with joy through complicated verbal racecourses, the tougher the better.

I would like to do a fourth, optional, set of these exercises before bed. I want to be the exemplary model patient, I want to heal up the fastest of anyone on this planet. But I'm too tired and decide just to go to sleep instead. Dr. Jay has my number all right.

Pain

"The surgery will be very painful," warns Dr. Jay. "I'll do what I can to keep you comfortable. So in addition to the general anesthetic for the hour the operation will take, I'll order an anesthetic block for your right arm." (The block couldn't be used for the second operation, so close to the first.) "This will last between twelve and twenty-four hours; as soon as you feel it beginning to wear off, take two Vicodin so that will kick in and take over." I have found that even doctors who tell us to expect pain—or worse afflictions (like many, we have dealt with the cancer scare and the heart attack alarm, fortunately false)—are deliberately not very specific. They tell us just what we need to know to be able to cope with the problem at hand, and no more. Perhaps suffering is so individual that to say more would be misleading; why complicate what is already difficult enough?

I don't know how much pain or what kind to expect. Everyone winces at the mention of "torn rotator cuff"; what do they know that I don't? During the pre-op months, on the pain scale of smiley to agonized faces that seem to adorn every room and cubicle in the hospital, I have experienced the full range, usually near the end that signals discomfort rather than the other pole of intense suffering. When we leave the hospital, I feel—surprise—no pain, though I am aware that this is transitory. As the shoulder block begins to dissipate, I realize that I am holding my own hand. It feels like sculptured marble—long, delicate fingers; smooth, alabaster skin—which alters in contour and texture much less sculptural as the feeling returns.

I hold onto the soothing memory of that one-handed touch as I am soon overcome by nausea and vertigo, side effects of the Vicodin. My husband calls Dr. Jay—what to do? We can't get the alternative, Anaprox, without an opiate clearance that the doctor needs to provide. Even then it will cost our insurance $174 to fill the prescription—$4.35 per pill. "One Anaprox is equivalent to two Aleve," says the doctor, "Why don't you just use that?" This cheap generic alternative (6.5 cents per pill) works well enough, with no side effects, to permit a couple of hours of fitful sleep.

"Why do you repeatedly hit your head on the wall?" went one of my father's jokes, whose punch line seems strangely apropos now—"Because it feels so good when you stop." It is such a relief not to experience the nausea, the vertigo, the itching, the overall grogginess, the anticipation of all of these, that I go cold turkey and never thereafter use any pain medicine except the occasional Aleve. I never do figure out where my pain falls on some abstract scale. It's not disabling, and during the daytimes I can usually find sufficient distraction to keep from dwelling on it. I mostly don't talk about pain either before or after either surgery except for the occasional yelp, "Ouch!" when an untoward motion catches me unaware. I'm not trying to be heroic. Although I come from a stiff-upper-lip family that tolerates no whining or special pleading, I figure there are worse things in the world, and I need to concentrate on recovery, as well as on the work that keeps coming in apace, however slowly I am actually able to do it.

Long Nights: Patient Still at Work, 3

For weeks I can't lie down in comfort. Being supine exacerbates the shoulder pain and causes every muscle in my body to tense up, so I spend the nights in a recliner chair. Trade named "Stressless," this chair has embraced a quarter century of family and friends, and, until now, it has fulfilled its name. It accommodates so many angles of repose that everyone who sits in it goes to sleep, whether they want to or not, except for the grandchildren, who like to swivel around and around, bouncing as they go. Its contours, comfortable though svelte, have seen us through the usual ordinary family's assortment of colds and flu, fretfulness and anxiety, surgeries minor and more demanding, and—since we've moved to Connecticut—three bouts of Lyme disease and the aftereffects of a brown recluse spider bite.

The hilltop views from the chair are ever soothing. Woods leafy in summer thin out in winter to reveal a Grandma Moses scene susceptible to a Robert Frost interpretation: beyond the brook that bounds our property, a farm in the valley, red barn, cows and horses stamping in the snow, wood smoke wisping into the evergreens beyond. On clear nights, the bare oaks in our yard sparkle with necklaces of stars; through the branches, a rosy glow emanates from the Hartford suburbs, twenty-five miles away. Buoyed by history and scenery, well tucked in by Martin, I expect to be able to sleep well. But as the hours, then the nights followed by more nights, pass with excruciating slowness, I realize that I cannot.

The sentences in the paragraph you are reading can be arranged in any order except for the last two, and they will accurately represent any of the forty-one consecutive nights I spend in the Stressless chair, time out of time. The room's too hot, too cold. The down comforter slides off, and I can't reach it unless I hoist myself erect with my free arm from a reclining position, thereby disturbing the careful arrangements of chair, footstool, pillows, nightgown, and bathrobe. Sometimes the avalanche of textiles in motion—only the sling is still—knocks off the books and papers piled on the table near the chair. My arm begins to ache. I itch. The nightgown twists, the robe wads up, cold air sneaks in above the kneesocks. There isn't much latitude to move around in the chair; I have to remain fairly erect to keep pressure off my shoulder. I'm uncomfortable and can't squirm to an agreeable posture no matter what I try. I fear I'll tip the chair over. My arm throbs. Should I take an Aleve? Have I had one recently? I should have written down when I took one, except that my hand hurts when I try to write. I feel a draft. After the first two nights, I resolve not to ask Martin, in our bed in an adjacent room, for help, though he still rises at intervals, from concern. He has to do so much extra work during the days that he should be exempt from night duty; after all, it's not a matter of life and death. I read. I listen to CDs—music, novels, nonfiction; the words drift in and out. The room's too cold; my shoulder hurts. I try not to look at the clock, and to gauge the day's arrival by the changing color in the sky. I await the NPR news broadcasts that begin at 5 A.M. and continue for four hours; maybe some sleep will creep in unannounced. Fortunately this semester all my classes and major committee meetings are in the coherent afternoons. Sometimes they last into the evening and steal hours from the long, dark nights.

The only real relaxation my body experiences during this time is in the hospital bed during my second surgery, when I am sedated. After I regain consciousness, I ask to stay there an extra hour just to get some rest. On the way home from the hospital, we buy, in a fabric store, some triangular foam wedges that, when positioned under pillows on the bed, approximate the hospital bed's comfortable angle and allow me to stretch out, supine, until the shoulder pain kicks in again—a useful transition to a good night's sleep. Why did we have to figure out for ourselves what must be common knowledge in the profession?

Fine

When I walked around campus with my arm in a sling, with mincing steps to avoid slipping on the ice-coated sidewalks instead of my usual stride, tilting to the left so if I fell I'd land on my free arm, I was greeted by colleagues and students with the familiar "Hi, how are you?" Couldn't they see the sling and its bulky "pillow" support? As I'd start to explain how I actually was, they'd race on past, so I quickly learned to answer, "Fine." "That's good," they'd say, disappearing beyond the snowbanks. Passers-by registered only what they wanted to hear and to see; if I'd declared, "I just murdered my grandmother," they'd have heard, "Fine," and again replied automatically, "That's good."

As Yogi Berra might have said, the process of recuperation and rehabilitation is "90 percent mental. The other half is physical." Six months after I've written the rest of this essay and I'm able, once again, to reenter the world as able-bodied—a term itself endowed with new significance—I can tackle the ending. As Everypatient, I've told stories here that I couldn't disclose to my own doctors, therapists, or hospital staff in an atmosphere rushed, overworked, and public. For even in medical contexts, there's pressure to say "fine," not to sweat the seemingly small stuff, especially if the problem is commonplace, the treatment routine, the recuperation relatively short, the outcome expected to be favorable. No drama here, no life-and-death struggle, no medical brinkmanship or surgical daring required. Ho-hum. Even the pain and suffering are ordinary, requiring neither heroism nor bravery; who cares about passive fortitude? As human beings, we all get a turn—maybe more than one—on the medical hot seat, no exemptions allowed. In writing, as in life, victim art is déclassé, if not downright taboo. Yet we love to hear and tell love stories, same old same old but ever new over and over; why not tales of disability, temporary as well as permanent? We do not have to be victimized by—or in—these stories.

Over the years, I have tried to give analyses of pertinent medical issues, mostly articles from the *New York Times* or health newsletters, to medical staff during routine office visits. Each time, my offerings have been politely declined. Do professionals value material only from professional sources? (Do I listen to my students? You bet, it's the easiest way to understand how to help them.) Do professionals have the time, or the desire, to process the material I proffer? (Do I follow student suggestions? When they're to the point, when they elicit improvements in either the students' work or mine.) Although I believe I have been (with one exception) respected as a patient, in every medical setting I have heard the time clock ticking and felt that I am using up too much of it. So I cannot show this essay to those kind people in the doctor's office and the hospital who could supply the answers that might indeed, alleviate pain and stress and enable patients to really mean it when we say we're "fine, just fine." Dare I hope that they'll read an authoritative version, clad in respectable print rather than a skimpy hospital johnny, and get the point?

The single mark of disrespect (other than the manager of the physical therapy clinic, who persists in calling me "young lady" rather than by my name, which he thereby does not have to learn), is that I have been classified as a patient "noncompliant" with the physical therapy. Is this label, usually reserved, my therapist explains, for teenage jocks who rush back to team sports and blow off the prescribed therapy, appropriate for one who conscientiously does each and every exercise as dictated? No, *noncompliant* is a way to blame the victim. If it's all my fault that my exercising destroyed the initial repair and required a second surgery, then I do not have a legal case should I decide to sue. Right? The pressure, subtly conveyed by this negative characterization, is to deter this route of redress. And I, usually quick to question authority, to defend the defeated and the downtrodden, author of a book on assertiveness for women, surprise myself by passively complying with the intimations of this label.

Why did I take this, well, lying down? I've pondered this decision, as have some of my more litigious friends. For several reasons: we live in a small town, I had the best doctor in the area and I was going to need him for the repair operation, which had to be performed immediately. I did not have the time to shop around. Or the energy, either psychic or physical, to mount a case. I had to concentrate on survival, recovery, and my job. And I knew, at least believed, I would recover, fully; that my body would again function at full capability; and that I'd be able to teach and write and play again, as usual. If I was going to be fine, what was the point of suing, and agitating my already jittery equilibrium in the process? There were and remain causes far more worthy of attention and money than whether I endured extra weeks of pain and suffering and, oh yes, additional risk, as the consequence of a second operation. Why should I expect particular sympathy from a judge, or jury, for such an ordinary problem?

So, also unusual for me, I bit my tongue. I complied fully and cheerfully, once again, with the requisite therapy; only this time both the therapist and I understood that we were not going for the burn. During orthopedist appointments, I willingly plowed through long books in the reception room in expectation that the good news would be worth the wait. And it was. I recovered fully, as anticipated, and have recommended both Dr. Jay and the therapist to others. End of story. Or is it? The same friends tell me it's not too late to sue. But I am immersed in writing another book, a new collection of new, true stories—this time with both hands—and gearing up for the vacation we couldn't take last winter. Except for the heightened responsiveness to others' sufferings that I hope will last as long as I live and plans for teaching a course in disability autobiography, this story is over.

Nevertheless I could interpret this experience from a variety of philosophical and theoretical perspectives, but which ones? So many are possible, singly or in combination: stoic, existential, Christian, Buddhist, postmodern, feminist, anti-ageist, disability studies, and more. But I resist the temptation to tie my analysis to a particular school of theory. I figure that readers will understand, in their hearts and in their bones, the private as well as the public dimensions of this narrative, even if our stories differ in the particulars. Likewise I resist the temptation to relax, to take good health for granted, to assume that the dues I've paid will last a lifetime. I run through the therapy exercises, add new ones. I measure our doorways to see whether they can accommodate a wheelchair, buy a new *Merck Manual,* resume the daily swim. Everything's just fine.

Coming Home

On the Road

My husband and I are travelers without borders; wherever we are together is home. We come home to our legal residence when duty calls, despite the alluring prospect of eternal vagabondism epitomized by Toad of *The Wind in the Willows*. This rakish amphibian, jaunty, utterly irresponsible yet eternally cheerful, racketing about in his gaily painted gypsy wagon, articulates the traveler's joyous creed: "Travel, change, interest, excitement! The whole world before you ... Glorious, stirring sight! The poetry of motion! ... The only way to travel! Here today—in next week tomorrow! Villages skipped, towns and cities jumped—always somebody else's horizon! O bliss! O poop-poop! O my! O my!" (29, 38).

Martin and I have traveled together ever since we spent the summer of our marriage and all our money—a cool thousand dollars, one-third of our prospective annual income—exploring Europe. Money well spent, despite the admonitions of people who cautioned, "But you'll have nothing to show for it." From the Brussels World's Fair, lunching on leftover wedding cake, to a *Wild Strawberries* setting in Sweden, to our spooky subway ride from West to East Berlin where we stalked its silent rubble, we fancied ourselves Meriwether Lewis and Sacagawea in quest of new worlds. We would always travel, as our sons—participants, willing and otherwise, in many subsequent trips on Fly-by-Night-Air—were later to learn. O bliss! O my!

We travel light; what won't fit into a small suitcase apiece and a backpack stays home. In the spirit of Toad, we continue to escape from jobs, house, bills, the duties of good citizenship. Our current travel is, however, more upscale than the dingy B and Bs of that wedding journey, reeking of the bacon grease that saturated the invariable breakfast of eggs and bacon and baked beans on toast, aka "nasty food," as one disgruntled proprietor, a former pub owner, described her repast. We abandon the split-second schedule that rules our lives from 8 A.M. to midnight, hours riddled with minutiae as well as major matters. We escape even from the gym and daily infusions of the *New*

York Times and NPR, though these are as hard to leave as a predictable supply of chocolate.

We do not abandon those we love, family and select friends, but we put ourselves deliberately out of touch. Our children know where to reach us, and our neighbors and secretary know how to reach our children and the fire department, though no one has ever called—yet—to alert us to crises at home. Our infrequent postcards bear no return address, as befits itinerant scribes. We use no Blackberry, fax, or e-mail, though we once tried to send a message from an Internet café in Tibet, just for the novelty, but it vanished in the altitude.

The cell phone is turned off until we come to a full stop on the return runway and call daughter-in-law Sara, whose harbor-front office is perilously close to Logan Airport, to come and pick us up. By then, if school's about to begin, I'll have experienced one or more anxiety dreams. Have I ordered the books? Where's the classroom? What am I teaching, anyway? And the headaches, nascent migraine included, will have begun again. "Welcome home," says the customs officer.

Home Again, Home Again: Stage 1

We always come home in two stages, like deep-sea divers gradually acclimatizing ourselves to reentry. On departing, we have driven 73.42 miles from our home in Connecticut to Laird's in Needham, a Boston suburb, to leave our car and catch up on family news before Laird or Sara takes us to the airport. When their children, Beth and Paul, were preschoolers, they often came along to experience the thrill of Terminal B or C, but as adolescents they have other things to do—school, soccer, music lessons. . . . This is the home to which we first arrive on our return.

At this point it would be dramatic to insert a story about the Return Trip from Hell to arouse reader sympathy, if not schadenfreude. To make sure you're on our side, feeling smug at having stayed at home, snug by the fireside, I could tell you how we languished in fetid jails with no language or lawyers at the ready, our passports confiscated, and bereft of all hope, only to be rescued at the last minute by. . . . And that we were met at international arrivals by Interpol agents, anxious relatives, paparazzi. But that is the stuff of fiction, and this is a true story.

In truth, therefore, I confess that our return in January from our most recent trip to an oddly snowless Boston was unremarkable. We were spared the extreme weather that socked it to fellow travelers in the rest of the country—ice, snow, lightning, heavy rain; flights missed or delayed, sometimes for four or five days; wayward luggage stranded in some distant airport. That we had in fact just spent considerable time in Costa Rica—a more recent trip than the one you read about in "The Dinner Hours"—slogging through rain forests, soaked to the skin, on narrow footbridges over engorged rivers when we weren't whitewater rafting or kayaking doesn't count. We asked for it, just as we asked for crocodiles, monkeys, and iguanas. However—and I am aware that the travel gods will note this for future retaliation—like our January return, our recent flights have occurred in good weather, and our baggage has come along for the ride.

So despite the rapture of reunion with our luggage, surpassed only by the joy of seeing our family, we look just like all the other travelers at the arrivals gate: rumpled, messy, tired, hungry, dressed in the wrong clothes for weather at the destination. What a pleasure it is to come home to people who belong where they are, comfortable, at ease except for the agitation to clear out fast so the minivan won't get towed. People who speak the same language, the language of home. We know we can count on a good meal, this time homemade chili over rice, with cornbread and a green salad, themed to the country we just came from. If we wish, a hot bath and a warm bed. No one expects presents, but they want to hear about adventures, animals, sights and scenery and sounds. Thanks to the digital camera they gave me for a recent birthday, and Martin's omnipresent sketchbook, they can now see the pictures right away and make copies for themselves.

We anticipate coming home to order, cleanliness, predictability. We hope that if there are surprises, they will be pleasant—Paul's team's victory in an improvisatory dramatic competition, Beth's learning "Stopping by Woods" by heart. But that is not always the case. Two years ago, Laird met us looking so worn, his hair beginning to grey, that our first words were "What's wrong?" "Three days after you left for Spain, Paul had an emergency appendectomy . . . at midnight." That was ten days ago. "He just came home from the hospital this morning." "Why didn't you tell us?" we asked. "We'd have come right home." Laird smiled, "That's why we didn't call. We didn't want to spoil your trip. And we asked Bard not to tell you, either."

Yet even without surprises, I am disoriented. With part of my mind I am anticipating returning to our house, and I am making mental lists of things to do—and not do—when we get there. Laundry. Mail. Groceries. Class to meet. Of course. "Take home the extra set of car keys"; we had left them at Laird's on our last trip. "Don't wash the passports"; another casualty of recent jet lag. I know, too, that we will return to news we do not want to know— friends' worsening health, even death, imminent before we went away.

Suppose the house has burned down, as our neighbor's dream house did eight years ago; it took them a year to rebuild. This sad experience—they lost everything three days before Christmas, and their dog died—led us to install a security system. Nevertheless, as we are homeward bound, I realize that I have forgotten to unplug the USB with all the new manuscripts on it and take it and the CDs with photos and more manuscripts to the office. Yes, they could be retrieved, but what a lot of work.... What a lot of nonsense. Somebody surely would have told us about a house fire. Unless they didn't want to spoil our trip.

Part of my mind is, however, still on vacation. I observe my country through alien eyes. The Atlantic winter light at Boston's forty-second parallel is a timorous reflection of Puntarenas's Pacific sunshine at the eighth parallel. I would even welcome a return of steamy-washcloth-slap-in-the-face humidity, instead of New England's congealing dampness. Even though I could barely understand the Spanish in which we were cocooned for nearly three weeks, English now sounds weird, grating fricatives and sharp consonants, a cacophony of cell phones. Magnificent tall trees—mahogany, balsa, guanacaste, walking palm—have been replaced by skyscrapers, their ornamental plantings bundled against the cold. No birds sing. And the people. So tall. So big, bulking up into so much space, moving so fast. What am I doing here? I want to go away again, as the hoboes' song of the open road says, "where they hung the jerk that invented work," "where there ain't no snow and the rain don't fall, and the wind don't blow." But the Big Rock Candy Mountains are nowhere on this earthly map, and our car is headed, inevitably, for home.

You Can't Go Home Again

Ever since my parents kicked me out of the home I grew up in when I went to England to marry Martin, I observed them through alien eyes as well, for to come back to New Hampshire was not only to enter another country but an alien space. The comfortable rented house in postcard-pristine Durham where I grew up, four bedrooms, one whole bathroom and two half baths, and a basement rec room for ping-pong next to the greenhouse, had been sold and carted off in big sections, Mom said, to make room for a new road. With no forwarding address, I never saw it again. Only the large rock, now shrunken, was left in what had been the front yard, near the tree where the remaining boards of our old tree house dangled iguana-like from the branches.

My father, true to his resolve never to own a home of his own—"It will tie you down to the same place forever"—rented the only place he could find, across the town line, in Lee, not Durham, another country. It would be temporary. As soon as Pop retired from the university, my parents would light out for the Big Rock Candy Mountains and never look back. They hated that house, with reason. Five cramped rooms and a minuscule bath near a noisy highway intersection, the backyard dropping off into a wetland that bred scraggly sumac and mosquitoes, kitty-corner from the main scenic attraction, a gravel pit full of rusting, dinosaur-shaped excavation equipment. The big rocks, little rocks, and dust made literal the metaphor that to visit my parents was to come home to a terrain riddled with land mines.

Although my parents could have spiffed up the house inside, they did not. They simply crammed all their furniture from the larger dwelling into the smaller one; a mix of early Depression-era and recent fire sale that, despite my mother's large canvases from her painting classes, would have been right at home in the No-Tell Motel. The couch, which Mom had reupholstered in shiny pink satin ("It was on sale"), was so slippery that sitters slid right off. The beds' deep troughs trapped unwary sleepers, though we took to bringing our own pillows to avoid heritage germs in the lumpy wads my parents used. Why my parents kept fifty-year-old lamps whose bare-wire cords sparked and sputtered every time they turned on the lights is as inexplicable as why they stayed in that house for twenty-five years. We would occasionally slip them a new lamp, and Mom eventually accepted a new mattress for her bed.

This was the house to which Martin and I brought our children to visit, once a year, from the time they were three and five until they had summer internships in college. My parents treated us like wayfaring strangers, hoboes, perhaps, from a gritty Johnny Cash version of "Big Rock Candy Mountain" rather than lilting Burl Ives, with none of the jokes or nuances of intimacy that as a child I had believed held our family together, rock solid. During every visit, Martin put up both with my father's silence and with his disparaging commentary about Jews, New Yorkers (aka Martin's parents, whom we shielded from meeting him), as well as psychologists and other social scientists—all of whom he stereotyped, and for whom he had nothing but contempt. For Martin understood that I desperately wanted my parents to know and love our children while they were growing up. And they did, or so I would like to believe.

With my parents we went to the beach, York, or Ogunquit, which had the best sand for walking and castle building and the shallowest shore for swimming. Around Wheelwright Pond we paddled "the Black Swan," a kayak my father had built from a kit, rowing upstream all the time instead of across a flat surface, because the seats were too low and he insisted on using canoe rather than kayak paddles. Could they also have been on sale? Every year, we hiked longer and longer distances in the White Mountains as the children's stamina increased. We were "climbing Mt. Oedipus," observed Martin, who kept my mother company at the base. Every year, my father's foothold was shakier, his descent more reckless, heedlessly running over the rocks on and off the trails until, at seventy-four, when the boys were teenagers, he skidded on a long, steep swath of loose gravel and tumbled down and down, his torn pants blushing crimson.

Bard and Laird loved these expeditions, except for the terror of that last mile down the last mountain. They also—they tell me as adults—enjoyed happy hours of throwing rocks in the gravel pit, accompanied by one or another grandparent, something they never got to do at home, getting sweaty and covered with dust. They say, too, that they were happy to spend the nights in sleeping bags on cots on the tiny screened porch, where they would awake covered in morning mist and mosquito bites. The alternative was to sleep in the basement, where the four of us spent only a single night in 1967, the first time after I insisted on visiting with the children.

The mildewed, low-ceilinged room of raw concrete was hung with sheets to partition the sleeping areas. Martin and I in my parents' nuptial bed with original mattress from 1929, the boys in my brother's Army surplus, double-decker mattresses (vintage 1943), were wedged between my father's work-bench and gallon jugs of unlabeled, toxic-smelling chemicals from his lab. Even though it was summer, the water heater ran off the furnace, which racketed up at half-hour intervals all night long, as did the water pump every time someone upstairs turned on the water or flushed the toilet. "We're moving to a motel," Martin announced to my parents the next morning. On the spot, they decided they could share Pop's bedroom so we could have the twin beds (circa 1938) above ground in Mom's room—even though, they observed, my brother and his family always slept in the basement without a murmur.

Whether these guest quarters contributed to any of Burke's four divorces is a matter of conjecture. Why Martin endured these visits—New Hampshire was a stop during various camping and research trips, and he could have stayed in more congenial quarters—is clear. He was there to protect me, even at the cost of enduring behavior that he would never have tolerated from any-one else. He was also there to tend me when I was sick, for I often arrived at the Lee house with food poisoning, rarely experienced anywhere else dur-ing our travels the world over. In that state I fainted repeatedly, a hazard to myself, so I had to stay in bed. I remember once coming to consciousness to hear Mom telling Martin, "Nobody ever took care of me in my whole life the way you take care of Lynn." She was right. But try as he might, he could not insulate me from my own lifelong vulnerability to my parents' insults, or their indifference. After every visit, we sought new territory with relief and exhila-ration; only the children wanted to stay longer.

Over the years, it seemed that when we were out of my parents' sight, we were generally out of mind. They never initiated phone calls, although Mom usually replied to my weekly letters. After initial visits to each new baby—Mom sent a sumptuous layette to our firstborn—they came to our home only once, in St. Louis, when the boys were ten and twelve, on the way to my mother's fiftieth high school reunion. The Christmas gifts they sent every year were so unremarkable, except for a set of homemade, tie-dyed place mats, that I finally started reciprocating in kind, recycling others' presents (today it would be euphemized as "regifting") when we went to visit. But after my father discovered a gift card—"Love from Chuck and Eunice," our St. Louis next-door neighbors—concealed behind a two-pound scented candle with a gravel-textured holder, out of shame I proffered only new gifts thereafter. In addition we gave them gifts from the heart: our children's drawings and poems, copies of each of my published books and articles, and Martin's handmade ceramic stamp for embossing cookies. We proffered useful mementoes from our travels, no kitsch: a small, hexagonal, brass Swiss clock; a Scottish wool blanket; Israeli throw pillows. We ordered a blue down comforter from a *New Yorker* ad and, later, a bathrobe to match. These all returned to our house after my parents died, courtesy of my sister, the estate executor, along with every one of my publications, uncut and unread.

My parents never invited us to visit, never said they were sorry when we left, and never made plans to see us anywhere else, for instance, at other relatives' houses, except to attend my doctoral graduation in Ann Arbor, class of '63, which incidentally was Martin's as well. I used to think that among my parents' three offspring and their families, our family was singled out for particular neglect, but as I write this I am not so sure. They never went out of their way to see Burke or Linda or their families either, except for my mother's desperate flight to California to try to prevent Burke's first divorce. Although my father enjoyed visits with his Detroit relatives, my mother, a most reluctant traveler, could never relax or sleep well anywhere except in her own bed. Nor did my parents ever engineer a family reunion, or go to any. Laird's wedding, when he was twenty-five, was the first time my siblings and my mother and I (my father was dead by then) had been together since Burke's first wedding, thirty-one years earlier, and for this Martin and I had made the arrangements.

Could what we had interpreted as prolonged hostility to Martin over the years, and their annoyance at my harping on health and safety and comfort, ours as well as theirs, simply have been indifference? Emotional atrophy from life in general? Could they have been jealous? Or angry? All of the above? Or perhaps none. To discuss their attitude with them was taboo, though on one stifling summer visit they had even seemed grateful when I tore off the cover of their feeble air conditioner—it had been so robust when we gave it to them—and cleaned off inch-deep dust from the filter. Voilá!

Nevertheless every week throughout the thirteen years between his retirement and his death, my father wrote to Mildred, his older unmarried sister in Detroit. Another aunt passed the letters along to me after Mildred died, a decade ago; I read them through once but cannot yet bear to tackle them again. He lamented, early and often, that his serpent's-tooth children didn't care, they had their own lives that excluded him and my mother, that he longed for the easy camaraderie with his own children that he experienced with his brother and sisters in Detroit. Mildred's answers unfailingly came back, "You're misreading the universe. They love you, they do," with proof positive. These he always rebutted, saying this neglect ultimately didn't matter, because civilization as he had known it during his carefree college days was on the verge of collapse anyway.

Pop's stern and rigid countenance resembled New Hampshire's stern emblem, the Old Man of the Mountain, a rugged profile comprised of five ledges on Cannon Mountain, a peak we had often climbed. Throughout the twentieth century, the Old Man was held together with cables and spikes, in an attempt to counteract the centuries-old battering of wind, snow, sleet, and rain, the cycles of freeze and thaw. In 2003 this granite visage finally collapsed. Yet in 2004 coin-operated viewfinders were installed at the base of the mountain. Visitors peering into the machines would see not the sheared-off mountainside that might be expected, but images of the Old Man before his demise. What Old Man am I seeing here? And through what lens?

Home Again, Home Again: Stage 2

We arrive home in Connecticut to find our house profiled against a starry sky, no snow to shovel, the Christmas wreath still looking crisp with a big cranberry bow topped by a varnished gingerbread cookie that Rhys, our youngest grandchild, had decorated with gumdrops the year before, when he was two. The front porch looks freshly swept, and we bring the luggage into a house that springs to attention when we turn on the front hall lights. The answering machine is flashing red; we will pick up the messages tomorrow. A peek at the 578 e-mails scrolling in—fewer than usual, because many people knew we were away and wouldn't have written—reveals, amidst the spam, predictable notices and good news. From other friends, the ominous subject lines: "tumor the size of a grapefruit," "hot spots, alas not tropical," "memorial service." These, too, can wait until tomorrow; having been in transit for eighteen hours, we can't handle the grief at this late hour.

The moonlight is filtering through the bank of floor-to-ceiling living room windows that front the woods, bright and deep, and the skylights. It illuminates the house that looks new, and strange to our travelers' eyes, even cleaner than we left it for the west coast friends who would stay awhile in our

The "Bloom hug" that gave rise to baby Rhys's observation, "We make a flower. Each one is a petal." This particular hug, which started us off, was at Bard's Ph.D. graduation from MIT in 1989. The setting is the parking lot of Joyce Chen's restaurant in Cambridge, Massachusetts.

absence. If this were a hotel, would we want to stay here? Yes we would, no question. We make the rounds; except for one plant, a chrysanthemum that has succumbed to a fungus, and beds that are so vaguely made up we can't tell whether the guests slept here or not, the house exudes order, and calm.

Something, however, is amiss; we could never come home to perfection. I can't figure it out, dashing about in my parka, making heaps of travel paraphernalia and clothes, all dirty, as I fish through our suitcases in search of my toilet kit. With this exertion, I can see my breath. And then the mystery is solved. Our friends, ever thoughtful, have not only turned down the thermostat, they have turned off the furnace—brand new, replaced providentially just before we left—and the house has been without heat for a week. Thanks to a winter a dozen degrees warmer than usual, passive solar construction, and R-68 insulation, the house is still a shade above freezing, and we have come home on what is turning into the coldest night of the year just in time to keep the pipes from bursting. As the furnace blasts into action, we decide to unpack; it's too cold to go to sleep. We put the passports, good to go until October 2, 2015, at the ready on my dresser, and the car keys likewise out of harm's way. We sort the clothes for the morning laundry, brew tea, leave a litter of plastic bags, ecology brochures, unsent postcards, and ticket stubs in our wake. I make sure the materials for the class I'll teach tomorrow are in good order.

In keeping with my wish to live free, and thus to die, with no regrets—my variation on New Hampshire's motto—I keep my house in order, and significant human relationships as well. I like to resolve difficulties—mechanical, intellectual, and especially personal—within twenty-four hours. Yet you have just read how my parents' intractable resistance to intimacy frustrated that resolve, year after year, with unintended gifts to me of power and, though it has taken a lifetime, perspective. When I was a child, I would stare at the titles on a long row of my father's chemistry journals, *The Crucible.* I did not know then the meaning of the word that I have since come to understand intimately, the vessel in which the refiner's fire burns away the dross, concentrates the pure essence, makes the whole stronger. I hope I have become that person.

I sustain the fiction that as long as I have a manuscript in progress, a class to teach, another trip in the offing, I will not die. Those rain forests, these woods are so lovely I do not want to leave this earth. I cannot bear to think that the space next to me in the bed that Martin and I have shared for nearly fifty years (with, as needed, the best new mattresses and box springs money can buy) will ever be empty. Or the space next to him. Our house is warm. We take swift showers, and, pulling up the blue down comforter, intertwined we fall asleep, yet again. Welcome home.

Works Cited

Alcott, Louisa May. *Little Women*. 1868. Reprint, Chicago: Goldsmith, n.d.

American Psychologist 55, no. 1 (2001) and 56, no. 3 (2001).

Anonymous review of Pete Hamill, *A Drinking Life*. http://www.moderation.org/review.shtml

Avakian, Arlene Voski, ed. *Through the Kitchen Window: Women Writers Explore the Intimate Meanings of Food and Cooking*. Boston: Beacon Press, 1997.

Behar, Ruth. "Dare We Say 'I'? Bringing the Personal into Scholarship." *Chronicle of Higher Education*, June 29, 1994, B1–2.

_____. *The Vulnerable Observer: Anthropology That Breaks Your Heart*. Boston: Beacon, 1996.

Bloom, Lynn Z. *Composition Studies as a Creative Art: Teaching, Writing, Scholarship, Administration*. Logan: Utah State University Press, 1998.

_____. *Doctor Spock: Biography of a Conservative Radical*. Indianapolis: Bobbs-Merrill, 1972.

_____. *Fact and Artifact: Writing Nonfiction*. 2d ed. Englewood Cliffs, N.J.: Prentice Hall, 1994.

_____. "Finding a Family, Finding a Voice: A Writing Teacher Teaches Writing Teachers." 1990. Reprinted in Bloom, *Composition Studies as a Creative Art*, 15–24.

_____. "Growing Up with Doctor Spock: An Auto/Biography." *a/b: Autobiography Studies* 8, (Fall 1993): 271–85.

_____. "How Literary Biographers Use Their Subjects' Works: A Study of Biographical Method." Ph.D. diss., University of Michigan, 1963.

_____. "Textual Terror, Textual Power." 1995. Reprinted in Bloom, *Composition Studies as a Creative Art*, 54–63.

_____. "Why I Wrote, Why I Write." *Maryland English Journal* 23, no. 1 (1989): 26–30.

Bloom, Lynn Z., Donald A. Daiker, and Edward M. White, eds. *Composition Studies in the New Millennium: Rereading the Past, Rewriting the Future*. Carbondale: Southern Illinois University Press, 2003.

Brubach, Holly. "How Dry I Am: The Drinking Memoir Now Has an Obligatory Ending." *New York Times Men's Fashion Magazine*, March 12, 2006, 90.

Chomsky, Noam. *Syntactic Structures*. The Hague, Netherlands: Mouton, 1957.

Chopin, Kate. *The Awakening*. 1899. In *Complete Works of Kate Chopin*. Edited by Per Seyersted. Baton Rouge: Louisiana State University Press, 1969.

Crick, Bernard. *George Orwell*. Boston: Little, Brown. 1980.

Croce, Arlene. "Discussing the Undiscussable." *New Yorker*, December 26, 1994–January 2, 1995, 54–60.

Works Cited

Crouter, Natalie. *Forbidden Diary: A Record of Wartime Internment, 1941–45.* Edited by Lynn Z. Bloom. New York: Burt Franklin, 1980. Reissued as part of *North American Women's Diaries and Letters,* Alexandria, Va.: Alexander Street Press, 2001 (CD format).

Cunningham, Michael. *The Hours.* New York: Farrar, Straus, Giroux, 1998.

Didion, Joan. "On Keeping a Notebook." In *Slouching towards Bethlehem,* 131–41. New York: Delta, 1968.

_____. "Why I Write." 1976. Reprinted in *Essay Connection,* 3d ed., edited by Lynn Z. Bloom, 43–50. Lexington, Mass.: D. C. Heath, 1991.

Dillard, Annie. "To Fashion a Text." In *Inventing the Truth: The Art and Craft of Memoir,* edited by William Zinsser, 55–76. Boston: Houghton Mifflin, 1987.

Drape, Joe. "After 8 Months Filled by Hope, Setback Ends Barbaro's Battle." *New York Times,* January 30, 2007, A1, 17.

Eakin, Paul John. "'The Unseemly Profession': Privacy, Inviolate Personality, and the Ethics of Life Writing." In *How Our Lives Become Stories: Making Selves,* 142–86. Ithaca, N.Y.: Cornell University Press, 1999.

Ede, Lisa, ed. *On Writing Research: The Braddock Essays 1975–1998.* Boston: Bedford / St. Martin's, 1999.

Ede, Lisa, and Andrea Lunsford. "Audience Addressed / Audience Invoked: The Role of Audience in Composition Theory and Pedagogy." *College Composition and Communication* 35 (May 1984): 155–71.

Elbow, Peter. "Closing My Eyes as I Speak: An Argument for Ignoring Audience." *College English* 49 (January 1987): 50–69.

_____. "Introduction: About Voice and Writing." In *Landmark Essays on Voice and Writing,* edited by Peter Elbow, xi–xlvii. Davis, Calif.: Hermagoras Press, 1994.

_____. "Ranking, Evaluating, and Liking: Sorting Out Three Forms of Judgement." *College English* 55 (February 1993): 187–206.

_____. "Reflections on Academic Discourse: How It Relates to Freshmen and Colleagues." *College English* 53 (February 1991): 135–55.

_____. "Three Mysteries at the Heart of Writing." In Bloom, Daiker, and White, *Composition Studies in the New Millennium,* 10–27.

_____. *Writing with Power: Techniques for Mastering the Writing Process.* New York: Oxford University Press, 1981.

Eliot, T. S. "Tradition and the Individual Talent." In *The Sacred Wood.* 1920. Reprinted in *The Critical Tradition: Classic Texts and Contemporary Trends,* 2d ed., edited by David H. Richter, 498–503. Boston: Bedford / St. Martin's, 1998.

Emig, Janet. *The Composing Processes of Twelfth Graders.* Research report no. 13. Urbana, Ill.: NCTE, 1971.

Farris, Christine, and Chris M. Anson, eds. *Under Construction: Working at the Intersections of Composition Theory, Research, and Practice.* Logan: Utah State University Press, 1998.

Fisher, M. F. K. *An Alphabet for Gourmets.* 1949. Reprinted in *The Art of Eating,* 573–744. New York: Macmillan, 1990.

_____. *The Gastronomical Me.* 1943. Reprinted in *Art of Eating,* 351–572.

_____. *With Bold Knife and Fork.* New York: Putnam's/Paragon, 1968.

Flaherty, Alice Weaver. "Writing Like Crazy: A Word on the Brain." *Chronicle of Higher Education*, November 21, 2003, B6–9.

Franklin, Benjamin. *The Autobiography of Benjamin Franklin*. 1793. Edited by Leonard W. Larabee, Ralph L. Ketcham, Helen C. Boatfield, and Helene H. Fineman. New Haven, Conn.: Yale University Press, 1964.

Freedman, Diane P., and Olivia Frey, eds. *Autobiographical Writing across the Disciplines*. Durham, N.C., and London: Duke University Press, 2003.

Frey, James. *A Million Little Pieces*. New York: Doubleday, 2003.

Frey, Olivia. "Beyond Literary Darwinism: Women's Voices and Critical Discourse." *College English* 52 (September 1990): 507–26.

Gass, William H. "The Art of Self: Autobiography in an Age of Narcissism." *Harper's*, May 1994, 43–52.

———. "Emerson and the Essay." 1982. Reprinted in *Habitations of the Word: Essays*, 9–49. New York: Simon and Schuster, 1985.

Geertz, Clifford. "Blurred Genres: The Refiguration of Social Thought." In *Local Knowledge: Further Essays in Interpretive Anthropology*, 19–35. New York: Basic Books, 1983.

———. *Works and Lives: The Anthropologist as Author*. Stanford, Calif.: Stanford University Press, 1988.

Gerard, Philip. *Creative Nonfiction: Researching and Crafting Stories of Real Life*. Cincinnati: Story Press, 1996.

Gere, Anne R., ed. *Into the Field: Sites of Composition Studies*. New York: MLA, 1993.

Gorman, James. "Ants, Better with a Dose of Humanity (and Humor)." *New York Times*, April 25, 2006, D3.

Graff, Gerald. "The University and the Prevention of Culture." In *Criticism in the University*, edited by Gerald Graff and Reginald Gibbons, 62–82. Evanston, Ill.: Northwestern University Press, 1985.

Grahame, Kenneth. *The Wind in the Willows*. 1908. Reprint, New York: Scribner's, 1965.

Gurganus, Alan (as told to Naomi Epel). "I Dreamed the Story of a Dream." 1993. Reprinted in *The Best Writing on Writing*, edited by Jack Heffron, 85–95. Cincinnati: Story Press, 1994.

Gutkind, Lee, ed. "A Million Little Choices: The ABCs of CNF." Special issue, *Creative Nonfiction*, no. 29 (2006).

Haber, Barbara. *From Hardtack to Home Fries: An Uncommon History of American Cooks and Meals*. New York: Free Press, 2002.

Heath, Shirley Brice. *Ways with Words: Language, Life, and Work in Communities and Classrooms*. Cambridge, England: Cambridge University Press, 1983.

Hemley, Robin. *Turning Life into Fiction*. Cincinnati: Story Press, 1994.

Holdstein, Deobrah H., and David Bleich, eds. *Personal Effects: The Social Character of Scholarly Writing*. Logan: Utah State University Press, 2001.

Inge, M. Thomas. Letter. *PMLA* 104 (October 1989): 904.

Inness, Sherrie A., ed. *Pilaf, Pozole, and Pad Thai: American Women and Ethnic Food*. Amherst: University of Massachusetts Press, 2001.

JAEPL: The Journal of the Assembly for Expanded Perspectives on Learning 9 (2003–4).

Jamieson, Sandra. "Composition Readers and the Construction of Identity." In *Writing in Multicultural Settings,* edited by Carol Severino, Juan C. Guerra, and Johnnella E. Butler, 150–71. New York: MLA, 1997.

Johnson, Edgar. *Charles Dickens: His Tragedy and Triumph.* 2 vols. New York: Simon and Schuster, 1952.

Joyce, James. "The Dead." In *Dubliners.* 1914. Reprint, New York: Random House, n.d., 224–88.

———. *Ulysses.* 1922. Reprint, New York: Random House, 1934.

Kirsch, Gesa. "Ethics and the Future of Composition Research." In Bloom, Daiker, and White, *Composition Studies in the New Millennium,* 129–41.

Kirsch, Gesa, and Patricia A. Sullivan, eds. *Methods and Methodology in Composition Research.* Carbondale: Southern Illinois University Press, 1992.

Kosok, Ana. Review of *A Drinking Life: A Memoir,* by Pete Hamill. http://www.moderation.org/review.shtml.

Lauer, Janice, and J. William Asher. *Composition Research: Empirical Designs.* New York: Oxford University Press, 1988.

Lawrence, D. H. "Benjamin Franklin." In *Studies in Classic American Literature.* 1923. Reprint, New York: Viking, 1964, 9–21.

Lejeune, Philippe. "The Autobiographical Pact." In *On Autobiography,* edited by Paul John Eakin, translated by Katherine Leary, 119–37. Minneapolis: University of Minnesota Press, 1989.

Leonardi, Susan J. "Recipes for Reading: Summer Pasta, Lobster à la Riseholme, and Key Lime Pie." *PMLA* 104 (May 1989): 340–47.

Lunsford, Andrea, and Robert Connors. *The St. Martin's Handbook.* 2d ed. New York: St. Martin's, 1992.

MacDonald, Susan Peck. "The Literary Argument and Its Discursive Conventions." In *The Writing Scholar: Studies in Academic Discourse,* edited by Walter Nash, 31–62. Vol. 3, *Written Communication Annual.* Newbury Park, Calif.: Sage, 1990.

McFeeley, Mary Drake. *Can She Bake a Cherry Pie? American Women and the Kitchen in the Twentieth Century.* Amherst: University of Massachusetts Press, 2000.

Marius, Richard. *A Writer's Companion.* 3d ed. New York: McGraw-Hill, 1995.

Marranca, Bonnie, ed. *A Slice of Life: Contemporary Writers on Food.* Woodstock, N.Y.: Overlook/Duckworth, 2003.

Miller, Arthur. *Death of a Salesman.* 1949. Reprint, New York: Penguin, 1976.

Miller, Nancy K. *Bequest and Betrayal: Memoirs of a Parent's Death.* 1996. Bloomington: Indiana University Press, 2000.

———. "Getting Personal: Autobiography as Cultural Criticism." In *Getting Personal: Feminist Occasions and Other Autobiographical Acts,* 1–31. New York: Routledge, 1991.

———. "My Father's Penis." In *Getting Personal,* 143–47.

Milstein, Sarah. "Using E-Mail to Count Connections." *New York Times,* Dec. 20, 2001. www.nytimes.com/doo1/12/20/technology/circuits/20STUD.html.

Mishler, Elliott G. "Meaning in Context: Is There Any Other Kind?" *Harvard Educational Review* 49 (1979): 1–19.

Montanari, Massimo. *Food Is Culture.* 2004. Trans. Albert Sonnenfeld. New York: Columbia University Press, 2006.

Nesteruk, Jeffrey. "Fatherhood, in Theory and Practice." *Chronicle of Higher Education,* February 11, 2005, B5.

Norris, Kathleen. *Amazing Grace: A Vocabulary of Faith.* New York: Riverhead, 1998.

North, Stephen M. *The Making of Knowledge in Composition: Portrait of an Emerging Field.* Upper Montclair, N.J.: Boynton Cook, 1987.

Oates, Joyce Carol. "Where Are You Going? Where Have You Been?" 1966. Reprinted in *The Norton Anthology of Literature by Women: The Tradition in English.* Edited by Sandra M. Gilbert and Susan Gobar, 1277–97. New York: W. W. Norton, 1985.

O'Brien, Tim. "How to Tell a True War Story." In *The Things They Carried.* 1990. Reprint, New York: Penguin, 1991, 75–91.

Ong, Walter J. "The Writer's Audience Is Always a Fiction." *PMLA* 90 (January 1975): 9–21.

Orwell, George. "Politics and the English Language." 1945. Reprinted in *Essays,* selected and with an introduction by John Carey, 954–67. New York: Knopf, 2002.

———. "Why I Write." 1946. Reprinted in *Essays,* 1079–85.

Park, Douglas B. "The Meanings of 'Audience.'" *College English* 44 (March 1982): 247–57.

Patai, Daphne. "Sick and Tired of Nouveau Solipsism." *Chronicle of Higher Education,* February 23, 1994, A52.

Plath, Sylvia. *The Journals of Sylvia Plath.* Edited by Ted Hughes and Frances McCollough. 1982. Reprint, New York: Ballantine, 1983.

Plimpton, George, and Max Steele. "James Thurber." In vol. 1, *Writers at Work: The Paris Review Interviews,* edited by Malcolm Cowley, 82–98. New York: Viking, 1959.

Roney, Stephen K. "Postmodernist Prose and George Orwell." *Academic Questions* 15 (Spring 2002): 13–23.

Roorbach, Bill. *Writing Life Stories.* Cincinnati: Story Press, 1998.

Rose, Phyllis. "The Coming of the French." *American Scholar* 74 (Winter 2005): 59–67.

Root, Robert. "The Experimental Art." *JAEPL* 9 (Winter 2003–4): 12–19.

Sanders, Scott Russell. "The Singular First Person." In *Secrets of the Universe: Scenes from the Journey Home,* 187–204. Boston: Beacon Press, 1991.

———. "Under the Influence: Paying the Price of My Father's Booze." In *Secrets of the Universe,* 3–23.

Scholes, Robert. *Textual Power: Literary Theory and the Teaching of English.* New Haven, Conn.: Yale University Press, 1985.

Shaughnessy, Mina P. *Errors and Expectations: A Guide for the Teacher of Basic Writing.* New York: Oxford University Press, 1977.

Shepard, Alan, John McMillan, and Gary Tate, eds. *Coming to Class: Pedagogy and the Social Class of Teachers.* Portsmouth, N.H.: Heinemann, Boynton/Cook, 1998.

Shields, Carol. *Larry's Party.* New York: Viking, 1997.

Shuman, R. Baird. Letter. *PMLA* 104 October 1989): 904.

Sinklos, Richard. "I Cannot Tell a Lie (from an Amplification)." *New York Times, Week in Review,* February 5, 2006, 3.

Smith, Dave. "A Few Sighs on the Subject of Editing, etc." 2001. In *Spreading the Word: Editors on Poetry,* rev. ed., compiled by Stephen Corey and Warren Slesinger, 12–21. Beaufort, S.C.: Bench Press, 2001.

Smith, Sidonie, and Julia Watson. *Reading Autobiography: A Guide for Interpreting Life Narratives.* Minneapolis: University of Minnesota Press, 2001.

Solomon, Deborah. "Mr. Bodacious." *New York Times Magazine,* November 16, 2003, 42–46.

Spinner, Jenny. "An Interview with Sam Pickering." *Fourth Genre* 5 (Spring 2003): 192–207.

Strunk, William, Jr., and E. B. White. *The Elements of Style.* 1979. 4th ed. Reprint, Needham, Mass.: Allyn and Bacon, 2000.

Tate, Gary, and Edward P. J. Corbett, eds. *The Writing Teacher's Sourcebook.* New York: Oxford University Press, 1981, 1988.

Theophano, Janet. *Eat My Words: Reading Women's Lives through the Cookbooks They Wrote.* New York: Palgrave, 2002.

Tisdale, Sallie. *The Best Thing I Ever Tasted: The Secret of Food.* New York: Riverhead, 2000.

Tompkins, Jane. "Me and My Shadow." 1987. Reprinted in *Feminisms: An Anthology of Literary Theory and Criticism,* 2d ed., edited by Robyn R. Warhol and Diane Price Herndl, 1103–16. New Brunswick: Rutgers University Press, 1997.

Trimmer, Josph M. *Narration as Knowledge: Tales of the Teaching Life.* Portsmouth, N.H.: Heinemann, Boynton/Cook, 1997.

Van Doren, Carl. *Swift.* New York: Viking, 1930.

Wallace, David Foster. "Getting Away from Already Being Pretty Much Away from It All." In *A Supposedly Fun Thing I'll Never Do Again: Essays and Arguments,* 83–137. Boston: Little, Brown, 1997.

White, E. B. Foreword. *Essays of E. B. White,* vii–ix. New York: Harper, 1977.

White, Edward M. *Teaching and Assessing Writing.* 1985. 2nd ed., San Francisco: Jossey, Bass, 1994.

Widmer, Ted. "So Help Me God." *American Scholar* 74 (Winter 2005): 29–41.

Williams, J. W. "Measuring Shoulder Function with the Shoulder Pain and Disability Index." *Journal of Rheumatology* 22, no. 4 (1995): 727–32.

Wolfe, Tom. "The New Journalism." In *The New Journalism with an Anthology,* edited by Tom Wolfe and E. W. Johnson, 3–52. New York: Harper and Row, 1973.

Woolf, Virginia. *To the Lighthouse.* 1927. Reprint, New York: Harcourt, Brace & World, 1955.

About the Author

LYNN Z. BLOOM is Board of Trustees Distinguished Professor and Aetna Chair of Writing at the University of Connecticut in Storrs. She learned how to write from Dr. Seuss, fun; Strunk and E. B. White, elegant simplicity; Art Eastman, nitpicking revision; and Benjamin Spock, precision. As Spock told her in an interview for *Doctor Spock: Biography of a Conservative Radical,* her first book, "If you don't write clearly, someone could die." These precepts govern her teaching—previously at Butler University, the University of New Mexico, the College of William and Mary, and Virginia Commonwealth University. They also inform the heart, soul, and human voice of her writing: autobiography, including essays collected in *Composition Studies as a Creative Art* and now in *Seven Deadly Virtues;* textbooks such as *The Essay Connection;* and research on nonfiction, including "The Essay Canon" and "Consuming Prose: The Delectable Rhetoric of Food Writing." "(Im)Patient," which appears in this collection, was named a Notable Essay of 2005 in *Best American Essays.*